Elites and Economic Development:
Comparative Studies on the Political
Economy of Latin American Cities

Latin American Monographs, No. 41
Institute of Latin American Studies
The University of Texas at Austin

Elites and Economic Development

Comparative Studies on the Political Economy of Latin American Cities

by John Walton

Institute of Latin American Studies
The University of Texas at Austin

International Standard Book Number 0-292-72017-3 (cloth)
0-292-72018-1 (paper)
Library of Congress Catalog Card Number 75-620108

The Latin American Monographs Series
is distributed for the Institute of
Latin American Studies by:
  University of Texas Press
  P. O. Box 7819
  Austin, Texas 78712

To Pris,
     Florence,
     Ginger, and
     Whitney,
     family and friends

Contents

Tables and Map

Tables

Map

Elites and Economic Development:
Comparative Studies on the Political
Economy of Latin American Cities

Preface

Looking back on a journey that began almost a decade ago, I am impressed anew by the observation that social research is less a kind of work that one "executes" than a commitment to a way of life with an autonomy of its own; an engagement that, once begun, takes one in geographical and intellectual directions never anticipated at the outset. In those years, from the initial field work to the writing of the final chapter, my thoughts have continued to change. The study reported here bears little resemblance to the one planned in 1967, and the results that were down on paper by late 1969 have undergone extensive reinterpretation since then. It is therefore unlikely that in another decade I will view these materials exactly as I do now. In many senses a book of social research and theory is a working document only artificially fixed in time and space with a date and two covers. Nevertheless, journeys must end somewhere, if not for reasons of saturation and fatigue, then because of the judgment that further wandering might obscure the broader course of the venture.

Initially I had planned a study of power and developmental politics in Guadalajara, Mexico, and Cali, Colombia, following out my earlier research interests in United States urban politics. I was convinced then, and continue to be, that one of the greatest shortcomings of sociological research and theorizing is a parochialism born of the limited interest in and academic rewards attached to comparative studies. My intention was, and is, to study, not the exotic ways of Latin America, but comparative issues of power and politics. Latin America simply provided a congenial setting for a kind of study that, in principle, could have been conducted in a variety of national-urban places. In the comparative study the central question I hoped to get at was, In what way does the distribution of political power promote or retard economic development, and why? As will become evident in the text, this very general question was motivated by my fascination for locating some empirical answers to the radical challenge to conventional, structural-functional theories of change and devel-

3

opment issued by scholars like Paul Baran, Frantz Fanon, Andre Gunder Frank, Celso Furtado, Irving Louis Horowitz, Gunnar Myrdal, Raúl Prebisch, and many others. In retrospect, and bowing toward neither partisan-advocacy sociology nor illusions of total objectivity, I would judge that my mind was open on these issues, partly out of the naïve belief that some rapprochement was possible. Though I am now convinced that the radical approach is vastly superior to conventional evolutionary theory, the ultimate aim of this study is to build new theory under the broad canopy of structuralist thinking.

During the summer of 1967 I conducted some pilot work in Mexico City while attending a seminar at the University of the Americas on the economic development of Mexico. With the immeasurable assistance of a grant from the Ford Foundation–sponsored Council for Intersocietal Studies at Northwestern University, its director, Richard D. Schwartz, and my departmental chairman, Raymond W. Mack, I was able to spend the calendar year of 1968 in Latin America. Although by this time I had thought about extending the study from two to four urban areas, it was impossible to plan on that before acquiring some feeling for the pace of work that could be maintained in the field.

After some reorientation in Mexico City I began work in Guadalajara in early 1968. By and large I received extensive cooperation from local leaders and organizations. This being my first site, I was still not altogether sure what I was doing, but having departed Northwestern with a generous stipend carrying only the presumption that I would be doing research, I felt obliged to persevere. But things did begin to take shape, owing largely to the tolerance and assistance of José Luis Reyna at El Colegio de México and, in Guadalajara, Elías and Elsa Dau, Alfonso Dau, Sigfried Herkommer, Harold Hughes, Jorge Garabay, Juan Delgado Navarro, and many others.

By June much was completed and I moved on to Cali, where I was greatly assisted by the kindness and expertise of José Castro Borrero. Others who went out of their way to help included Bernardo Garcés Córdoba, Arlene and Harrinson McKay, Dr. Leonardo Sinisterra, and Reynaldo Scarpetta. Finally, my gratitude and respects to the memory of Manuel Caravajal, the most universally recognized and respected leader in Cali, whose unselfish devotion to development guaranteed him a prominent place in Colombian history of this century.

Because of the courtesy and cooperation extended me by everyone in Cali, the work went rapidly. By October I found my research agenda complete and decided to pursue the four-city plan by moving on to Medellín. With the help of an old friend, Fr. Guillermo Saldarriaga, and the Industrialists' Association I was able to complete a research plan in Medellín comparable in outline to the Guadalajara and Cali work, though somewhat reduced in scope, by December of 1968.

Thanks to supplemental funds from the Council for Intersocietal Studies I was able to round out the four-city study with field work in Monterrey, Mexico, during the summer of 1969 on a scale comparable with the Medellín research. In Monterrey I enjoyed the assistance of Juan Carlos, Roberto Garza Sada, Jr., Héctor Luis de León, Antonio L. Rodríguez, Edgardo Reyes Salcido, and some fifty other leaders who generously cooperated with my questioning.

Much has been said, justifiably and otherwise, about the difficulties of conducting social research in Latin America, particularly on politically sensitive issues as dealt with here, but also, more recently, on all manner of topics. Although I went into the field with the criminal debacle of Project Camelot and a Colombian analog, "Operation Simpático," very much on my mind as potential reasons for distrust and noncooperation, I must admit that, in more than three hundred formal interviews and as many more research-related conversations, my fears in this regard proved to be unfounded. Indeed, having gained the confidence of some respondents I broached the subject myself, only to discover that local concern about the possibly subversive or espionage motives of a North American researcher was minimal. I mention this datum with a sense of ambiguity, since I personally condemn espionage or counterinsurgency under the guise of research and hope, without great optimism, that United States intelligence has extricated itself from academic front organizations. Nevertheless, I think this experience is worth reporting for several reasons. First, by way of proviso, my experience may have been unique because I was interviewing established leaders in two countries thus far less concerned about academic espionage than, say, Chile, though justifiable antagonism is growing. Second, I operated as a more-or-less free agent working with the phonebook and a few initial connections, and avoiding potential entanglements associated with a staff of interviewers or any local university ties. This is not to say that I tried to be secretive; indeed, I accepted invitations to meet with local groups to talk about the research and tried to be as candid as I could about my intentions when quizzed by informants. In short, the place, style, and candor of research may have had a lot to do with allaying suspicion. But I report the experience for reasons other than these tactical or methodological observations. What I would like to convey is the suggestion that the difficulties of research in Latin America may be overrated; that distrust is less in evidence than is generally believed, *not* because of the unselfish professional interests of social scientists, but, on the contrary, because of the simple good manners of Latin Americans and their desire to register somewhere their understanding of developmental problems. When talking with a United States researcher these people were not distrustful but genuinely cooperative, not suspicious but self-confident, less interested in the potential doings of the CIA than in the actual policies of United States trade and aid. I do not wish to leave the impression that research in Latin America is virgin territory or that North American investigators are uncritically received. And, indeed, my impression is that things are now more difficult than they were in 1968. I do want to suggest that the Latins I worked with were gracious and generally alacritous to talk about developmental issues of mutual concern when the purposes were clear and there was some expectation that their judgments would reach a wider audience. Against proper strictures on the disingenuous use of research, it seems to me that the responsibility of the social scientist and the formula for continued reception in Latin America is the faithful reporting of the ideas and aspirations that constitute the standpoint of the other.

With that in mind, it is my hope that this book will be read as a piece of research and theory inextricably tied to issues of policy at home and abroad. If such does prove to be the case, any credit that may result should be broadly apportioned. My debt is, first, to all of the Mexicans and Colombians who lent support during the eighteen months of field work and in subsequent correspondence related to some initial reports of my results that were circulated to those interested in following the study. Second, I am grateful to Northwestern University for logistical support and a style of administrative tolerance that has allowed me to come and go as the dictates of the work seemed to demand. My good friends and great bosses Raymond W. Mack and Charles C. Moskos are specially acknowledged. Also, to my colleagues and students in the Department of Sociology I am notably appreciative of the good counsel and humor that have helped enliven my interest in sociological work. As students, co-workers, and Colombian scholars in their own right, Carlos Dávila and Enrique Ogliastri have given me much help and satisfaction. The University of Texas at Austin provided me with additional funds for the data analysis and manuscript typing, ably completed by Tamara Belden. As a visiting professor at Texas during 1971–1972, I enjoyed the assistance of the Department of Sociology, the Institute of Latin American Studies, and several students working on related projects, including Robert Driscole and Thomas J. Rosser.

Finally, my greatest debt is to my wife, Priscilla, who participated at every stage of the research, setting up interviews and collecting data in the field, acting as an ambassador in a culture she knew better than I, and, later, assisting in the organization of historical data. Without her the study probably would have been completed, but on a reduced scale. She deserves much of the credit and will, I am sure, happily take it.

1. The Organization of Inquiry

AN ORIENTATION TO THE POLITICAL ECONOMY OF
DEVELOPMENT

It is now nearly twenty years since the community of North American
social scientists returned to the problem of international development as a
major concern of research and theory. The word "returned" is used advisedly, since the causes and consequences of industrial development were
central themes in classical social theory at the hands of Marx, Weber,
Durkheim, Spencer, Schumpeter, Veblen, and many others. For reasons
that would require a treatise on the sociology of knowledge to explain
adequately, this classical vision of the main drift of modern society lay
dormant for a period of years in North American social science until its
post–World War II awakening.

Clearly the rekindled interest in development was occasioned by broader social changes: a new role for the United States in world affairs, the
rapid emergence of new nations in Asia and Africa to join the ranks of the
older members of the Third World—principally the Latin American re-
publics—the Cold War, and, not unrelated, expanding sources of support
for cross-national research. Alongside these were changes of a more internal sort taking place in social science, principally a growing awareness of
the parochialism and narrow empiricism born of home-grown pragmatism
and the enthusiastic reception of European positivism.

The distinctive feature of this post-war resurgence of interest in problems of development and industrialization was the fact that classical concerns were internationalized and advanced upon by a phalanx of social
scientists of every description. Social anthropologists, benefiting from previous cross-cultural experience, shifted their attention from describing
primitive societies to analyzing development and change in peasant communities and urban slums. Social psychologists turned to questions of indi-

vidual modernism and achievement. Political scientists focused on nation-building and the comparative study of institutions such as governments, parties, and interest groups. Historians probed into the murky past of these countries too often assumed to have no past. Demographers profiled the structure of population and its changes. Sociologists took up questions of race, stratification, mobility, and elites. Development economists produced data to assess classical economic theory and also forged into the field of "noneconomic" aspects of economic development. Geographers were on hand and often extended the limits of convention by studying migration and settlement patterns. No discipline was slighted. Students of business administration mixed with linguists; disciplines frequently intersected in studies of bureaucracy, the military, the labor force, the community, the diffusion of innovations, international law and trade, policy-making, and so forth.

As might be expected, this proliferation of interests rapidly assumed chaotic proportions. It was not only the fact that so many people were dealing with so many aspects of the problem. More to the point was the fact that their orientations were encapsulated. As Horowitz aptly notes,

> Almost unfailingly, development is written about from the particular standpoint of "the science of" politics, economics, sociology, anthropology or psychology. The standpoint is derived from the author's professional commitments rather than from the developmental process as such.[1]

Yet this substantive and theoretical disarray was to be anticipated. For one thing, there was no consensus on a "paradigm" or overarching theoretical orientation. Interestingly, where it was possible to detect "schools of thought" or at least theoretical affinities, these tended to cluster around the ideas of a few classical thinkers. For example, the influential collection by Almond and Coleman, *The Politics of the Developing Areas*,[2] was an early attempt at integration around the guiding metaphors of structural-functional theory. This theory derived largely from the work of Talcott Parsons and, in turn, relied on his understanding of Weber and Durkheim. Although this orientation attracted, and continues to attract, many sociologists and political scientists and a few economists, it fell short of its ambition to unify social science approaches.[3] Similarly, some economists and social psychologists developed theories of entrepreneurship and achievement that owed much to both Weber and Schumpeter.[4] A steadfast orientation is the neo-Marxist, nurtured in the lean years by Paul Baran and recently regaining a position of importance commensurate with the rest of our classical legacy.[5]

Notable, however, in each of these contemporary schools is the distinctively modern stamp they give to classical positions, as well as the easy permeability of the boundaries that would seem to separate them. To this we must add the fact that much of the literature does not fit into these discernable approaches. Indeed, attempts to fashion a single, general orientation turn out to be hopelessly eclectic.[6] In Hirschman's words,

> The intensive study of economic development has had one discouraging result: it has produced an ever lengthening list of factors and conditions, of obstacles and prerequisites. The direction of the inquiry has proceeded from thoroughly objective, tangible, and quantitative phenomena to more and more subjective, intangible and unmeasurable ones.[7]

Clearly another reason for this eclectic confusion is the fact that the concept of "development" has no clear referent. Notions like development, industrialization, modernization, and even social mobilization are often used interchangeably. Indicative is the statement in a major work by Levy that "anyone who feels strongly that the term modernization *must mean* something other than its explicit definition here should feel free to substitute any other term or symbol provided he does so consistently."[8] Against this total flexibility with which the consistent reader may substitute any meaning he likes for the concept, other writers prefer a narrow identification of development with industrialization.[9] For the moment, the point is not that one definition or another may be preferable but simply that we can expect little theoretical or substantive integration of a field the scope and content of which cannot be consensually agreed upon. Two astronomers who define, respectively, their field as the study of everything in the heavens and the study of telescopes will find little in common theoretically.

But the sociology of development should not be left at this impasse, for there may be greater potential for integration than the foregoing observations would indicate. One salient characteristic of the "second decade of developmental studies" is a certain progress in critical awareness. Not more than a decade ago the guiding metaphors that managed to capture what consensus did exist relied on broad evolutionary precepts.[10] Development and modernization were viewed as change processes that followed a "Western model." Developing nations moved along a continuum from "traditional" to "modern," albeit in irregular jolts and on tangents. The points along this continuum were marked by such historical experiences of Western nations as urbanization, secularization, mass education, industrialization, and democratization.[11] Social structures moved in the direction of "structural differentiation" as individuals in tandem adopted the rationality of "modern man."[12] The end product of the process was predicted to be a growing psychic and social uniformity.

Recently, however, the trend in research has been toward qualifying these global metaphors through an emphasis on variability within the developmental process and the special circumstances that confront currently industrializing societies in contrast to more advanced states.

More specifically, this critical mood has directly challenged many of the guiding assumptions of evolutionary functionalism. For instance, the distinction between "traditional" and "modern" has been questioned on the grounds of causal adequacy and empirical fit. Practices typically associated with each notion appear to have *both* positive and negative influences on development, and these practices are routinely encountered in societies that span the developmental continuum; "traditional" industrial urbanites may be as common as "rational" rural peasants.[13] The applicability of Western models to today's Third World is alleged to be quite limited because of a number of historical dissimilarities; there is also the argument that developed nations deliberately perpetuate backwardness through self-serving neo-colonial relations. Even more fundamental to the critical mood is the fact that structural-functional evolutionary theories were never very successful in the twin senses of stimulating new discovery and charting the direction of social change.

Another salient characteristic of the "second decade of development studies" has been the growing popularity of an alternative paradigm variously labeled the neo-Marxist, structuralist approach,[14] or dependency theory.[15] Taking some liberties with Kuhn's analysis of scientific revolutions,[16] the critical mood that reacted to structural-functional analyses of development and modernization began to produce a number of "anomalies" or results not easily accommodated by the approach. If, for example, social and economic development was to have been the necessary consequence of urbanization, technological diffusion, communications, and the differentiation of social structures, then why do Third World societies that have been the objects of these influences find themselves underdeveloped (and underdeveloping) today? Why do standard indicators of economic development show that while the scope and activities of transnational corporations continue to grow (representing an ever increasing proportion of the GNPs of the advanced nations), Third World economies either stagnate or "develop" in the direction of greater social and economic inequality? Why are the political systems of these countries, which we were told would become more "integrative" and "democratized," still rent by the conflicts of class struggle and neo-colonialism?

In response to such disquieting questions, the late 1960s witnessed an increasing interest in the theory of structural dependency, particularly among Third World scholars and in certain circles within the United States. This approach, of course, was not new, having been central to the writing of Baran and the European Marxists. Moreover, with respect to certain key arguments such as the widening gulf between advanced and underdeveloped countries, it accorded with the influential Prebisch thesis on "terms of trade"[17] and Myrdal's "cumulative and circular causation."[18] What was new, however, was the fact that a younger generation of scholars from diverse national backgrounds began to elaborate and research the theory of structural dependency, reaching in the process a receptive international audience.

Central to the dependency perspective was the observation that advanced metropolitan states and underdeveloped satellite countries or colonies operate in a single, interrelated world economic system. The development of the former cannot be understood apart from the underdevelopment of the latter. Satellite countries do not have "dual economies" (one modern and dynamic, the other traditional and stagnant) but economic and social systems that are integrated (or malintegrated) according to the nature of their incorporation into colonial and neo-colonial networks. Societies that once enjoyed periods of relative prosperity often have subsequently underdeveloped with the global spread of commercial, industrial, and technological capitalism that depends increasingly on the extraction of surplus from the periphery. The underdevelopment, or misdevelopment, of Third World nations is seen as being caused by structural relationships between them and the advanced nations that dominate world economies. Fundamentally, these center-periphery relationships are characterized in terms of bilateral inequality as described by Dos Santos:

> By dependence we mean a situation in which the economy of certain countries is conditioned by the development and expansion of another economy to which the former is subjected. The relation of interdependence between two or more economies, and between these and world trade, assumes the form of dependence when some countries (the dominant ones) can expand and can be self-sustaining, while other countries (the dependent ones) can do this only as a reflection of that expansion, which can have either a positive or a negative effect on their immediate development.[19]

One of the better-known versions of the theory is found in the work of Frank. His work is useful in that it presents a series of hypotheses capable of being tested. Stated bluntly, the first hypothesis is that "the satellites experience their greatest economic development and especially their most classically capitalist industrial development if and when their ties to the metropolis are weakest."[20] Second, the extent and nature of the impact of dependency on developing areas will vary with the historical period in which they embark on the process of modern industrial growth. Third, internal differentiation of privilege will be observable between economic sectors and elites corresponding to the extent of their metropolitan ties.

Since Frank's initial work, other students of this perspective have begun to stress the *differential consequences* that arise out of the interaction between forms of imperialism and the *variable* internal conditions of Third World countries. That is, the approach is moving, at least theoretically, from a general orientation to the statement of testable, contingent relationships. A critical step in this direction was the recognition that exclusive focus on "metropolitan ties" led to a rather monolithic understanding of the development process. Noting that classical Marxist theories "have not considered the subject of imperialism from the point of view of the dependent countries," Dos Santos argues cogently that

> dependence is not an "external factor" as is often thought. . . . The international situation in which that movement produces itself is taken as a general condition but not as the demiurge of the national process, because the manner in which that situation acts upon national reality is determined by the internal components of that reality. . . . It is necessary to go beyond a unilateral perspective which limits itself to analyzing the problem from the point of view of the hegemonic centers and it is necessary to integrate the peripheral zones into the whole of the analysis as part of a system of socio-economic relations on a world scale. . . . Dependence conditions a certain internal structure which redefines it as a function of the structural possibilities of diverse national economies. . . . Even if these national economies do not condition relations of dependence in general, they limit their possibilities of expansion, or rather, they redefine them at the level of their concrete functioning. . . . We must study the manner in which dependent national economies structure themselves internally (and how they do this within the context of the world system) and the role they play in the development of the world system.[21]

Applying the same reasoning to more specific levels of analysis, Dos Santos broaches the problem of structures of power and domination with the observation that "external domination is impractical in principle. Domination is only possible when it finds support in national sectors which benefit from it."[22] Consequently he argues for the need to analyze the "articulation between the dominant interests in the hegemonic center and the dominant interests in the dependent societies."

Several writers reflect this prescription in their analyses of the origins and consequences of various elite types. Furtado, for example, distinguishes between urban and rural elites in Latin America's colonial era.

In this way, a ruling class was formed made up of two groups with interests which were distinct but not necessarily in conflict. On the one hand there was a group of land owners vested with considerable power over the population in their domain, and on the other hand there were those elements whose wealth was derived from commerce and other activities principally urban in character.[23]

Alliances between the latter "progressive faction of the ruling class" and government accounted for the expansion of Latin American exports. A closely parallel interpretation by Cardoso discusses the differences between entrepreneurial elites of rural origins and those of the trading and mining sectors with respect to their contributions to industrialization and dependency. Among a series of influences he credits economic development to the "economic action of the non-landowning groups, which succeeded in controlling the state to some extent."[24]

Finally, as in the case of elite studies, the dependency perspective is being applied to many other substantive issues such as migration,[25] urbanization,[26] social stratification,[27] labor markets,[28] and indigenous communities.[29] Yet, while these are encouraging indications of the perspective's vitality, many questions await systematic research.

To return to the earlier point about the potential for an integrated approach to the sociology of development, it would now appear that in the critical reaction to conventional theories and in the dependency approach there exist the elements for a more exacting, if delimited, framework for inquiry. In this work we shall advance one such integrated perspective, focused on the *political economy of development*. Needless to say, other analysts would probably fashion different strategies, depending on their evaluation of the theoretical literature and their substantive concerns. But the watershed of the first decade of development studies seems to suggest precisely the utility of limited conceptual frameworks wherein the emphasis may be laid on the linkages between a specific set of factors and mechanisms that are important to, if not definitive of, the developmental process. The political economy of development is elected as such an approach in this work because it seems to capture some of the more intriguing and less researched features of the Third World.

The orientation of this study is based on a convergent set of theoretical perspectives derived from this critical reaction to evolutionary thinking and dependency theory. Most fundamentally we will be concerned with developing a framework based on a limited number of interrelated factors that are judged theoretically to be crucial to the developmental process and, subsequently, with evaluating their interplay in comparative research. In that sense the study conforms with Moore's judgment that ". . .

what is needed, and is mostly not at hand, is the construction of limited-alternative or typological sequences where total generalization is improper."[30]

Five theoretical perspectives are combined to organize this approach and orient the empirical research. First, it is assumed that societies differ in the way in which they experience the developmental process according to *sequence and timing of change.* Bendix notes that "once industrialization has occurred anywhere, this fact alone alters the international environment of all societies. There is a sense in which it is true to say that because of timing and sequence industrialization cannot occur in the same way twice."[31] In a similar vein, dependency theorists such as O'Connor,[32] Castells,[33] and Dos Santos[34] identify distinct stages in the expansion of Western capitalism and trace these to differential impacts on the underdeveloped periphery. Finding merit in such observations, the present study deliberately compares cases with differing historical experiences of development. Where the factors of timing and sequence do appear to condition the nature of the developmental process, explanations are sought as one basis for limited generalization.

The second theoretical perspective is that *social stratification and power* constitute the critical structural factors intervening between historical changes and particular patterns of development. Social stratification may be seen as both a cause and a consequence of the developmental process, depending on one's analytical perspective. In this study, social stratification will be treated principally as an intervening, causal variable conditioning the developmental process generally and the distribution of power specifically. Class structure and power structure are not regarded as isomorphic, but they are assumed to be closely related, the nature and extent of that relationship being empirically problematic.

Illustrative of the importance attached to these considerations is the statement by Hoselitz that

> since there seems to exist a considerable body of empirical evidence that in presently underdeveloped countries economic leadership is concentrated among a group of people who also control political power, a reallocation of patterns of responsibility and authority demands a shift of political power from the present political elite to a different one and the simultaneous reshuffling of the status system of the society.[35]

Many observers share this belief. Bendix illustrates how the comparative study of ruling groups is critical in accounting for historical patterns of development.[36] Nash proposes that an extreme polarization of wealth and power is inimical to development, although under other circumstances "the more organized the group holding political power, the easier it is to embark on development programs."[37] The same point can be drawn from a different, conflict-oriented perspective:

> The chief fact to be recognized is that very few "have" sectors of a society are willing to pay the full price for rapid economic progress. . . . Where economic and political power is concentrated in the hands of a small group, whose main interest is in the preservation of the status quo, prospects for economic progress are very slight unless a social revolution effects a shift in the distribution of income and power.[38]

While differing with some of these writers on the theoretical primacy of social class, dependency theorists, as we have seen, lay heavy emphasis on questions of stratification and power.

Third, and more specifically, this study assumes that in the contemporary Third World economic development is best understood as an outcome of *the political process and the functions of the state.* In many senses economic development is *the* issue shaping the political process and, conversely, the state is so heavily involved in promoting development that economic change is embedded in a matrix of political influences. In contrast to developed "economic societies," Third World nations, in Horowitz's view, are "political societies . . . [in which] the economy becomes the dependent variable in the operations of the State."[39] In a more general vein Moore observes: "That the State in a country now seeking rapid economic revolution will exercise a major degree of control by comparison with the earliest models of industrialization seems clear, and this forms another basis for generalization."[40]

Fourth, it is assumed that in this sequence of factors affecting the developmental process the ultimate influence is found in the *capacity for decision-making.* Timing and sequence of industrialization, structures of stratification and power, developmental roles of the state and politics, all of these ultimately register their effect by means of what actors are able to do within a socially structured context. To state it differently, just as it is essential to understand the structure of social power and the institutions through which it operates, so, too, is it necessary to understand how power is actually used in concrete historical situations. Similarly constituted elite groups may take widely varying courses of action depending on their particular circumstances, goals, and opposition and on the organization of non-elite groups. Indeed, elites may differ widely in their very ability to make decisions. Hirschman's analysis in *The Strategy of Economic Development* is based on the capacity for decision-making as the key to development.

> Our diagnosis is simply that countries fail to take advantage of their development potential because, for reasons largely related to their image of change,

they find it difficult to take the decisions needed for development in the required number and with the required speed. . . . The shortages of "pre-requisites" of production are interpreted as a manifestation of the basic deficiency in organization. . . . We have identified the ability to make such decisions as the scarce resource which conditions all other scarcities and difficulties in underdeveloped countries.[41]

Although Hirschman does not discuss the relationship between elite structure and decision-making capacity nor produce a theoretical analysis of conditions that would promote more effective organization, this approach focuses attention on the actual workings of the political process and dovetails with the theoretical orientation.

Finally, it is assumed that contemporary developing societies cannot be understood from an intranational or intraregional standpoint that presumes a large measure of autonomous control over the area's economic fortunes. Rather these societies must be understood as embedded in a network of *dependent and interdependent relations* spanning local, regional, national, and international levels. While this would appear to be a point of easy agreement, it is mainly within the structural dependency approach that we encounter serious efforts to deal with its implications. Yet it is precisely here that research is most needed to fill in the substantive features that account for variable patterns of center-periphery relations.

These five interrelated theoretical ideas characterize the present orientation to the political economy of development. Since they derive from critical discussions, they represent, in many senses, deficiencies and omissions in earlier thinking that this study attempts to rectify. That is done in two ways; first, by explicitly building them into the analysis and, second, by doing so in a comparative study that will allow some empirical assessments of their actual consequences. The framework poses the following kinds of questions: If timing and sequence of industrialization are important, what are some of the essential categories or time-related differences, and what are the distinguishing features of developmental experiences that were begun under these different conditions? If different configurations of social power are basic concerns, what types emerge here and how are they related to more and less successful development? If metropolitan ties have variable impacts depending on the "internal" conditions of less developed societies, what are those conditions associated with more and less autonomous or dependent development?

THE COMPARATIVE DESIGN AND RESEARCH METHODS

This research deals with the process of economic development in Latin

America. That choice was informed by a variety of considerations that boil down to personal interest and a special attraction to that part of the world, together with the fact that Latin America reflects most of the conditions typically associated with underdevelopment. Next, the selection of research sites within Latin America was influenced by the twin considerations of national context and subnational, regional variation as these reflect features of the theoretical framework.

At the national level, Mexico and Colombia were selected for comparison of a number of parallels. Fundamental was the fact that while these two countries differ with respect to the degree of economic development attained, they may be noninvidiously compared. Mexico's growth rate has been one of the more impressive among Third World nations. United Nations figures indicate that between 1960 and 1965 the annual growth rate of Mexico's GNP was 6.0 percent, 2.6 percent per capita. But Colombia has kept pace, occupying the intermediate range among Latin American nations, with its GNP increasing at the rate of 4.5 percent, 1.7 percent per capita, during the same years.[42] A recent analysis also indicates that the two countries have fairly comparable import structures, a key consideration in the analysis of national development.[43]

Politically, Mexico and Colombia have had comparable experiences of stability in recent years—Mexico since the 1930s under a post-revolutionary, one-party government, Colombia since the late 1950s under a unique National Front government in which the Liberal and Conservative parties alternate in the presidency every four years and divide equally all other elective and appointive posts. Generally these countries share the common historical experiences of Spanish colonization, wars of independence, and subsequent North American economic domination, as well as a common language and all that is entailed by the notion of Hispanic-American culture. Needless to say, there are fundamental differences between the two countries that are equally important to the research design. A great deal will be said about this later. Our concern here is simply to indicate those parallels that do exist and that enhance the comparative design.

The second factor influencing the selection of research sites concerns regional variation. Comment is required on this criterion since it represents one of the unique aspects of the design.

Until recently it has been conventional to regard nations as the appropriate units of analysis for comparative studies of economic development. There is, however, increasing recognition that this focus may obscure the critical processes and factors that condition development. Several points support the argument. First, it has been noted that wide disparities between sectoral and regional development within given nations render suspect, or at least undifferentiating, the use of the nation as a unit of analysis.[44] Regional "growth poles" may account for the bulk of a nation's development effort and differ vastly from other areas within the same geopolitical unit. Second, and by implication, subnational regions often constitute "natural areas" whose development has depended more on local, or local-international, factors than on national conditions. For example, theoretical explanations of successful or unsuccessful development often rely on regional analyses of location, ethnicity, or class structure.[45] Third, comparative regional studies allow conditional assessments of national policies where they have their most concrete manifestations, at the local level. Finally, systematic methods of subnational regional analysis, if they can be developed, will permit broader comparisons within and across nations. Horowitz argues in a similar vein regarding units of analysis:

> Social science has been unable to generate an adequate literature at the level of comparative international development. . . . Even work done within a broad-ranging rubric, such as international relations, smuggles in nationalistic orientations, or isolates factors for analysis such that comparisons across national lines provide precious little predictive or explanatory power. The heart of the problem seems to be the assumption that the nation is at all times and in every way the critical organizing pivot in the behavior of men and their societies. In point of fact, the role of the nation itself should be carefully measured in terms of other variables that may have equal or even greater explanatory value, such as urbanization, industrialization, and population.[46]

Comparative studies based on urban or regional units allow for the introduction of urbanization, industrialization, modes of production, regional or racial sentiments, national policy, foreign influences, and so forth as variables whose actual impact could be assessed across cases.

For these reasons, regional areas were adopted as the units of analysis in the comparative study. This allowed subsequent comparisons along several dimensions, i.e., intranational comparisons of regions sharing common contextual attributes; cross-national comparisons of regions sharing common developmental experiences; cross-national comparisons per se; and serial comparisons of regions. All of this requires some clarification of what defines a "region." As the term is employed here, a (subnational) region embodies an urban area and its dependent rural surroundings. The surroundings are dependent both politically and economically on the urban center. Quartered in the urban center are the political and economic institutions that have the greatest impact on life in the surrounding area, through markets and trade or through the provision of public services and the exercise of political authority. The urban center, in turn, shapes the contours of the region by its own dependency on the surroundings for supply of needed goods and services. These reciprocal sources of power and dependency engender a social-psychological identification of people with the region. Indicative of this are regional names that apply equally to places and groups of people. Where reciprocal ties of power and dependence begin to weaken, the periphery of the region is found, and probably the frontier of another, though obviously we can expect buffer zones, no man's lands, and nested boxes of regions, depending on the particular forms of power and dependence. At the operational level in this study, a region comprises a large urban center and its surroundings, coinciding, roughly, with the state or department of which the city serves as the capital.

Earlier we stressed the importance of timing and sequence in the development process. When and by what sequence of events a region experiences development were noted as conditions that can shape the process in very special ways. Accordingly, this dimension of historical timing was built into the design.

With respect to these considerations Mexico and Colombia provided the crucial requirements for the design. A unique demographic parallel exists between the two countries. In each the largest city is the capital. Outside of both capitals are two important cities of nearly equal size, the second and third cities, only distantly rivaled in size and importance by all those that follow. Further, in both countries one of these cities has traditionally been an industrial center, whereas the second has only recently begun the transition from being the commercial trading center of an agricultural hinterland toward greater industrialization. The four regions, denoted by the names of their central cities, are the industrial centers of Monterrey in the state of Nuevo León, Mexico, and Medellín in the department of Antioquia, Colombia, and the transitional cities of Guadalajara in the state of Jalisco, Mexico, and Cali in the department of Valle del Cauca, Colombia. The cases and how they fit the dimensions of the research design are summarized in Table 1.

We turn next to a description of the procedures employed in the field studies of each of these regions. Following from the issues raised in the theoretical orientation, our first specific methodological task was to identify the elites or decision-makers in the development process and the key institutional bases of power through which they operated. More precisely, several tasks were suggested: identification of elites and key development-related organizations, analysis of the linkages between and among elites and organizations, and description of the actual decision-making process. By focusing attention on elites we endeavor to trace one important kind of influence on the development process. And although elites may often pro-

TABLE 1

THE COMPARATIVE DESIGN: DIMENSIONS AND REGIONAL CASES

National Economic and Political Characteristics

		More developed. One-party, post-revolutionary. (Mexico)	Less developed. Two-party, National Front. (Colombia)
Economic Development History	Early industrialization	Monterrey, Nuevo León (1,200,000)*	Medellín, Antioquia (1,000,000)
	Transition to Industrialization	Guadalajara, Jalisco (1,300,000)	Cali, Valle del Cauca (900,000)

*Population estimates for the urban center of the region, 1968.

vide the critical influences, we do not assume that they provide the only ones.

The methods employed here were adopted from those used in North American studies of community power and decision-making and involve a multi-stage, standard interviewing procedure.[47] First, interviews were conducted with a number of persons occupying important positions in public- and private-sector organizations directly concerned with "development activities" in a broad sense. The criteria for inclusion of organizations in this universe were that the organization have a constituency (i.e., that it "represent" a set of people) and a mandate (legal or chartered) to concern itself with activities broadly affecting economic development. Operationally the following kinds of organizations qualified: in the public sector, municipal- and state-level agencies in charge of economic planning, urban services, public works, housing, agriculture, the treasury, education, public credit, federally-sponsored regional planning, et cetera; in the private sector, the bankers' associations, chambers of commerce, industrial associations, agricultural interest groups, employers' associations, unions, private-sector planning and educational institutions, merchants' associations, societies of engineers, architects, et cetera. The universe was defined in such a way as to exclude only private firms, service clubs, social and cultural or religious groups, and the like. It was, therefore, fairly exhaustive of the local organization infrastructure. Typically these organizations had a first and second officer, president and director or manager and secretary. When this was the case, both were interviewed; for all organizations the top executive officer was interviewed. This first sample of organizational heads will be referred to as the "subleaders."

At this stage all respondents were given a structured interview that covered autobiographical information, attitudinal questions, perceptions of influential persons and organizations in the region, perceptions of important development projects realized or in progress in the region, persons and organizations participating in these projects, major problems facing the region, and appropriate roles of the public and private sectors in the promotion of development.

The second and third stages of the method built on the initial one. As a first approximation of the top elites or "influentials," the nominations by subleaders of important people in the region were tabulated. Those persons most frequently nominated were designated as influentials. In the second stage these influentials were located and given the same standard interview, including items wherein they could make their own nominations for important persons, organizations, and projects. The third stage of the method tabulated the most frequently mentioned development-related projects of importance in the area according to the judgments of subleaders and influentials. These projects then became the focus of case studies that entailed both unstructured interviewing of "activity participants" (identified in the earlier interviews and from participant referrals) and the use of a variety of documents describing project histories. In each of those project case studies an effort was made to identify important participants and illuminate the decision-making process.

To supplement these data from the interviewing and project case study procedures, a wide range of additional materials were collected: histories, items dealing with economic performance and national economic and political conditions, and, generally, whatever could be located that appeared to be of potential value.

Having said all this, we must now enter one important qualification. A set of practical considerations, involving mostly time and money, suggested the unfeasibility of pursuing this complex design with equal intensity in all four regional areas. Consequently, it was decided to economize by adopting a "more intensive" procedure in two areas and a "less intensive" one in the other two. Because, in some senses, the transitional cases were more complicated (i.e., more in flux and less endowed with supplementary data sources), Guadalajara and Cali were the objects of the more intensive procedure and Monterrey and Medellín of the less intensive. Specifically, this entailed fewer subleader interviews, fewer influential interviews, and fewer project case studies in the latter two cases. With those differences, however, the general procedure followed in the four regions was the same. In the chapters that follow, material from the four will be considered uniformly and with equal confidence, since there is evidence indicating that the procedures differ only in detail, not in substantive thrust. For example, patterns identified in the early going of the more intensive method were not altered in later investigation. Simply more detail was uncovered, suggesting that the major outlines could be provided by the shorter method. Moreover, histories and published material on social, political, and economic characteristics were more elaborate for Monterrey and Medellín, thus balancing somewhat the disparities in field work. Table 2 summarizes the total numbers of interviewees at each stage of the procedure in the four regions.

THE CONCEPT OF DEVELOPMENT

The term "development" has been subject to such diverse and vague usages that one may rightfully wonder whether different authors employing the term are talking about anything even closely equivalent. The gamut of usages runs from narrowly-conceived quantitative conceptions of economic performance to global social changes in a direction preferred by the

TABLE 2. INTERVIEWEES

Region	1. Public Sector Subleaders	2. Private Sector Subleaders	3. Influentials	4. Subtotal	5. Projects Studied	6. Activity Partici-pants	7. Total (4+6)
Guadalajara	31	34	18	83	5	25	108
Cali	31	39	17	87	5	20	107
Monterrey	22	20	(4)*	42	2	8	50
Medellín	19	21	(4)*	40	2	6	46
Total	103	114	35	252	14	59	311

*In Monterrey and Medellín the second step of the method was dropped, i.e., no unique set of interviews with influentials was incorporated. The numbers in parentheses indicate that some influentials were also positional leaders and were interviewed in that capacity in the first stage. Since these numbers are duplications they do not figure in the row and column sums. However, some activity participants were also subleaders or influentials. When such persons were involved in and knowledgeable about a project, separate, unstructured interviews were conducted with them on a second visit. Thus the total N of 311 refers to distinct interviews, not persons.

observer, e.g., toward greater affluence or democratic politics. In most cases the definition is imbued with a strong normative component; implicit is the unquestioned suggestion that development is desirable, the road to progress and the good life. Yet writers often shy away from the value-laden implications of their definitions, preferring to seek scientific immunity in the myth of a "value-free" stance. The fact that a given definition of development implies an endorsement of particular policies compatible with that definition is seldom confronted openly.

In recent years, social scientists have increasingly come to recognize that the separation of fact and value is an illusion; that scientific inquiry inevitably entails value choices regarding what problems are to be investigated, what standpoint they are viewed from, what evidence is to be trusted, and what the evidence suggests should be done about the problems. But to recognize that value neutrality is an impossibility does not mean that we have to abandon the possibility of honestly objective and accurate investigation, provided those terms are properly understood. The fact that the researcher is somehow involved in his subject matter does not mean that his analysis must be in error; it does mean that his standpoint (like any other) will be partial to certain features of the situation. To use a conventional illustration, according to one's sympathies one may study crime from the point of view of the criminal or of the law enforcement agencies. Obviously such polar perspectives on the same phenomenon will produce different accounts, but neither need be inaccurate provided that the researcher follows the scientific norms of honest and faithful description of the subject matter. Social scientists feel that the best way to deal with the inevitable interplay of facts and values is to make their normative commitments explicit for themselves and others. Once there is open recognition of the chosen perspective and of the possible sources of bias, objectivity within the perspective can then be pursued.

Coming back to the problem of defining "development," we can now appreciate that any definition must contend with the dual objective of making explicit both its scope and its value premises. In that endeavor let us first clarify what development is not. Development is not to be equated with the sheer growth or increase in scale of a society. Though frequently employed, this approach ignores distributional consequences and fails to answer the question, What kind of growth? Nor is development to be thought of as social change per se, since that notion is vague and directionless. Finally, development is not to be understood as industrialization or "westernization," terms that connote only portions of particular developmental experiences.

Development is defined here as a process of change in the social, economic, and political organization of a society, the principal consequences of which are higher absolute levels of efficient output as well as a broader distribution of benefits. Greater resources and their broader distribution enhance the degree of equality and the range of individual choice that characterize a society and, therefore, enter into the definition as consequences.[48] Development is a generic term and includes, at a minimum, the more specific manifestations of economic, political, and social development. Each of these terms designates a set of societal institutions engaged in the "production" of goods and services, the development of which can be judged by the social organizational arrangements that govern the level and distributional availability of their "products." The development of these institutional spheres results in an enhanced capacity to deal with the human and physical environment among a broader segment of the society.

More specifically, *economic development*, which can be measured fairly well, refers to real increases in material welfare (including but not restricted to income) and greater equality in its distribution. The definition contrasts with others such as "real increase in productivity per head," increases in real income per capita, or an elevated gross product, in that it adds to the emphasis on absolute scale of income and productivity an equal concern for how material benefits are distributed. By implication the definition must include quantitative and qualitative indicators of economic performance and raise as a problematic empirical question the extent to which these go hand in hand, something that has been too readily assumed by researchers employing strictly quantitative measures. Operationally, this study will attempt to measure both aggregate economic indicators of development, with data on gross product, per capita income, and industrialization, and distributional or quality of life indicators such as income distribution, local control of enterprise and profit, and the availability of services, housing, and education. More will be said later about how such indices can be constructed.

In light of our previous remarks, some comments on the normative implications of this definition are required. An egalitarian bias is contained in the general notion of development and in its economic species. A more developed society is characterized by both a higher absolute level of productivity and a more equitable distribution of benefits. This implies that we must weigh (equally) the two dimensions of development and recognize possible conflicts between them. Methodological procedures for doing this will be attended to later. Normatively the definition means that changes that enhance productivity to the detriment of distributional welfare are instances not of development but of retrogression. Changes that enhance productivity but leave distributional consequences unaffected may represent only small gains in development. Each of these statements would probably win easy intellectual agreement, despite the fact that real life analogs seem to produce interminable debates over their merits. More troublesome, perhaps, is the converse. Changes that enhance distributional welfare to the detriment of productivity are regarded here as instances not of development but of retrogression; and changes that enhance distributional welfare but leave productivity unaffected may represent only small gains in development (productivity being distinguished from profit). Although it is tempting to equivocate at this point by saying that sacrifices in productivity that promote material welfare may be morally justified and, therefore, should be termed development, we shall be consistent with the definition in placing equal emphasis on both dimensions. And since we can imagine sources of conflict between the two dimensions—though these are by no means inevitable and may be infrequent empirically—our definition of development will not coincide with various observers' notions of "good."

Two additional notions merit brief comment. Increasingly, students of economic dependency are using the term "misdevelopment" to refer to situations in which the resources of a society are exploited in ways that mainly benefit advanced imperial states and work to the detriment of most segments of that society. Illustrations are abundant but generally involve a very unbalanced economy in which one resource (e.g., agricultural or mineral) is exploited by a small group of local and foreign interests for export to the neglect of other potential sources of development—classic historical examples include Chilean copper, Bolivian tin, Cuban oil and sugar. Whether such conditions of structural dependency are *the* basic problems of development can be debated (and will be later). It seems hardly debatable that such conditions are crucial and must be addressed by our definitions. Although misdevelopment is recognized and treated in this study, it seems to require no special definition, since our conception of development, particularly its distributional emphasis, avoids the pitfalls encountered by narrowly quantitative conceptions that are trapped into regarding misdevelopment (which may raise the GNP and per capita income) as development.

Finally, contemporary observers of various ideological persuasions recognize that a society may be "underdeveloping" or getting poorer for a variety of reasons that include both internal (e.g., population growth) and external (e.g., terms of trade) factors. This, of course, is no profound revelation, but it deserves mention as a corrective to the assumption of unilinear progress contained in evolutionary theories. Again the notion requires no special definition here, since it is easily incorporated in the definition of development based on process. Social science is understandably committed to the value of "progress"; laudable as that may be, it should not blind us to the fact that events are often moving "backwards."

ORGANIZATION OF THE STUDY

The chapters that follow conform generally to the points in our framework for the political economy of development. Chapter 2 offers a brief history of each of the urban centers, with particular attention focused on the theoretically salient conditions, timing of industrialization, and socioeconomic or class structure. Beyond that, the discussion will attempt to convey a feeling for the social life and modernizing experiences of these four regions. The results of the comparative study are reported in the next four chapters. Chapter 3 deals with structures of power and influence, with special attention given to both the constituency of ruling groups and the organizational structure through which they operate. Chapter 4 examines the social backgrounds and developmental ideologies of decision-makers in the four regions. In chapter 5 we take up a number of concrete instances of developmental issues that figured importantly in the recent political life of the areas. Here our theoretical concern is centered on both the priorities and the efficiency of decision-making. Chapter 6 deals with the consequences of all the foregoing factors in terms of quantitative and qualitative developmental accomplishments. Finally, chapter 7 summarizes the results in a more general fashion and stacks them up against several contemporary theoretical interpretations. Finding most of these inadequate to the task of explaining the comparative developmental experiences of the four regions, we suggest some new interpretations for subsequent evaluation. In the spirit of the present chapter we close with some thoughts on the political implications of the study.

2. Social Structure and Economic
Growth in Four Cities of Latin America

The four urban regions that provide the basis of this comparative study present a broad and varied panorama of developmental experiences. Guadalajara and Cali have in the past twenty-five years been the objects of an explosive urbanization taking place in what were earlier rather bucolic trading centers. Most industry is of post–World War II vintage and the service sectors continue to dominate economic life. By contrast, Monterrey and Medellín are distinctive national showcases, justly famed for their early industrialization and independent regional ethos. Yet closer analysis belies the facile assumption that the development of the four regions corresponds systematically to the timing of industrialization. The pattern is a good deal more complex; each area has its distinctive accomplishments and on a number of economic indicators their positions are juxtaposed. The purpose of this chapter is to convey something of the historical experience of economic growth in the regions and to describe their social structures. In the discussion we shall set the stage for the field research and attend to aspects of the first two items of the theoretical framework.

GUADALAJARA, JALISCO, MEXICO

Guadalajara and its environs, the first of our four cases, represents a transitional economy within a more developed nation. Since the first official census of 1895 the state of Jalisco has been among the most populous in Mexico—the largest from 1895 to 1930 and second or third ever since. From the time of that first census, and probably from a good deal earlier, Guadalajara has consistently maintained its status as Mexico's second city.[1] As such it has played a dominant role in the commercial and administrative affairs of western Mexico and served as the "corridor of the north-

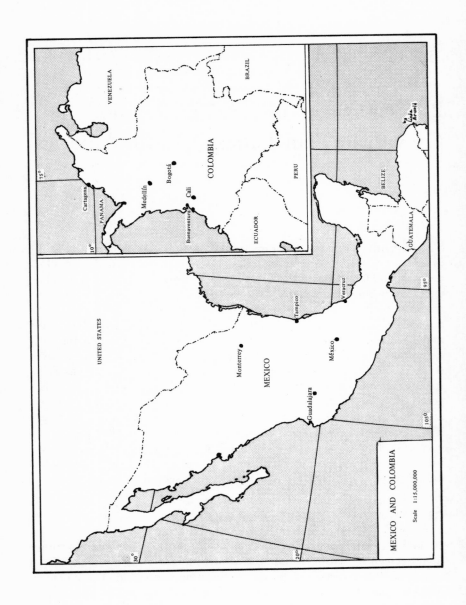

MEXICO AND COLOMBIA   Scale 1:15,000,000

west" between Mexico City and the United States border. Guadalajara has always maintained a well-deserved reputation as one of the most beautiful of Latin American cities. The imprint of the Spanish colonial era is unmistakable in the present layout and architecture of the city, a somewhat remarkable though deliberate achievement given its rapid twentieth-century growth. In some senses the colonial era also left its mark on the city's social structure, although a torrid history of conflict and revolution has created a region of great contrasts along dimensions from the geographic and rural-urban to the economic and social. In many respects Guadalajara is an enigma, though it shares its enigmatic characteristics with other developing areas. It is a region engaged in the "struggle for modernity,"[2] yet struggling with tools fashioned by its historical legacy. Like the rest of Mexico it has put its faith in the revolution, often discovering the painful irony that with modernity closer at hand the aspirations of the revolution are ever more distant.

Followers of Hernán Cortés, the Spanish conqueror of Mexico, first settled the Valley of Atemajac in 1531. After some indecision about the most appropriate location, Guadalajara was founded on its present site in 1542, becoming the administrative center of a vast territory known as Nueva Galicia. In 1546 the Bishopric of Guadalajara was established, followed in 1548 by the *audiencia* (or legal court of the crown); these and the *ayuntamiento* (or municipal government) formed the three pillars of the colonial political system. With gradual success the Spaniards were able to subdue the indigenous Indian population, although revolts persisted for the next two hundred years and a number of free Indian villages survived.

The local economy rested on agriculture, particularly livestock, corn, wheat, and cotton. Agricultural production was organized on the basis of the hacienda system, which entailed several characteristics of social and economic importance. Original settlers were granted *encomiendas* that included both land and an Indian tenant-slave labor force. Strictly speaking, these were not owned by the *hacendado* but held in trust for the crown. In practice, however, they tended to become hereditary fiefs. Indians were commandeered to work as cultivators and domestics, in exchange for which they were provided a small plot of their own. From an economic standpoint the hacienda was notably self-sufficient, providing for the needs of the manor and demanding from, or providing to, the outside world very little. Only the *hacendado* entered into the money economy, through the sale of surplus crops. Once subdued, the Indians received paternalistic treatment of their physical and spiritual needs without having to venture off the lands. In the same sense in which Elkins characterizes North American slavery, the hacienda, from an economic and sociological standpoint, was a "total institution."[3]

The principal occupation of the city of Guadalajara was administering the legal and religious affairs of the vast territory. Commerce, then as now, was fundamental, although colonial economic policy limited its potential. All exports, which included precious metals and agricultural products, were transported to Mexico City, and all imports came from Spain through the same intermediary. Interregional trade was discouraged within both Mexico and the Spanish Empire. The policy, of course, was designed in the interests of Spain and required that the colonies remain underdeveloped and dependent on Spanish imports. Only in the primitive skills of pottery, weaving, tanning, and kindred activities did any artisan industry develop. Regional growth was also stifled by geographical isolation and poor communications.

In political matters the colonial system was even less efficient. Conflicts of authority were endemic to the relations between Guadalajara and Mexico City as well as between local centers of the church, military, and civilian government. Out of these grew a sentiment for regional autonomy that later fueled the independence movement of 1810–1821. In this first of several Mexican revolutions, Guadalajara and Jalisco were to play an important role. The call-to-arms of the wars of independence was issued by Miguel Hidalgo, a fiery priest if a poor military tactician, closely identified with the Indian cause. On September 16, 1810, Hidalgo proclaimed the independence of New Spain in his "grito de Dolores" and on December 6 issued the "Guadalajara Manifesto," which called for the elimination of taxes and slavery and the return of lands to the Indians.[4] Concerning the occasion of this manifesto, it has been observed that "Hidalgo's chief triumph came in the western city of Guadalajara, where he received a royal welcome and was granted the title of Serene Highness."[5]

The economic effects of the wars of independence on Guadalajara were evidently mixed. Hostilities in the countryside produced a heavy urban migration. Prewar population estimates for the city are sketchy but the figure probably stood at around 25,000. One source indicates that by 1823 it had reached 46,804 and by 1827 some 60,000; another, perhaps more reliable, report places the figures at 45,500 in 1838 and 75,000 in 1857.[6] This, of course, led to an expansion of the city's construction industry and commercial potential. The independence-minded local government opened the nearby port of San Blas, whose commercial use was prohibited during the colonial era, but which now permitted trade with Peru, Panama, and the Philippines on more advantageous terms. It is reported that from 1815 to 1819 the Guadalajara customs house realized a fourfold increase in revenues.[7] But widespread fighting during the independence period also brought economic reversals. Evidently the mining industry was hardest hit, but also "the thriving textile industry in Querétaro and in

Guadalajara could no longer be sustained in the absence of raw cotton shipments, and in 1820 these centers produced less than half their accustomed output."[8] Yet these setbacks were probably temporary, and it appears on balance that the first quarter of the nineteenth century brought the beginnings of disinvolvement with the colonial economy.

By the 1840s, traditional industrial activity based on artisan and textile manufactures was being amplified. In 1840 two new textile factories were established. A paper factory begun in 1842 in the town of Tapalpa represented the state's first important industry outside of Guadalajara. Two larger installations for the production of textiles were begun in 1843 and 1844 respectively. Guadalajara was said to have some of the largest factories in the country, including five devoted to textiles, two to paper, and others to liquors, beer, cigarettes, crockery, starch, and soap, in addition to numerous smaller artisan crafts.[9]

But these events were only the very early signs of change in an economic order that by and large retained its colonial character after independence.

It [independence] was, in essence, a minor change at the top, a substitution of the conservative creole for the conservative peninsular and a continuation of the social system created by the class-conscious Spaniard during three hundred years of rule. . . . The government was in the hands of a group whose every intent was to re-create, in all respects save that of political personalities, the dominant colonial patterns.[10]

Nowhere was this more evident than in the rural sectors. It is estimated that in 1855 75 percent of Jalisco's population still lived on ranches and haciendas and in towns of less than 25,000.[11] The lack of agricultural technology and adequate transportation systems prevented the marketing of potentially profitable yields in the urban centers. Much of this arrested development was blamed on the class structure and the indolence of the rural elite.

Of the [non-Indian] ranchers, a small group divided and retained for themselves the greatest part of the product from agricultural activities. *Hacendados*, owners of extensive lands, fearing bandits and insurrections, resided in the cities for most of the year, the largest number being in Guadalajara. They preferred the life of luxury to opulence; the expansion of their domains, not their cultivation, was their pleasure. . . . Technical progress, social reform, democracy and heresy were their favorite abhorrences. Their ideals: in the technical, the use of the old; in the social, the established order; in politics, a strong man able to run the army, and an army sufficient to maintain order; and in ecclesiastical matters, a clergy that repressed Protestants and free thinkers, practiced asceticism, sustained the sect with splendor, and pompously administered the sacraments. In short the reality around them ruled over by Santa Anna. The only alterations desired by the rural landowners could be reduced to two: contain the abuses of the military and the economic concupiscence of the high clergy. It suffices to say that the *hacendados* stood in the ranks of the conservative party.[12]

Under such circumstances, agricultural workers and their families, who made up 90 percent of the rural population, lived in great poverty. Family incomes, estimated at seventy-five pesos a year, were barely sufficient to purchase minimal amounts of corn, beans, chiles, butter, salt, and cloth for making clothes. Medical expenses, baptisms, weddings, and other special expenses were covered with loans from the hacienda that could never be repaid and left the peasant in perpetual debt peonage.

Although this depiction of the class structure applies to the majority of the population, several important qualifications should be made. In Jalisco, more so than in many parts of Mexico, there also existed a class of smallholding agricultural proprietors, though as a rule these Indian and mestizo small farmers occupied the poorest lands. Similarly, in the cities there were small merchants and shopkeepers. No doubt the vast number of administrative functions performed in Guadalajara generated a class of government-church-military bureaucrats. With the city's emphasis on education at all levels, there were probably a moderate-sized educational bureaucracy and a student population. Moreover, given the state of manufacturing technology, much of the region's "industrial" output was produced by small-scale artisans. In short, between the extremes of the upper-class landowners, clergy, and politicians and the lower-class Indian-mestizo peasantry there was an intermediate stratum that, though not sizeable or politically influential, lent a certain distinctiveness to Guadalajara, in contrast to most of Mexico at this time.

Jalisco shared moderately in the material progress of the Porfiriato period (1876–1910). The most important boon was clearly the railroad that linked Guadalajara to Mexico City and other urban centers in 1888, ameliorating one of the oldest problems of regional development. The new service stimulated trade with Mexico City, particularly in textiles, yet at the same time it further emphasized centralization and dependence in trade by eclipsing potential regional commerce, notably through the port of San Blas. In some senses the railroad streamlined colonial trade dependence on the capital.

Nevertheless, industry was expanding, and by 1880 the city counted some eighty furniture makers, twelve each of carriage and candle factories, four each of book binderies, gilding shops, and soap factories, numerous textile mills, and other establishments producing silk, apparel, china, glass, starch, paper, tobacco, beer, tequila, and many other products.[13] Local businessmen interested in the possibilities of further manufacturing held their first industrial exposition in 1888. In the sixty years prior to 1900, Guadalajara's population increase was said to be "enormous," arriving at 101,208 by the turn of the century and at ever-increasing growth rates per annum.[14]

In contrast to its role in earlier periods of national upheaval, Jalisco's part in the revolution of 1910 was relatively minor. Several factors seem to account for this unexpected circumstance. In the first place, Guadalajara was somewhat distant from the geopolitical center of the revolution, which was Mexico City, its surrounding states, and the northern states that served as staging areas for insurgent forces. Second, in Jalisco the conditions motivating the revolution, such as foreign economic control and complete *latifundia* domination of the countryside, were *relatively* less pernicious than in other states, such as Morelos. Although the class structure was far from egalitarian, there is still merit in the observation that "small rural proprietors, students, wage workers on the haciendas and in commerce, professionals and the greater part of the public officials considered themselves, in the majority and with pride, as of the middle class."[15] Finally, Jalisco's political culture was more disposed to the passions of political theory than revolution. In a somewhat defensive tract in reaction to the charge that Jalisco was outside of the revolutionary mainstream, Zuno observes that the great contribution of Guadalajara's liberal intellectuals was in providing the ideas for social reorganization.[16]

Yet this is not to imply that Guadalajara was quiescent during the revolutionary period of 1910–1917. In the early years there were extensive demonstrations against the government by students and socialist workers.[17] Federal troops occupied the area to protect the larger haciendas and the much-resented monopolistic electricity company. Although local forces were said to be ineffective against these federal troops, the railway system was seized and put in the service of Carranza's insurgents to the north. In July of 1914 Guadalajara came under the control of the revolutionary movement when Obregón routed federal troops. A counterattack early in 1915 against Pancho Villa's army, then resident in Guadalajara, produced the fiercest fighting in the area. With the revolutionary victory of 1917, several prominent figures from Jalisco received important positions in Carranza's new government.

It was the aftermath of the revolution that brought the decisive changes shaping Guadalajara's contemporary political economy. The main effect of these changes can be summarized with the observation that a revolutionary political party broke the back of the landowner-church elite and replaced it as the ruling class.

Concerning the church, the Constitution of 1917 reflected the strong anticlerical mood of the revolutionaries, who, for the most part correctly, perceived the church as the bulwark of the old order. Most important, the church was prevented from holding any real property. The immediate post-revolutionary years witnessed protracted conflict between the new government and Jalisco's clergy, terminating ultimately in the bloody Cristero rebellion of 1927, which led President Calles to deport all of Guadalajara's bishops and church leaders.[18]

The second major act in the dismantling of the old order was land reform. Once official determination to pursue land reform became clear, the security of land tenure and agricultural investment evaporated, discouraging further investment. "When wholesale expropriation of land began to take place and made farm land a precarious investment, the large landowners salvaged what assets they could and fled to such cities as Mexico City, Guadalajara and Monterrey. They invested their savings in real estate, industry and commerce."[19]

With respect to the effects of land reform in Jalisco, some careful appraisals are in order. Aside from obvious political considerations and special concessions to revolutionary heroes, Mexican land reform was guided by practical norms such as existing inequities of distribution, arability of land, and the number of tenants prior to parcelization. All of these factors influenced the size and number of plots awarded. Comprehensive national figures indicate that in 1915 the typical size (inequality) of holdings in Jalisco was below the average and that a higher percentage of those holdings were under cultivation or in use.[20] For example, 1933 figures show that in Jalisco private large (1,000 hectares or more) farms represented 58 percent of the land and 2 percent of the farms, while on a national basis they were 83 percent of the land and 2.2 percent of the farms. Similarly, Jalisco ranked only fifteenth among thirty-two Mexican states and territories in arable land, but fourth in the amount of that land in use. Thus, by national standards the picture is unmistakably one of smaller and more productive patterns of land tenure. Nevertheless, by 1944 Jalisco ranked eighth in the amount of land distributed and third in the number of recipients.[21] These observations taken together—i.e., that land reform was, on the average, more extensive in an area where it was "needed" less— suggest that rural Jalisco was affected substantially by land reform and that a debilitating form of social and economic organization inherited from colonial days was effectively dismantled. And, of course, the great significance of this lay in the fact that it was accomplished in a head-on clash between the revolutionary party and the landowners.

These were the fruits of the revolution in Jalisco. The church maintained its strong following but lost its economic power and its decisive influence in politics. The large landowners repaired to the cities, often acquiring urban properties and commercial interests, while the smallholders gained control of the countryside. The old order was broken, and into the breach stepped the representatives of a new ruling class drawn from the ranks of the revolutionary party and the rapidly growing community of merchants and industrialists.

The political situation in Jalisco began to stabilize in direct proportion to the consolidation of power nationally under the revolutionary party. It was during the widely commended, and occasionally feared, governorship of J. Jesús González Gallo (1947–1953) that Guadalajara entered the modern era. González Gallo is reported to have been a forceful and visionary leader with strong ties to the federal government. The major ambition of his regime was modernization of the city of Guadalajara, whose population was expanding with such rapidity that existing urban services were under serious strain. (See table 2.) To meet the crisis the governor, with substantial help from the federal treasury, launched a series of urban infrastructure projects, including widening the principal thoroughfares of the city, a new railroad station, a central bus terminal, a beautified civic center, low-cost housing, sanitary services and drainage, and a major hydro-electric system designed to meet the critically dwindling supply of water and power.

This program of urban reconstruction was characterized by many dramatic events. During the widening of one of the streets it was discovered that the proposed route would pass directly through the headquarters of the federally owned telephone company. Undaunted in their ambitions, local officials commissioned an engineering firm to raise the building from its foundations and, without disrupting telephone service, move it backward some sixty feet, allowing the street to pass. In the civic center, several square blocks around the main cathedral were razed and replaced with elegant plazas. Local legend has it that González Gallo was able to achieve this by eliciting the archbishop's aid to obtain the land in exchange for a promise that the finished plazas around the cathedral would form the shape of a cross. These are just two examples of the costly attention given to the urban beautification program for which Guadalajara has become justly renowned.

As table 3 indicates, these years also witnessed a rapid rate of population growth. From 1940 to 1960 Jalisco was second only to the Federal District in terms of the percentage of the population living in urban (2,500 or more) places. From 1940 to 1950 the mean annual increase in Guadalajara's population was 4.9 percent and from 1950 to 1960 some 6.4

TABLE 3

POPULATION OF GUADALAJARA AND JALISCO IN SELECTED YEARS

	Guadalajara Population	Percent Increase	Jalisco Population	Percent Increase
1885	91,685			
1895	93,934	8.5		
1900	101,208	20.5	1,153,891	
1910	119,468	18.0	1,208,855	4.7
1921	143,376	20.0	1,191,957	- 1.4
1930	179,556	25.2	1,255,346	5.3
1940	229,234	27.7	1,418,310	13.0
1950	377,016	64.5	1,746,777	23.1
1960	736,800	95.4	2,443,261	39.9
1968	1,250,000	69.6	3,300,000	35.1

SOURCES: María Teresa Gutiérrez, *Geodemografía del Estado de Jalisco*, and *Jalisco ofrece.*

percent, and in each of these ten-year periods the increase due to urban migration was greater than that stemming from natural increase (3.0 of the 4.9 figure from 1940 to 1950 and 3.7 of the 6.4 from 1950 to 1960).[22]

Naturally this urban growth was a stimulus to commerce and the construction industry. But at the same time a variety of new enterprises were taking root. Table 4 indicates a steady increase in new business ventures since 1941, with the exception of several years in the mid-fifties that correspond to the crisis in electrical power supply. Since 1962 activity has accelerated but on a pre-existing broad base; another tabulation indicates that by 1965 there were 8,672 industrial establishments in the state of Jalisco doing over five billion pesos annually in the value of production.[23]

The principal industrial activities in Guadalajara are food products, beverages, textiles, shoes, animal feed, metal plating, industrial lubricants, and metal products. A growing number of foreign-owned firms have been attracted to the city owing to its hospitable environs and infrastructure capacities (i.e., industrial sites, gas, water, electricity). Although no precise estimates are available, foreign ownership or control is evident in perhaps a third of the larger enterprises, such as Kodak, Sears, Corn Products, Nestlé, Ralston Purina, Anderson Clayton, Burroughs, Motorola, Phillip Morris, Celanese, and Union Carbide. More typical, however, is the presence of firms owned by Monterrey and Mexico City interests. With several

TABLE 4

NEW ENTERPRISES ESTABLISHED AND CAPITAL
INVESTED IN JALISCO, 1941–1967

Years	Number of Enterprises	Capital Invested (Pesos)
1941–43	33	18,005,000
1944–46	75	31,298,500
1947–49	30	17,865,000
1950–52	37	51,930,325
1953–55	25	47,480,000
1956–58	21	67,778,800
1959–61	34	63,605,000
1962–64	65	371,706,000
1965–67	34	572,829,000
	354	1,242,497,625

SOURCE: *Jalisco ofrece*, p. 37.

notable exceptions in shoes, food oils, textiles, apparel, construction, metal products, soft drinks, and tequila, it would appear that nearly half of the larger investments are not locally controlled.

A second outstanding characteristic of Guadalajara industry is its small to medium size and the dispersion of its ownership, particularly in artisan crafts and light manufacturing. When the nine major industrial activities in Guadalajara and Monterrey are compared, Guadalajara has about three times as many establishments (253 versus 77), with about a third of the value of production (769,048,000 versus 2,028,633,000 pesos), and roughly a fourth of the capital invested (583,796,000 versus 2,277,631,000 pesos), or a ratio of less than 1 to 10 in the capital invested per firm. As we shall see, the comparison with Monterrey may be somewhat unfair, given the latter's dramatic history of industrial development. But these figures do accurately reflect a pattern of dispersed ownership and small- to medium-sized firms as characteristic features of Guadalajara's industrial structure.

Concerning the overall economic structure of Jalisco, table 5 indicates that over the years the labor force occupied in primary activities has steadily declined, with manufacturing ("transformation") and construction industries, along with commerce and services, picking up the surplus. The sectoral distribution of gross product presented in table 6 has

TABLE 5

POPULATION ECONOMICALLY ACTIVE IN JALISCO (In Percent)

Year	Agriculture, Livestock, Fishing	Industry				Commerce	Trans-portaion	Services	Unspecified and Unemployed	Total (N)
		Extrac-tive	Trans-formation	Construc-tion	Elec-tricity, Gas					
1947	60.16	0.34	12.09	2.89	0.25	9.02	2.38	8.20	4.64	99.97 (516,870)
1957	54.19	0.51	14.79	4.06	0.33	10.39	3.00	11.18	1.55	100.00 (684,998)
1967	45.44	1.02	17.22	5.31	0.31	12.54	3.84	14.12	0.18	99.98 (989,026)

SOURCE: Jalisco, Mexico: estimates of the State Department of Economics based on census data.

TABLE 6

ORIGIN OF GROSS REGIONAL PRODUCT IN JALISCO
AT CONSTANT PRICES (In Percent)

	1957	1967
Primary sector	18.60	20.28
Agriculture	10.27	12.48
Livestock	7.74	7.40
Forestry	0.54	0.30
Fishing	0.05	0.10
Secondary sector	25.10	27.13
Mining	1.36	1.73
Transformation	20.40	21.58
Construction	2.61	3.24
Electric	0.73	0.58
Tertiary sector	56.30	52.59
Commerce	17.88	21.48
Services	7.59	9.79
Banking	5.96	4.94
Government	12.56	7.04
Communication and Transportation	12.31	9.34

SOURCE: Jalisco, Mexico: estimates of the State Department of Economics.

changed only slightly in the ten-year period covered. Agricultural and manufacturing activities make about the same contribution and, as is characteristic of developing economies, the tertiary sector is dominant. This, too, is particularly characteristic of Guadalajara, long a center of commerce, administration, and other services.

Two final observations on the regional economy help to round out this description. First, investor mentality in Guadalajara has always been noticeably conservative, preferring land and fixed rentals to higher-risk industrial investment. The amount of money locally on deposit in savings accounts is said to be quite high in contrast to that in other cities and has frequently been a point of the development-minded politicians' criticism of the business community. No doubt this financial conservatism has structural roots in the special "rationality" generated by an agriculturally-based society. Second, according to Mendoza, Jalisco's food-processing industry represents about 60 percent of all manufacturing, and the peculiar disadvantage of this lies in the fact that about 80 percent of the inputs to this industry are in the form of primary goods, inhibiting any notable industrial integration or economically stimulating backward and forward linkage effects.[24] One of the principal features of Guadalajara's economic development to date is its structural rigidity, based on the disproportionate importance of food processing, and, conversely, the relative dearth of linkages among manufacturing enterprises.

This description of contemporary economic organization suggests the existence of a relatively open and egalitarian class structure by national standards. In the rural sector, undoubtedly, there still exists extensive poverty, particularly in *ejido* and Indian communities. Nevertheless, historic patterns of land tenure coupled with land reform imply a proportionately large number of small proprietors. In the city there is a sizeable urban proletariat made up of construction workers, street vendors, transportation workers, and similar unskilled persons. But, again, the economic structure generates a substantial lower-middle- to middle-class stratum peopled by artisans, small-scale industrialists, merchants, public employees, and salaried employees in commerce and industry. Finally, the absence of large agricultural or industrial interests means that the upper class is less in evidence than in other major cities. This speculation (and it must be speculation in the absence of systematic studies of class structure) appears to be borne out by comparative national figures on income distribution indicating a smaller proportion of Guadalajara's population at either of the extremes of wealth and poverty.[25] Thus, when contrasted with the nation as a whole and with other major urban centers, the middle sectors are better represented in Guadalajara's class structure.

Events of the last forty years have brought great changes in the historically separatist and antagonistic relationship between Jalisco and Mexico City. With the consolidation of political power under the one-party system the national government strengthened its presence in localities throughout the republic. In Jalisco it aggressively intervened to break up the old elite through the application of land and church reform laws. Later, particularly after the regime of González Gallo, the federal government became an active partner in local development through the provision of extensive infrastructure projects, including, among the several already mentioned, a much improved system of rail, highway, and air communications bringing Guadalajara and the capital into ever closer contact.

Moreover, following the destruction of the old order a new elite of politician-developmentalists grew up in the void. Since, under the one-party system, the careers of these "new men of power" depended on their favor in Mexico City and their ability to implement federally planned developmental schemes, cooperative state-national relationships were self-sustaining. In this respect Jalisco seemed to excel, many of its ex-governors and political leaders going on to higher posts in national politics. A closely related change took place with respect to the public and private sectors. In Guadalajara the bulk of the new economic investments in industry and commerce were post-revolutionary, coming on a scene increasingly under the control of the political party elite. This in turn required that the private sector accept federal authority and assistance. Public-private collaboration was not only the most prudent course but, increasingly, the only alternative. And the new economic community found enough aspirations for local development in common with the public sector for them to be able to work together in relative harmony.

In addition to this trend toward federal-local convergence, Jalisco retains many of its distinctive regional traits. The church is still probably more influential than in other sections of the country; Guadalajara is the home of Mexico's only cardinal. In matters of general economic and social policy the residents of Guadalajara appear more conservative than those of other major cities. Similarly, the city maintains its traditional role as a center of cultural activities and education, with four universities that draw students from a number of surrounding states. Among Jalisco's most revered native sons are a number of nationally- and in some cases world-famed muralists, poets, writers, and artisans.

MONTERREY, NUEVO LEÓN, MEXICO

Monterrey, our second case, represents the design parameters of early industrialization within a more developed national context. To Mexicans generally and to the people of Nuevo León, or the *regiomontanos* as they proudly identify themselves, Monterrey represents a great deal more. The city's early and frankly spectacular achievements in the area of industrialization have led to chronicles that describe it variously as an "industrial miracle," "the Chicago of Mexico," and "the Sultan of the North." A strong sense of austere pragmatism attributes this miracle, not to divine Providence, but to "the work of men in short sleeves," an example of Mexican effort and ingenuity. The psychological significance of these laurels for a developing nation are undeniable. Yet the facts of Monterrey's development are much more complex. Like the rest of our cases, Monterrey does not constitute a model of developmental achievement; its historical path has been unique and its accomplishments mixed. Against a background of substantial material progress the city has lagged in several critical fields of human welfare. Moreover, the numbers who have shared in the miracle may be fewer than is desirable.

Northeastern Mexico was settled roughly fifty years after the conquest of the central region. The first reported exploration of the area was in 1577, but hostile Indian clans and unpredictable climatic conditions, alternating between droughts and floods, resisted any permanent settlement until 1596, when Monterrey was founded on its present site. The first provincial governor was appointed in 1599, with the territory placed under the military, civil, and judicial jurisdiction of Mexico City but under the ecclesiastical governance of the Bishopric of Guadalajara. In these early years the most serious problem of the nascent colonial town was a legion of Indians engaged in settled agriculture and organized in loosely federated tribes that fiercely resisted domination. Indian wars were chronic through 1650 as the town was attempting to gain a foothold on the territory and, indeed, persisted with regularity until the 1800s.

The region developed very gradually during the eighteenth century. After modest beginnings the mining industry was vitalized by a rich silver strike in 1757 that was soon followed by others. Though still a relatively somnolent colonial town, Monterrey began to function as a trade and distribution center for the mining areas. Perhaps because of Monterrey's remoteness from Mexico City, commercial activity departed from the colonial pattern of dependency. One important early source of trade was in contraband such as tobacco, consumer goods, and firearms introduced into Mexico from the north via Monterrey.[26] Similarly the gulf coast port of Soto la Marina, opened in 1781, provided local traders a unique resource, because the rest of the country was required to send and receive all goods via Mexico City and the port of Vera Cruz.

Nevertheless, Monterrey entered the wars of independence a relatively isolated and inconsequential colonial town. The mainstay of the economy was agriculture, principally livestock, corn, beans, sugar cane, and wheat. While this economy was notably humble, it had the distinct potential advantage of lying at the margins of the colonial ambit. In agriculture the hacienda system was not prevalent, due to poor soil conditions and a relatively indomitable Indian population. For the most part, large estates could not be profitably operated, slave labor was difficult to consign, and neither justified the risks of defending extensive properties against hostilities. Conversely, opportunities in commerce were increasing in a region somewhat unfettered by colonial imposition of dependence.

By 1824 the city numbered 11,044. The ports of Tampico and Matamoros had been opened, giving Monterrey a decisive advantage in controlling the trade of the northeast between the sea and the interior, an area that contributed reasonably to the domestic economy but was distinguished by its export trade.[27] As noted in Montemayor's definitive history of Monterrey, the economy of the region was based on agriculture (the cultivation of beans, corn, sugar cane) and cattle raising; nevertheless, a specialized artisan industry was forming, dedicated to a variety of activities: shoemakers, carpenters, blacksmiths, tailors, potters, tanners, silversmiths, stone masons, weavers, sailmakers, barbers, bakers, seamstresses, fireworks makers. At the time, commerce was gaining importance: in 1824, fourteen clothing stores and thirty grocery stores are mentioned; in 1831 there were thirty-one of the former and eighty-five of the latter. Foreign-made apparel was sold and well liked by the population, and Mexican clothing was also desired, though on a lesser scale.[28]

This experience of peace and prosperity during the first quarter-century of Mexican independence reached an end when Monterrey became embroiled in the Mexican-American War. Indeed, the years of 1846–1876 were as chaotic for the northeast as they were for the rest of the country.

One of the earliest battles of the Mexican-American War was fought squarely in the city, where Zachary Taylor's army was met by the patriotically aroused citizenry of Nuevo León. For five days during September of 1846 the pitched conflict raged, and when it was over the North Americans victoriously occupied the devastated and depopulated city. During the twenty months of the occupation the economy stagnated and the city fell into further disrepair. Yet the talisman of Monterrey's early history was still working. The nationally disastrous loss of half the Mexican territory to the United States was ironically beneficial to Monterrey. The city now became Mexico's closest important commercial link to the United States border, which resulted in new trade opportunities and enhancement of the traffic in contraband.

In the post-war years the states of Coahuila and Nuevo León came increasingly under the control of the regional caudillo Santiago Vidaurri, who promoted political stability and commercial expansion by establishing Monterrey as the customs control center for the nation's northern ports and frontier.[29] It was during this period that the first important industries were established in Monterrey—the first sugar mill in 1853 and, with Vidaurri's support, the first textile mill in 1854. Population growth kept apace of these changes, reaching a reported 26,000 in 1856.[30]

In these years Monterrey's independence from the federal government grew more evident for economic and political reasons. Vidaurri was often in conflict with Benito Juárez over the role of the northeast in the new nation. This ill will was heightened when an Austin, Texas, newspaper story was circulated in Mexico claiming that Vidaurri planned to promote an independent Nuevo León–Coahuila state to unite with Texas in a new republic to be called Sierra Madre.[31] Although the story was probably untrue, it was nevertheless true that Monterrey's spirit of political autonomy ran high. Most notably, it was fueled by economic prosperity derived from the substantial export trade between regional port cities and the Atlantic-blockaded Confederate States of America during the (North American) Civil War of 1861–1865.

Yet by 1866 another economic crisis had befallen the city. Industrial development had not progressed beyond the sugar and textile mills established more than a decade earlier. Commerce was in a slump because of the end of the United States Civil War and the destruction of several important market centers and commercial houses during the war with France. The mining industry in the Sierra had declined seriously, with a consequent reduced demand for commercial trade. Moreover, local commercial enterprises were now suffering from the trade in contraband that cut seriously into the internal consumer market. Public works had been neglected and the urban environment was a shambles. But it was in response to these fortunes that Monterrey began on its course of industrialization. Indeed, Vizcaya's excellent analysis, *The Origins of the Industrialization of Monterrey*, dates the period of Monterrey's entry into a modern industrial economy from 1867 to 1920.

Several important changes were afoot during the early transition period. In the field of communications Monterrey was tied into the national telegraph system in 1869, and by 1876 a network of roads connected the city to Piedras Negras in the north, the port city of Matamoros to the east, and Mexico City southward.[32] In 1872 a second important textile mill was established, followed by a third in 1874. In the ensuing years these three mills (La Fama, El Porvenir, La Leona) expanded and adopted more modern technology, thus representing for some the real beginnings of industrialization.[33] In 1873 the state began the first systematic statistical accounting, reporting the population of Nuevo León at 178,872 and Monterrey at 33,811.[34] Another estimate placed the city at about 30,000 in 1880.[35]

The changes that laid the foundation for industrialization began to accelerate in the 1880s. As we have seen, the thirty-five-year reign of Porfirio Díaz, which began in 1876, placed heavy emphasis on infrastructure works, notably railroads. The railway construction begun in Monterrey in 1881 had a significant impact on the region. By 1884 rail links were established with Saltillo and with Laredo on the United States border and by 1898 with the entire national system via the port of Tampico and Mexico City. Interestingly, the railroad had divergent effects on Monterrey's economy. It sounded the death knell of commerce by opening the region to Mexico City markets and suppliers as well as by providing easy access to the border, with regular "shoppers' trains" from Monterrey commuting to the free trade zone. Local consumers were reported to be putting off major purchases until these trips, when they could obtain the preferred United States manufactured goods of every description. Conversely, inexpensive railway transport was soon to provide an important advantage to industry for shipping exports to the gulf coast and consumer goods throughout the country.

From a political standpoint, the most crucial cause of the imminent industrial boom was the appointment of General Bernardo Reyes as the regional military commander and provisional governor in 1884. Although Reyes was dispatched by Díaz to maintain order in the recalcitrant region, he proved to be an enormously capable and popular administrator, remaining as the elected governor until 1909.

The Reyes administration is legendary in Nuevo León, and deservedly so. In his first year in office the new governor broadened the laws for industrial promotion through tax exemptions and, on his own initiative, granted some 1,300 urban properties to people intent on starting new businesses.[36] In politics his decisive achievement was to restore peace among factional groups. In administration he successfully attacked perennial problems by developing an excellent system of uniform tax collection and, with the increased public revenues, launched a number of badly needed urban works, including water supply, renovation of the central plaza, bridges, a penitentiary, a carriage-drawn municipal transportation system, and a number of colleges and secondary schools. And, of course, his greatest achievement lay in the active encouragement of new industry. Important to the governor's success was the fact that, unlike earlier regional leaders, he had strong support from the federal government. Reyes enjoyed great prestige for the honesty and efficiency of his government, and he used this resource in personal efforts to attract new industrial investment. As a result, there developed a climate of mutual confidence and close working relations between the public and private sectors unprecedented even for Monterrey. Reyes got results, and it was the governor himself who, surveying his work, dubbed Monterrey the Chicago of Mexico.

The fruits of all these efforts to convert Monterrey into an industrial center were borne between 1890 and 1900. The year of 1890 was probably the most dramatic in local history, since it witnessed the establishment of the two pillars of Monterrey's economy, the beer and steel industries. The initial steel mill was small and soon to be eclipsed by two mammoth firms in this field. But the brewery—Cervecería Cuauhtémoc—was to become the fountainhead of an industrial dynasty. The founders of this new enterprise were men of modest means acquired in commerce. When one of the co-founders (Isaac Garza) married the daughter of another (Consuelo Sada), the basis was established for a group of family capitalists that to this day plays the leading role in the region's industrial economy.[37]

In classical entrepreneurial fashion the Garza-Sada family became the "Monterrey Industrial Group" as their enterprises snowballed from beer to glass for the beer bottles, to the potash for manufacturing the glass for the bottles, and so forth. A number of forward linkages also were generated in packaging, merchandising, and finance, each with its own spinoffs. In addition to the fact that the Garza-Sada group was to become the dominant force in the industrialization of Monterrey, the case is important for three reasons. First, it indicates characteristically that the capital requirements for the new industry were met by the fortunes accumulated earlier in commerce. Second, it shows that Monterrey's industrial pioneers were, for the most part, people of middle-class origins, not poor but certainly not a privileged elite. Finally, as has been noted in more general discussions, the typically "traditional" extended family, with its inherent trust and capital-pooling capabilities, was a key instrument for Monterrey's modernization.[38]

In the same year the brewery was founded, ten other industries were begun, four in steel, smelting, and the manufacture of metal products and others devoted to furniture, apparel, cigarettes, soft drinks, soap, and bricks. By 1892 fourteen new factories were in operation, with investments of a million and one-half pesos and some 800 workers.[39] Unlike the Garza-Sada group, a number of these enterprises invited United States investors, including Daniel Guggenheim, who invested in one of the steel companies. Germans, Italians, and Spaniards also invested heavily, and for a time these foreign investors may have had controlling interests in the major firms. But, if that was temporarily true, it was short-lived as new locally-financed enterprises continued to spring up.[40] After the brewery, the second great industry was the Fundidora iron and steel mill established in 1900. Here, too, foreign capital participated, though the founder and holder of the controlling interest was Adolfo Prieto, a Spaniard who spent most of his life in Mexico. The keystone industries, Cuauhtémoc and Fundidora, were followed in the early years of the century by a variety of others in the familiar fields of metals, glass, textiles, apparel, furniture, soap, leather goods, food products, construction materials, bus and carriage bodies, and machinery, along with a plethora of artisan and satellite industries. Monterrey's industrial growth rate during this period was unparalleled; in 1906 there were nearly twenty thousand factory workers, and capital invested in industry approached forty billion pesos, increasing at a rate of 30 percent per year.[41] In 1910 Nuevo León led the nation in industrial production and, effectively, this means Monterrey, where nearly all of the important industry was located.[42]

The factors that explain Monterrey's luminary industrial achievements are several and derive from its own resources as well as its unique relations with the national and international economy. Taking these up in reverse order, we have already noted how Monterrey prospered in export trade from the opening of its ports in the 1820s, in the early traffic in contraband, and, later, in trade with the Confederate States. In 1890 Monterrey's trade with the United States was seriously affected by the passage of the McKinley Tariff Act, the first in a series of protectionist measures, which raised the duties on non-precious ores coming into the United States by some 50 percent. Although the act was designed to benefit United States mining interests, it also had the ironic consequence of stimulating the iron and steel industry in Monterrey, since the opportunity was presented for local smelting and refining of iron ore mined in the northeast and now denied an export market. Indicative of the international origins of Monterrey's heavy industry was the fact that among the early pioneers of steel mills in the region were the Guggenheims, whose Puebla, Colorado, plant had relied on iron ore from Chihuahua. With imported ore now at a prohibitive cost, Guggenheim and two other United States manufacturers of steel set up mills in the most likely Mexican site according to the criteria of raw material availability and export opportunities, and that was Monterrey. Fortunately, local capitalists were sufficiently solvent and astute to join in this new initiative and shortly take control of it.

Within the Mexican national context, industrialization in Monterrey also benefited from the policies of the Porfirio Díaz regime. The railroad opened up new internal markets for manufactured goods and provided easier access to export points on the United States border and the gulf coast. Even more directly, the massive construction projects that Díaz undertook spurred demand for local manufactures such as steel rails, passenger cars, structural steel, and related goods essential to infrastructure works. Finally, Díaz's measures to revive the moribund mining industry, albeit under foreign control, benefited Monterrey, which processed much of the ore and supplied the mines.

From a more exclusively local standpoint there were additional causes of Monterrey's industrialization. Clearly the city's location, a backwash in the colonial days, proved especially fortunate for subsequent commerce. Of fundamental historical importance was the relative immunity of the region from the debilitating dependence of colonialism. And this was due to circumstances beyond mere location. Although the proximity of seaports and their early use is of note, interregional trade was probably not great before independence. More important, it would seem, was the fact that the region was inhospitable to extensive agriculture and the self-sufficient hacienda system.

Vizcaya condenses his explanation of local development into the following words:

> The factors that provoked the industrialization of Monterrey can, consequently, be summarized as follows: a) external: 1) the McKinley Tariff, 2) construction of railroads, 3) abundance of foreign capital, 4) consolidation of the Porfirist [Díaz] regime; and b) internal: 1) industrial protection laws, 2) sources of capital already existent in the city, 3) availability of moderately skilled labor, 4) influence of General Bernardo Reyes, 5) proximity of Monterrey to the United States, 6) the greater amount of water than in other important northern cities of the country, and 7) the enterprising spirit of the *regiomontanos*.[43]

As Mexico's leading industrial center in 1910, Monterrey was only indirectly affected by the revolution and its aftermath. Most of the problems animating the revolution, such as land reform, foreign domination, political corruption, Díaz's tyranny, or the degradation of national pride, were relatively absent from Monterrey. The story of the revolution in Monterrey concerns less how the social order was transformed than how local industrialists and national revolutionaries came to terms.

This is not to say that the revolution had no impact locally. The city represented a valuable prize for adversary armies and in 1913 was the site of major fighting between the forces of Huerta and those of the revolutionary caudillo of the north, Carranza. Although Huerta's army prevailed in this encounter, it was routed from the city within a year by Pancho Villa, who terrified the local business elite and extorted from the Chamber of Commerce a large "donation" to support his troops.[44] Under these circumstances, many of Monterrey's merchants and industrialists went into exile in the United States.

When the revolution ended in 1917, Monterrey found itself in economic stagnation and unparalleled urban decay. The flight of the upper economic groups during the struggle had left the city functioning only slightly above a subsistence level, not that they could have prospered had they stayed, with the entire national economy at a standstill. Rural violence led to the migration of over 7,000 people to Monterrey, bringing the 1921 population to 88,479. This influx produced even greater strains on deficiencies in urban housing, services, and employment. Industrialists and merchants returned and reinitiated their activities, but they were skeptical of the intentions of the revolutionary government and cautious in new investment that might be lost to irresponsible socialist schemes, as they viewed some of the policies of the new order.

Nevertheless, these fears slowly abated with increasing signs of political stability. More important to the business community, government acquitted itself well with the passage of the Law for Protection of New Industries, which provided a 75 percent reduction of taxes for ten to twenty years, depending on the importance of the new enterprise. Under the encouragement of this measure, 150 new enterprises were begun.[45] By 1930 all growth indicators were up: the city's population had increased a remarkable 50 percent plus since 1921, reaching 137,387; a record 438 factories employed 24,350 workers, with over 153 million pesos invested and a weekly payroll of 730,500 pesos; average salaries were the highest in the country; banking and financial institutions were doing an unprecedented volume of business; and on the social side the percentage of the population enrolled in educational institutions was half again the national average, and amenities like the telephone were ten times more common in Monterrey than in the nation.[46]

Yet with all of these gains the industrialists who constituted the power structure of Monterrey were not reconciled to the leftist ways of the federal government. Prominent among their misgivings were the issues of "socialist education," that is, the federal monopoly in primary and secondary schools; "local democracy," or the right to select official party candidates for municipal and state office rather than having them imposed by Mexico City; and, particularly, federal labor law versus Monterrey's right to maintain "independent" (i.e., company) unions. Some of these concerns were pacified in February of 1936 when President Cárdenas came to Monterrey and met with a delegation from the economic community. The meeting was amicable, with local leaders evidently impressed by the president's handling of himself. A few concessions were granted by both sides. The president indicated that while his administration was forcefully committed to improving the lot of the worker through unionization, he also conceded that the Monterrey industrialists had nothing to be alarmed about. Local leaders reiterated their opposition to unions organized through the official party but acknowledged the problem of the worker and offered cooperation through the provision of low-cost housing.

In general, relations between Monterrey and the federal government continued to swing from peaceful coexistence to thinly-veiled antagonism. An unprecedented show of unity with the central authority came in 1938, when Cárdenas expropriated British and American oil interests in Mexico, turning oil into a nationalized industry. Ideological principles aside, the Monterrey group was patriotically inspired by the expulsion of the foreign capitalists and sponsored a huge public demonstration to convey their feelings. Yet in other matters they continued to regard the government as dangerously radical, particularly when several serious labor problems arose in the late 1930s. But the earlier response of withholding investment during periods of political uncertainty had been abandoned. According to Saldaña, the industrialists reasoned that, if a communist system was imposed, then they would need their strength to establish a new regime and, in short, should not cut their own throats.[47] But local anxiety was not justified by the actual course of events. "The 1930s witnessed the entrance of the state into ownership of such important industries as electric power and petroleum, but contrary to some detractors of Cárdenas, who tried to represent the Revolutionary as a Communist, his economic policies harmed few Mexican industrialists."[48]

In any event, Cárdenas's term was up in 1940, and he was followed by Avila Camacho, a man more to the tastes of the northeast. With the outbreak of World War II, Monterrey's economy began to boom as never before, and there was little time for political fretting. The following figures give some impression of the local impact of the war.[49]

	1937	1942	1946
Number of Industries	438	551	650
Capital Invested (in millions of pesos)	153	227	409

The number of local industries increased by half in nine years, while the capital invested increased about one and two-thirds times, indicating substantial growth, most of it in already existing firms. Notable among these, of course, was the steel industry supplying the United States war effort.

Thirty years after the revolution, Monterrey had made its peace with the new society and had returned to doing what it did best, coming out, as it had so often before, on top.

Monterrey's rapid expansion did not terminate with the war. Incredibly, capital invested in industry tripled between 1946 and 1950, passing the one billion mark; in the next fourteen years it increased more than six-fold and between 1964 and 1968 nearly doubled, reaching a figure of fourteen billion.

Population estimates indicate a parallel trend, with the metropolitan area nearly doubling in size between 1940 and 1950 and between 1950 and 1960, then beginning to taper off somewhat (table 7). In the larger context, Monterrey was growing much faster than Mexico as a whole and the state of Nuevo León, which implies, as the figures indicate, a growing concentration of the state's population in the capital city. This, in turn, is reflected in the fact that Nuevo León ranked third in the percentage of the

TABLE 7

POPULATION INCREASE OF THE MONTERREY METROPOLITAN AREA AND THE STATE OF NUEVO LEON

Year	Monterrey Metropolitan Area[a]	Percent Growth[a]	Percent Growth of Mexico[a]	State of Nuevo León[b]	Percent Growth	Metropolitan Area as % of State
1880	30,000	--	--	272,000	--	11.0
1900	62,000	--	--	328,000	20.6	18.9
1910	79,000	27	11	365,000	11.3	21.6
1921	88,000	11	- 6	336,500	- 7.8	26.2
1930	134,000	52	16	417,500	24.1	32.1
1940	186,000	39	19	541,000	30.0	34.4
1950	356,000	91	31	740,000	36.7	48.1
1960	680,000	91	34	1,079,000	45.8	63.0
1970	1,178,000	73	--	1,695,000	57.1	69.5

SOURCES: a)   Jorge Balán, Harley L. Browning, and Elizabeth Jelin, *Men in a Developing Society: Geographic and Social Mobility in Monterrey.*

            b)   *Censo General de Población* (various years).

population living in urban areas, behind Mexico City and Guadalajara in each of the censuses from 1940 to 1960.[50] Of course, much of this growth was due to migration. From 1940 to 1950 the average annual increase was 6.0 percent, 3.6 from immigration and 2.4 from natural increase. During those years Monterrey was increasing faster than Guadalajara and receiving a larger proportion of rural migrants. However, during the 1950–1960 period the situation was reversed: although Monterrey increased at a mean annual rate of 6.3 percent, 3.2 from immigration and 3.1 from natural increase, Guadalajara was slightly higher in terms of growth rate and the proportion of that due to immigration.[51] Interestingly, the most recent trend data on population and industrial growth seem to indicate a gradual slowing; that is, Monterrey is still growing, but growing less rapidly. It may be approaching a point of saturation of investment with respect to local opportunities and of population with respect to resources, jobs, and urban services. In regard to the former, Monterrey industrialists are reported to be investing in other cities with increasing regularity. Knowledgeable informants in Guadalajara report that Monterrey banks lend more money in the city than do local ones.

Monterrey, unlike Guadalajara and the other cities dealt with in this study, reflects an exceptionally large concentration of the labor force in manufacturing as opposed to commerce and services (table 8). Understandably, the agricultural labor force is small in the city, but it is quite reduced, in comparative terms, for the state as a whole. This reflects the low agricultural potential of Monterrey's arid and sparsely-settled hinterland and, conversely, the domination of industry in the general economy.

In table 9 the same pattern is documented, here with respect to the origin of the state's gross product. Regrettably, the only available study of sectoral productivity dates from 1955, and other data already presented would suggest that the contribution (and obviously the magnitude) of the industrial sector is underestimated. Nevertheless, the data show that manufacturing is by far the most productive activity (37.8 percent), followed at some distance by commerce (18.0 percent) and private and professional services (18.5 percent).

When Monterrey's economy is considered from the standpoint of social class structure, a pattern of marked inequality emerges. By national standards, income distribution is noticeably uneven. From the great fortunes of the families of the industrial groups to the destitute poverty of the unskilled migrant slum dwellers, Monterrey is well represented in the extremes of class structure. The middle sectors certainly exist among salaried employees in industry, independent professionals, artisans, and merchants, but their numbers are smaller than in other cities due to Monterrey's economic structure, in which public bureaucracy, retail trade, craft indus-

TABLE 8

DISTRIBUTION OF THE ECONOMICALLY ACTIVE LABOR FORCE IN NUEVO LEON AND METROPOLITAN MONTERREY FOR SELECTED YEARS (In Percent)

Sector	Nuevo León 1960	Metropolitan Monterrey 1966
Agriculture	10.1	1.2
Mining	0.8	0.7
Manufacturing	35.0	40.3
Construction[a]	8.4	7.6
Commerce	16.9	17.0
Transportation[b]	6.1	6.7
Services	22.3	24.7
Other and no information	0.4	1.9
Total	100.0	100.0

SOURCE: "Ocupación y salarios en Monterrey metropolitano, 1966."

[a] includes gas and electricity
[b] includes storage and communication

try, and agricultural smallholdings are reduced in importance. Moreover, better than 30 percent of the male labor force qualify as "unskilled" and about one-third are engaged in "pre-industrial" activities, both entailing low incomes.[52] Another analysis includes among the "urban proletariat" 37 percent of the total labor force.[53] When this evidence on the occupational structure is combined with an analysis of income distribution, the contours of class structure come into sharper relief. In a carefully executed study of income distribution in Monterrey, Puente Leyva[54] classified the population as shown in table 10.

Although some observers might quarrel with the labels given to social strata or the brief time span of the figures, this study is the best available. It not only indicates a marked division among income levels and a reduced middle sector but also suggests that income inequality is becoming more extreme. Of further and more persuasive note is the clear consistency among separate analyses of the occupational and class structure. There seems little doubt about the well-defined inequity of Monterrey's class structure.

To say that the class structure is well defined and based on marked

TABLE 9

GROSS TERRITORIAL PRODUCT BY SECTORS OF THE
ECONOMY OF NUEVO LEON, 1955 (In Millions of Pesos
and Percent)

	Gross Product	Percent
Primary Activities	*247.2*	*6.6*
Agriculture		
Forestry	108.2	2.9
Fishing		
Livestock	139.0	3.7
Extractive Industry	*60.5*	*1.6*
Mining	57.8	1.5
Petroleum	2.7	0.1
Industry	*1,532.8*	*41.1*
Electrical Energy	35.5	1.0
Construction	90.0	2.4
Manufacturing	1,407.3	37.8
Commerce and Services	*1,658.2*	*44.5*
Commerce	669.2	18.0
Banking and Insurance	44.7	1.2
Transportation and		
Communication	208.4	5.6
Private and Professional Services	*690.3*	*18.5*
Nonprofit Services		
Government	45.6	1.2
Housing (rents)	*228.6*	*6.1*
Total	3,727.3	100.0

SOURCE: *Estructura económica del noreste de México: Un análisis
regional, 1955*, p. 23.

inequities between strata is not, however, to deny the presence of social
mobility. One large-scale study in Monterrey found that opportunities for
occupational mobility were substantial and on the increase. The experience of occupational mobility was closely correlated with migration and
education among the lower occupational ranks,[55] suggesting that the mobile occupational structure has been fed by a steady stream of rural migrants.

TABLE 10

SOCIAL STRUCTURE OF MONTERREY'S POPULATION WITH REFERENCE TO PER CAPITA INCOME LEVEL

Social Strata	Monthly Income Range Per Capita (1965 – Pesos)	% of Total Population 1960		1965	
Indigents	119 and below	1.4		7.6	
Poor	120–155	21.6	34.4	15.0	51.2
Poor in Transition	155–223	11.4		28.6	
Middle Class (Non-Solvent)	224–326	33.2		15.9	
Middle Class (Solvent)	327–504	14.5		16.2	
Upper Class (Privileged)	505 and above	17.9	32.4	16.7	32.9

SOURCE: Jesús Puente Leyva, *Distribución del ingreso en un área urbana: El caso de Monterrey*, p. 21.

CALI, VALLE DEL CAUCA, COLOMBIA

Cali, with the surrounding Cauca Valley, represents our third case, described by the design parameters as a transitional economy within a less-developed nation. In a general sense these characteristics make Cali more typical of the conditions facing Latin American developing areas. But this is not to concede that the region is without its distinctive accomplishments. Again the picture is one of contrasts. Instances of classical Latin American problems such as the *latifundia*, urban overcrowding, and foreign economic incursion are found side by side with post–World War II industrial expansion, a lively commercial sector, and recent efforts to reform rural productivity.

Cali was founded in 1536 by Sebastián de Belalcázar, a lieutenant of Pizarro who pushed northward after the defeat of the Inca Empire in search of new lands and treasures for the Spanish Crown. In 1540 Belalcázar was appointed the first governor of a large and ill-defined area including the Cauca Valley and its mountainous perimeter, called the Province of Popayán after the colonial city some sixty miles to the south that served as the capital. Finding little gold in the region, the Spaniards laid claim to the fertile agricultural lands and the large Indian population under the *encomienda* system.

At an early date the pattern of social and economic organization based on the hacienda became apparent. In a standard work on the Cauca Valley, Crist notes with reference to the period around 1600: "Even at this early date the trend was unmistakable. The amount of land and the number of serfs on it were becoming the measure of wealth in the economic vacuum of the colony. The growth of the estates and the diminution in the size of subsistence plots resulted in the expansion of pastoralism over food crops and the increased pressure of the landlords on the serfs."[56] Beef production was lucrative, with easy transportation and extensive markets in Popayán and Quito to the south and the Antioquia-Chocó region to the north. As a result the large estates grew larger and more numerous, simultaneously driving the indigenous population off the good land and up the Andean slopes to cultivate intensively the poorer land. Yet the process was gradual and could have been reversed had it not been for the fact that under both the colonial regime and independence the valley was relegated to the role of a supplier of agricultural exports.

> Thus even toward the end of the colonial period the relatively small *haciendas* were still diversified. The saddest feature was that they were almost invariably sold to large landowners—many of them resident in Popayán—who were intent on increasing the extent of grazing lands for their cattle. The degree of diversification . . . had it been general, and had it continued, would have kept the economy of the valley healthy.[57]

Although cattle raising was the principal activity in the early years, the appearance of sugar cane plantations was noted as early as 1560, with exports from the sugar mills beginning by 1588. The most lucrative by-product of sugar was rum, which had a lively market in the mining areas to the north. Crist observes that "by 1760, sugar cane was the principal crop under cultivation in the valley, and the production of molasses and the extraction of *aguardiente* (spirits) was the basis of the economic life of the area."[58]

During the mid-1800s, migrants from Antioquia and other agriculturally poor regions began to settle small farms in the northern reaches of the valley, ignoring legal titles in a de facto land reform.[59] In these areas coffee was soon to become the principal cash crop, profitably cultivated on small plots. Particularly in those hilly areas not conducive to cattle or sugar production did small farms increase. In the valley proper some diversification of agriculture took place on the large estates, particularly with dairy farming, tobacco, rice, corn, bananas, beans, and cotton.

Although early population figures are sketchy, the city of Cali was growing slowly and, more important, assuming the leadership over the region formerly held by Popayán. This was due in part to the fact that regional sentiment and support for independence ran high in Cali, though clearly the city's locational advantage in regional commerce was fundamental. Eventually to be outdistanced, the nearby town of Palmira was also growing and by 1835 had a population of 8,173, slightly more than Cali's 7,866. Differential population growth rates are indicated by the 1938 figures of 44,788 and 101,883 for the two towns respectively. Most of this growth began only in the last quarter of the nineteenth century, continuing rapidly from then to the present.[60] Cali more than doubled between 1918 and 1938 and increased ninefold in the next thirty years.

It was only with the opening of the twentieth century that Cali began its industrial development. Perhaps the most widely noted event signaling this change was the installation, near Palmira, of a modern sugar refinery. Since 1864 James Eder, a Russian-American immigrant to Colombia, had been operating the first large-scale, steam-powered refinery in the area. In 1898, desirous of completely modernizing the operation, Eder brought heavy machinery from England to the seaport of Buenaventura, which, though scarcely sixty miles from Palmira, was accessible only by a mule trail over rugged and mountainous terrain. Even with 1,800 oxen and mules it took three years to haul the machinery to its destination at the La Manuelita plantation. In 1901 the first modern processing plant began to operate in the area. Yet, with a few exceptions, mostly in sugar refining, industrial development did not really get under way until the 1930s.

Among the factors contributing to the development of the region, Lloyd-Jones terms the rise of Cali as a distribution center the "original energizer." With the opening of the Panama Canal in 1914, Buenaventura began growing and by the late 1930s was Colombia's most active seaport. In the same period (1914–1915) a railway system was completed, making Cali a vital link between the coast and the thriving coffee regions northward in Antioquia and Caldas, which then found it more profitable to export via Buenaventura.[61] Cali naturally became the hub of commercial activity and a major internal distribution center. These events, too, were probably responsible for the rapid growth of the city's population after 1918. Although it was not until 1945 that the first motor road to Buenaventura was completed, by this time Cali was already linked to international airways, serving as a stopover for flights from the United States and Panama to Lima and Santiago.

Industrial development began in earnest in the 1930s and accelerated rapidly after World War II. It was based principally on the processing of agricultural products. In this group, food products were most important, followed by paper, beverages, textiles, rubber, confections, tobacco, wood, and leather. Gradually other industrial activities of a more diversified sort began to emerge, notably in chemicals, metal products, machinery and electronics, printing, and non-metallic minerals (e.g., lime and cement). In addition to the commercial and distribution-related factors already mentioned, several external conditions helped spur industrial development in Cali. Notably, the depression in the United States during the 1930s led to some diversification of agriculture and the processing of agricultural products. As in so many countries, World War II provided new opportunities for trade and the expansion of national industry. Internally, an excellent foreign exchange position protected industry, and the purchasing power of an expanding population combined to propel industrial growth in the postwar years.

This new industrial development had two important characteristics, First, among the important local industrial interests, few represented newly emergent or socially mobile groups. Rather, the same families who had made their fortunes in agriculture—especially in sugar, cattle, and dairy farming—simply extended their influence by moving into new pursuits. There were, of course, some exceptions to this pattern, particularly in the presence of German, Lebanese, and North American immigrant entrepreneurs. But fundamentally industrialization followed the familiar pattern of increasing the concentration of wealth and power. Second, the major part of the new industry was established and controlled by nonlocal interests. For example, Hagen reports that among the founders of the forty-four enterprises in Valle del Cauca having over one hundred employees in 1956, only eight were of local origin, while twenty came from other parts of Colombia (mainly Antioquia) and sixteen were of foreign origin.[62] Between 1945 and 1953 the number of manufacturing establishments in Valle del Cauca increased sevenfold; the number of manufacturing employees more than doubled; gross production increased eightfold; value added in manufacturing expanded sixteen times.[63] All of these trends appear to have continued on a steady rise until 1963, when a reversal of several years' duration set in, owing to stagnation of the construction industry, labor conflicts, and, quite probably, foreign exchange problems of the national economy.[64]

If one process could be singled out as the major determinant of Cali's contemporary character, it would have to be rapid urbanization (table 11).

Since 1912 the city has been growing at an astonishing rate, acquiring in the process a larger proportion of the residents of the entire department. In the most recent intercensal period, 1951–1964, the city grew by 124 percent while the department increased only 57 percent. Several sources indicate that Cali's population during the last decade increased at the rate of 8.3 percent per year. Evidently the majority of this was due to migration

TABLE 11

POPULATION OF CALI AND VALLE DEL CAUCA
IN SELECTED YEARS

Years	Cali	Percent Increase	Valle del Cauca	Percent Increase
1806	6,100	--		
1905	30,700	403		
1912	27,700	- 10		
1918	45,500	64		
1938	101,900	124	613,230	--
1951	284,200	179	1,106,927	80
1964	637,900	124	1,733,053	57

SOURCES: *Cali y el Valle del Cauca; XIII Censo Nacional de Población.*

(4.8 percent), since natural increase is estimated at 3.5 percent annually.[65] Rapid urbanization is also taking place in other cities within the department; in 1964 nearby Palmira had a population of 140,889 and was followed by four other towns of more than 50,000.

In global figures contemporary economic organization reflects several trends. Table 12 on labor-force characteristics shows that the population economically active in primary occupations (agriculture, livestock, et cetera) is declining while that in secondary (industrial) and tertiary (commerce, transportation, and services) occupations is growing. Following the pattern typical of developing countries, commerce and services are the fastest-growing sectors and employ the largest segment of the labor force.

In table 13, data on the regional gross product indicate that the proportional contribution of industry, particularly "transformation" or manufacturing industry, is growing at the expense of other sectors. Examined in more detail, the figures on agricultural productivity show that sugar is still king in the valley; in order of value follow livestock, coffee, cotton, soy beans, rice, and corn. The composition of industrial productivity reflects this agricultural base, with food products at the top of the list. Nevertheless, other branches of industrial activity are important, as the rank order of the top ten in gross production goes on to include chemicals, paper products, beverages, textiles, rubber (especially tires), metal products, confections, machinery and electrical equipment, and printing. In 1964 the department contained 20.8 percent of the national aggregate value of industry; perhaps 60 percent of this is located in Cali.[66]

TABLE 12

POPULATION ECONOMICALLY ACTIVE BY TYPE OF
ACTIVITY IN VALLE DEL CAUCA FOR VARIOUS
YEARS (In Percent)

	1951	1964
Agriculture, livestock, fishing	46.28	32.43
Extractive	1.11	1.30
Transformation	15.91	18.95
Construction	4.71	5.75
Electricity, gas	0.30	0.35
Commerce	7.38	11.98
Transportation	5.12	5.51
Services	15.20	19.81
Unspecified and unemployed	3.98	3.92
Total (N)	99.99	100.00
	(389,746)	(529,544)

SOURCE: National Census, 1951, 1964.

A problem alluded to before is the extent of foreign participation in and/or control of local industry. In Cali the presence of foreign industry is substantial, although data on its exact proportions are (by design) difficult to obtain. Holt cites a figure of "more than one hundred U.S. business firms in Cali," concentrated in pharmaceuticals, tires, chemicals, food processing, and textiles. Lloyd-Jones lists the top firms in these same areas, showing that about two-thirds are foreign.[67] Blasier observes that

> foreign control of manufacturing, especially North American, is large. A leading figure associated with the local association of manufacturers estimates that 40 percent of local manufacturing is foreign owned, and even this estimate may be low. Among the companies represented are: Alcan, Colgate-Palmolive, Gillette, Goodyear, Grace, Home Products, Quaker Oats and Squibb. Almost all of the top managements of these companies are North American.[68]

A Colombian promotional magazine distributed in the United States lists thirty-five large foreign firms operating in the Cauca Valley, adding to Blasier's list Abbott Laboratories, Armour Pharmaceutical, Baxter Laboratories, Miles Laboratories, Borden Chemical, Celanese Corporation, Chemetron Corporation, Olin Mathieson Chemical Corporation, Coca-

TABLE 13

ORIGIN OF GROSS REGIONAL PRODUCT IN
VALLE DEL CAUCA AT CONSTANT PRICES
(In Percent)

	1954	1964
Primary Sector	23.26	21.30
Agriculture	16.91	15.30
Livestock	4.19	3.90
Forestry	0.00	0.00
Fishing	--	--
Secondary Sector	27.64	32.20
Mining	0.38	0.90
Transformation	20.68	27.10
Construction	5.91	4.00
Electric	0.67	1.20
Tertiary Sector	49.08	45.50
Commerce	14.62	20.20
Services	9.04	10.30
Banking	2.20	1.60
Government	6.17	4.40
Communication and Transportation	17.05	9.00

SOURCE: *El por qué de un plan de desarrollo económico y social para el departamento del Valle del Cauca* (1965).

Cola, Container Corporation of America, Fleischman Distilling Corporation, B. F. Goodrich, U.S. Rubber, Johns-Manville, Johnson and Johnson, Nestlé, Phelps Dodge, Phillips Petroleum, Ralston Purina, Remington Rand, Sears Roebuck, Singer, and others.[69] A similar list published by the local Association of Industrialists contains fifty-five inclusions, adding, once again, many familiar names (e.g., Anderson Clayton, Corn Products, Mobil Oil, Shell Oil, Standard Brands, Union Carbide).[70]

Official national figures from 1964 showed that of 165 true corporations in the department, 22 or 13.3 percent were foreign.[71] But this figure is not broken down by size of firm and underestimates the number of firms as reported in other sources. A separate analysis of the sources of capital invested in the 25 top local firms, as indicated by Chamber of Commerce records, showed slightly over half were foreign-controlled.[72] These separate estimates suggest a figure of 40 to 50 percent of the major industrial firms under foreign control, a fact that is fundamental to any understanding of local economic development.

A final characteristic of contemporary economic organization is the fact that, despite the Cauca Valley's growing population, the land reform act of 1961, and limited efforts at agricultural diversification, large estates and extensive land use continue their historical predominance. According to an agricultural census of 1959, 2 percent of the farm owners control 43 percent of the land; smallholders (ten *hectares* or less, which is equivalent to twenty-five acres or less) represent 70 percent of the department's population but control less than 10 percent of the land.[73] This pattern is probably more extreme on the fertile valley floor around Cali. A recent study of the land tenure problem concluded that the *latifundia* system is still maintained through the political machinations of rural elites and that a strong positive correlation obtains between land quality, estate size, and extensive use.[74]

These principal features of socioeconomic organization are best summarized in their consequences on class structure. The rural sector is dominated by large landowning elites that employ the bulk of the population as agricultural workers (e.g., on sugar plantations and dairy farms). The smallholder or middle peasant class is quite reduced. A marginal urban proletariat has grown substantially in recent years and is partially absorbed in the tertiary sector, though still greatly underemployed. Manufacturing controlled by local and foreign elites is of recent origin and tends to be capital intensive, creating a small labor bourgeoisie in the midst of a much larger unskilled and migrant labor force. An urban middle sector exists in commerce, artisan industry, and various services including the public bureaucracies, but its numerical importance is small in contrast to the lower classes. In short, the pattern of social stratification is distinctively inegalitarian.

MEDELLÍN, ANTIOQUIA, COLOMBIA

The Antioqueño region of western Colombia occupies a prominent position in the annals of Latin American economic history. Its fame is due, in part, to a series of developmental achievements, from extensive gold mining in the sixteenth and seventeenth centuries to the boom in coffee and commerce of the nineteenth and rapid industrialization in the twentieth. Coupled with this is a subcultural reputation for independence and regional identity that, when combined with the economic achievements, gives rise to the depiction of an "entrepreneurial spirit" or "Protestant ethic," albeit among a strongly Catholic population. These and other unique features of the area have attracted the theoretical interests of a variety of Colombian and North American scholars. Characteristic of this interest and the region's complex history is the fact that two theories of development as far apart in style and ideology as Everett Hagen's social psychology and Andre Gunder Frank's neo-Marxism both cite Antioquia as a case supporting their thesis.[75] More important than these conflicting interpretations, however, is the welter of historical materials produced by this fascination with Antioquia. As we review that evidence it will become apparent that the Antioqueño legend requires critical scrutiny. At several points in its history, developmental progress has been noticeably absent, and its once pre-eminent role in the economy of Colombia has recently declined relative to other regions.

As was the case in so many areas of the New World, the first Spanish conquerors came to Antioquia in search of gold. Beginning in 1537, expeditions from the Cauca Valley and the Caribbean coastal city of Cartagena traversed the region repeatedly to establish mines and loot gold from Indian burial sites. In 1546 Jorge Robledo founded the first town in the area, Santa Fe de Antioquia, initially under the provincial jurisdiction of Popayán.

During these early years Antioquia's gold mines became the best known and most extensive in Latin America. Beginning from rich deposits discovered by the Indians, the Spaniards broadly extended their operations to other veins, placer diggings, and river bottoms. New towns grew up as deposits were found to the north of Santa Fe in Zaragosa, Remedios, and Cáceres. Perhaps the high point of mining in the colonial era was around 1580, when the Buritica mines near Santa Fe worked 300 Negro slaves and 1,500 Indians, while Zaragoza was said to have from 3,000 to 4,000 Negro slaves. Nevertheless, the boom was relatively short lived: "After a brief period of high returns which depended, in large measure, on Indian labor, productivity fell off sharply, yet the mining economy survived on a subsistence level throughout the colonial period."[76]

The early collapse of large-scale mining was owing to the lack of adequate technology and labor. From the technological standpoint, without blasting, pumps to remove water from shafts, and other vein-mining methods, only the most accessible ore could be retrieved before the site was "depleted." Further, this economy relied heavily on slave labor, which had to be fed at high costs and was especially susceptible to repeated epidemics. Thus, "the exhaustion of the labor force, not the gold, caused the decline."[77] These factors contributed to an important shift in the structure of the mining economy in favor of smallholders and individual operators. Gold was still plentiful in scattered placer sites and river beds, where its extraction promised modest profits to the small operator employing primitive techniques.

Changes in the mining economy were both anticipated and fortified by a series of mining ordinances that were passed in 1587 by local government and that would later become the basis for mining laws throughout the Andean area. Designed to rationalize production, these measures regulated the size and number of individual claim sites, required that claims be actively worked, and provided courts for settling disputes. These two events, the rise of a class of smallholders and the advent of political reforms to encourage their activities, were bellwether events in the region's early development.

Although mining was the basis of the economy in the early years, agriculture was obviously necessary to sustain it, and commerce arose to perform the intermediary function. The first permanent settlement near the present site of Medellín was established in 1616. A second village within the city's current limits came in 1646 and Medellín was formally designated a city in 1675. The town depended equally on mining and agriculture, providing livestock, raised in its surrounding valley, and other supplies to adjacent mining areas. For many years it was uncertain whether Medellín or Rionegro would become the central city of the region. Locational advantages vis-à-vis mining and agricultural zones as well as trade routes appear, much later, to have favored Medellín. A number of factors, including the isolation of the region, the supply needs of the mines, and the low productivity of agriculture, combined to place great emphasis on trade, and it was in Medellín that a new merchant class began to prosper most.

Yet throughout the eighteenth century Antioquia remained poor and underdeveloped.[78] The minority engaged in mining enjoyed an unequal share of the region's profits, but even these groups suffered from the lack of agricultural productivity and the consequent high cost of necessities.[79] An important epoch in regional history began in 1775 when Governor Juan Antonio Mon y Velarde instituted a series of reform laws to alter this situation, including the establishment of new towns in which families were granted town lots and farming land, a decree that everyone not engaged in mining plant a certain amount of corn, town commissions to oversee the administration of and compliance with these reforms, bonuses for cultivating new crops, production quotas, the establishment of trade schools, and vagrancy laws. The reforms were carefully planned, supervised in their implementation, and particularly comprehensive in scope. As Fajardo notes,

. . . an obscure provincial administrator, Mon y Velarde, almost two hundred years ago, stated in familiar language the principles of a theory of development that is being discovered in great contemporary treatises. . . . There is in it a theory of economic backwardness, of agrarian reform, of the market and prices and the role of technical innovation in agriculture. There is also a policy of massive education and even a policy of protection of the destitute, the humanistic inspiration of which contrasts with the cynicism and ethical neutrality of many "pure" models in the social sciences.[80]

Beyond that, the reforms seemed to have worked. Many new and prosperous agricultural settlements took root, and colonization of new territories was stimulated. Prices of food to miners declined, laying the basis for the subsequent revival of the industry. Again of crucial importance was the promotion, through political reforms, of a rural class structure of smallholders that paralleled changes in the mining economy and contrasted so vividly with the *latifundia* of other regions.

The reform laws, population pressures, and the general poverty already mentioned gave rise to an extensive colonization movement, with large numbers of settlers moving principally to the south, but also west and east from Antioquia into Caldas, Quindio, Tolima, Chocó, and the upper reaches of the Cauca Valley, extending the "Antioqueño Country" into portions of six of today's departmental entities. López Toro speaks of two periods of Antioqueño colonization, and, although some 56,000 people took up new residences during the first of these (1675–1787), it was during the second wave (1808–1870) that nearly 400,000 colonists settled in the areas indicated.[81] The economic and political implications of colonization were of great magnitude. Transportation routes were established, linking towns in formerly isolated areas. Small mining and agriculture prospered on holdings of limited size and sustained an active regional commercial network. In concluding his classic study of the period Parsons states:

To sum up, the extreme parcelization of the lands of recent Antioqueño settlement must be interpreted chiefly in the light of the recency of their occupation. Only the old granitic massif of the Rionegro-Medellín-Santa Rosa heartland was effectively incorporated into the colonial structure and even here the strong emphasis on mining and the scattered nature of the deposits did not favor the development of the deeply rooted feudal traditions which sprang from the agricultural and livestock haciendas in other parts of New Granada. . . . The concept of wealth, then, was not tied either to subject peoples or to the soil as much as to hard work and initiative. On the new volcanic lands to the south and west the extremely broken nature of the country, together with the coffee planters' proud, free, and independent spirit of self-determination combined to produce this anomaly of a democratic society of small holders on a continent dominated by traditional Latin latifundism.[82]

From these foundations the economy of Antioquia continued to grow after independence. Under liberalized trade policies merchants began importing English textiles and luxury goods, distributing them as far south as Quito. Commercial houses were maintained in Jamaica and London, representing Colombia's principal contact with the outside world. Free trade policies created pressures on the supply of gold, and it was at this time that foreign, mainly English, companies were invited in to modernize the mining industry. This was accomplished, returning Antioquia to a pre-eminent position among Colombian gold-producing areas, but at the cost of passing control of the largest mines over to foreign interests.[83] The trend was slow; it is estimated that until 1880 about three-fourths of the labor force (not the earnings) in mining were Colombian small operators.[84] Moreover, with the exception of these foreign incursions into mining, the great bulk of the economy was locally controlled.[85]

Gold provided the backbone of Antioqueño commercial expansion. Its great importance lay, not in mining per se, but in its function as a medium of exchange. In his critique of Hagen's social psychological interpretation of Antioquia's economic growth, Safford stresses the possession of gold as the principal source of commercial and financial power.

> Gold helped the Antioqueños a great deal in their domination of the economy, being a very useful kind of exchange in a country and an epoch of poor communications and primitive financial institutions. . . . Even after 1850, when many Colombian merchants had established their credit in England and France, gold remained a principal means of payment because of the meagerness of exports of other products. Obviously the merchants of Medellín had a clear advantage over their counterparts in Bogotá. The Antioqueños controlled the most important medium of exchange; the Bogotá merchants often had to resort to them in order to make payments abroad. . . . In domestic commerce Antioqueño gold also had an important role, because it gave the Medellín capitalists the most important source of credit.[86]

But if Antioquia's merchant class profited under liberal trade policies, the same could not be said of the country as a whole. In his economic history of Colombia, McGreevey argues "that the period of 1850–90 was one of stagnation and decline, resulting in large part from errors in policy decision."[87] Prominent among these errors were the promotion of monocrop agriculture for export (as in Cali) and extensive imports that depressed the artisan class by thwarting local production.

It was in the late nineteenth century that this period of economic stagnation was broken and Colombia took its most decisive step toward development with the introduction of coffee. Coffee cultivation was comparatively late in coming to Colombia. Produced in the Caribbean, Venezuela, and Costa Rica in the eighteenth century, it was not until 1860 that the first Colombian plantation was established and 1880 before the real coffee boom started. It was the Antioquia region, whose mountainous volcanic soils were especially well suited to coffee growing, that took the lead in producing this new export crop. The great developmental advantage of coffee was not only in its lively export market but, more profoundly, in the social organization of its production. The berry was well adapted to cultivation on Antioquia's small, owner-operated farms, even those comprised mainly of steep slopes. The trees did not require a great deal of attention nor the best pasture and crop land a small farmer might possess. As a result, the cultivator was able to raise simultaneously subsistence crops and coffee, the sale of which provided additional earnings and brought him, for the first time on any substantial scale, into the money economy. The reciprocal benefits of an agricultural cash economy for artisans and merchants were, of course, extensive.

In contrast to the organizational structure of coffee growing in Brazil or Central American countries a large share of total coffee production as well as a large number of producing farms were smallholder peasant operations. . . . This difference in the organizational structure of coffee production is a major explanation for the favorable impact of coffee growing on Colombian development. . . . From the point of view of economic and social change, the most important feature of the introduction of coffee as an export product was that it drew significant numbers of the population directly into the market. The older hacienda operations introduced only a small portion of the population into a money economy. Coffee production introduced a shifting over from non-market orientations for thousands of peasant families. Small-holders dealt directly with urban buyers of coffee and sellers of consumer goods.[88]

The economic effects of coffee production went far beyond the cultivator. Antioquia's well-established merchant class and commercial houses profited, but their prosperity redounded to the benefit of the larger society through a series of linkages that included the cash economy, greater internal demand, the diffusion of management skills, foreign exchange, import substitution, and, notably from the outset, expansion of the transportation system. Coffee, more than anything else, provided the impetus to merchants and government to solve the long-vexing problem of Antioquia's geographical isolation. Until the 1880s trade goods were transported by pack animals to such locations as the Cauca and Magdalena rivers, at which points they could be transferred to steamboats. Beginning in 1885 the construction of railway networks steadily reduced the time and cost of transportation between Medellín and export terminals in the coastal cities of Cartagena, Barranquilla, Santa Marta, and Buenaventura, as well as to the many points in between. The legacy of these "coffee railways" in terms of cost-reducing efficiency came in the 1920s as a stimulus to industrialization.

The first appearance of anything approximating an "industry" is difficult to mark precisely. Hagen mentions that in the 1860s Antioquia had breweries using advance methods, a cacao mill, pottery and ceramics, tanneries, and primitive shoe production. Textiles appeared in the 1870s and by the 1880s all of these had improved their methods and were joined by cigars, cigarettes, confections, and an iron works producing mining and agricultural equipment.[89] Production of Panama hats, tableware and crockery, light mining equipment, and coffee pulpers also occurred before the turn of the century.[90] The bulk of this was probably artisan industry and handicrafts carried on in small shops.

Antioquia's true entry into the industrial age is better dated between 1902 and 1907, when three textile factories were established in and around Medellín. Of course it was no accident that the founding of these industries coincided with the coffee boom, since many of the new industrialists had accumulated their capital in commerce. Best known of these former coffee merchants was Alejandro Echavarría, who in 1907 founded "Coltejer" (Compañía Colombiana de Tejidos), which was to become Antioquia's largest textile plant and, indeed, one of the largest national corporations in Latin America. Because of the accumulated wealth in Antioquia and the wide market available through substitution of English imports, textiles took the lead, Coltejer being followed by the next of the "big three," Fabricato and Tejicondor. But, while textiles were and continue to be central, other key industries arose in the early 1900s, including Colombia's first steel mill, cement, rubber, chemicals, glass, tobacco, beverages and liquors, and others. This industrialization expanded rapidly. Within ten years of its inception the textile industry was the largest in Colombia.[91] By 1918 Medellín was the leading manufacturing center in the country, a position it occupied until 1945.

Antioqueño industrialization followed two definitive paths. It was, for the most part, established and controlled by local capitalists with backgrounds in commerce and mining.[92] Foreign interests were clearly present, particularly in those fields to which they brought new technology such as mining and transportation, but they never overshadowed native entrepreneurs. "Perhaps half of the foreign capital was concentrated in transport facilities—mainly railroads. There was virtually no foreign investment in manufacturing: thus the earliest phase of industrial development was achieved almost completely without the assistance of foreign capital, re-

TABLE 14

POPULATION OF MEDELLIN AND ANTIOQUIA IN
SELECTED YEARS

Years	Medellín	% Increase	Antioquia	% Increase
1835	14,800	--	158,000	--
1869	29,765	101.1	--	--
1883	37,237	25.1	--	--
1905	59,815	60.6	650,000	311.3
1912	66,547	11.3	--	--
1918	79,146	18.9	823,000	26.7
1928	120,044	51.7	1,011,324	22.9
1938	168,266	40.2	1,188,587	17.5
1951	358,189	112.9	1,570,197	32.1
1964	772,886	115.8	2,477,299	57.8

SOURCES: *Medellín, Estudio general de la ciudad y su área circundante, 1969; Antioquia, Síntesis socioeconómico;* James J. Parsons, *Antioqueño Colonization in Western Colombia.*

quiring only the help of technicians who set up and operated the first mills for Colombian owners."[93]

Second, although industrialization came at a rapid pace, it did not bring in its wake the disruptive effects alleged by so much conventional theorizing.[94] Rather, industry came as a natural outgrowth of accumulated capital and opportunities for import substitution. The fervently Catholic labor force was not secularized by these trends toward modernization. Traditionally conservative beliefs persisted and were reinforced by the paternalistic institutional practices of the large textile companies, for example, church-run dormitories for female workers, cooperative stores, free medical services, and other social welfare benefits. As some commentators have pointed out, "traditionalism" may have contributed positively to the mobilization and commitment of the labor force.[95] "Solemn religious processions, festivals and masses frequently interrupt factory routine, and images and paintings of Jesus and Mary are everywhere in evidence in plants and offices. Management here has been remarkably successful in investing factory work with an esteem not common in older industrial lands."[96]

As for the recent features of the region's economy and society, Medellín's population, like that of most urban centers, has been increasing rapidly throughout the twentieth century. Table 14 indicates the rate of this urbanization. The department of Antioquia has become increasingly urbanized. In 1928, 28 percent of its inhabitants lived in towns of 1,500 or more; by 1964 the figure had risen to 53 percent. Further, in 1966 the single city of Medellín contained 33 percent of the population of Antioquia, while the city and its immediate environs of the Valley of Aburra (including the towns of Bello, Copacabana, Giradota, Estrella, and Caldas) contained 45 percent. The annual rate of population increase in Medellín and its surroundings between 1951 and 1964 is estimated at 6.0 percent, of which 2.9 stemmed from natural increase and 3.1 from immigration.[97] Although these figures are impressively high, it should be recalled that for recent years they are well below those of Cali.

The contemporary fame of Medellín rests, of course, on its industrialization. In 1966 the department of Antioquia registered 1,966 industrial establishments whose gross product occupied second place nationally behind Bogotá. Of this industry in the department, 92 percent of both the net investment and personnel occupied was located in Medellín and its immediate surroundings.[98] Textiles continue to dominate the economy, with 39 percent of the aggregate value of manufacturing, followed at some distance by beverages, apparel, food products, cement, chemicals, tobacco, metal products, machinery, and leather.

Despite this evidence of growth, Medellín has had its troubles in recent years. Since the post–World War II period, Bogotá has assumed the industrial leadership of the country that once was Medellín's. After the bounty years of 1954–1956 the development of the department has slowed markedly due to problems of the national economy and a likely saturation of local possibilities.[99] Nevertheless, it would be very short-sighted to predict any long-term reversals for this dynamic region. In the face of contemporary challenges, local groups have responded with characteristically innovative plans for the development of new agricultural zones, industrial diversification and decentralization, mixed public-private corporations for exploring new fields of enterprise, and a series of other measures.

Table 15 on labor force distribution in the department reflects a pattern of relative stability between 1951 and 1964. Primary activities have declined but continue to be the modal category, due, no doubt, to the continued importance of coffee and food processing. The manufacturing, commerce, and service sectors have made small gains. Regrettably, there are no data for Antioquia on the origin of the gross regional product by sectors that would serve as a basis for comparison with Cali. Indicators from selected sectors suggest that, although the value of Antioquia's gross product is higher than that of Valle del Cauca, the percentage distribution of the gross product by sector of origin is about the same. For example, in

TABLE 15

POPULATION ECONOMICALLY ACTIVE BY TYPE OF
ACTIVITY IN ANTIOQUIA FOR VARIOUS YEARS
(In Percent)

	1951	1964
Agriculture, livestock, fishing	50.8	44.8
Extractive	1.7	1.0
Transformation	14.4	16.1
Construction	4.4	4.9
Electricity, gas	0.4	0.2
Commerce	4.9	7.9
Transportation, communication	3.7	3.8
Services	15.0	16.9
Unspecified and unemployed	4.7	4.4
Total	100.00	100.00
	(478,210)	(658,845)

SOURCE: National Census, 1951, 1964.

1965 Antioquia derived 20.29 percent of its gross product from manufacturing, while the figure for Valle del Cauca was 20.10 percent.

We have already noted the relative absence of foreign ownership and control in Antioqueño industry. Another key feature of local enterprise, stemming perhaps from earlier experience in mining and commerce, is the large number of true corporations as opposed to "limited societies" or family-controlled businesses. Offical data from 1964 indicate that Antioquia had 265 such corporations, of which 7 (3.6 percent) were foreign, while Valle del Cauca had 165 with 22 (13.3 percent) foreign.[101] The figures may be taken as evidence of the more "modernized" industrial economy of Antioquia, in which ownership and corporate organization are more widely dispersed. Illustrative of this trend is Medellín's Coltejer, the largest textile plant in Latin America, with capital resources of 907 million Colombian pesos and "some 40,000 stockholders none of whom possesses over one percent of the stock."[102]

To sum up, the historical experience of economic development in Medellín requires a social-structural explanation.[103] With respect to the organization of production, the distributive pattern of land tenure and small-holdings in mining were fundamental. Out of these evolved a set of reciprocating demands that laid the basis for commerce and the entrepreneurial leadership of the merchant class. More than any single element, the relatively egalitarian class structure produced the complementarities and incentives for sustained development. From export trade and industrialization a distinct and powerful upper class emerged, but the majority of its members were not nobles but self-made men who arose from an equally distinct and extensive middle class. Political development, from the early mining ordinances to the reforms of Mon y Velarde and the self-governing new towns of the colonization era, provided a climate of conservative and civic-minded governance that contributed substantially to economic progress. It is undeniable, too, that a distinctive ethos of regional pride, achievement, and spirit of association emerged. But these were the social-psychological consequences of developmental achievements that had their own structural causes.

3. Comparative Perspectives on the Structure of Power

Using these historical sketches of the four regions as a baseline, we turn now to questions of contemporary social organization as revealed in our field research. In following the methods described in chapter 1, the first task is to characterize the structure of political power in the regions as it is seen through the eyes of organizational leaders. Subsequently we shall characterize these leaders and examine the ways in which they work through organizational networks in the making of developmental decisions. But those considerations await a description of elite groups and their relationship to the system of social stratification. From the standpoint of our theoretical orientation, we have thus far dealt with the historical experience of development and its consequences for the pattern of class structure. Continuing with an elaboration of that framework, we now address the question of power and social stratification.

AN APPROACH TO THE STUDY OF POWER IN LATIN AMERICAN CITIES

Studies of community power and decision-making in North American cities go back at least twenty years, to the publication of Floyd Hunter's well-known book *Community Power Structure*,[1] and even further if we consider the early community studies that dealt, *inter alia*, with local elites.[2] In the ensuing period this field grew both in volume (including by now many hundreds of titles)[3] and in sophistication. Early case studies, such as Hunter's, that challenged the egalitarian premises of local democracy drew rebuttals from the "pluralists," who claimed, at least for their case studies, that political influence was widely distributed among fluid coalitions of interest groups. The debate between these "elitist" and "pluralist" schools is so well known and widely chronicled that it requires no description here.[4] Suffice it to say that, although valuable theoretical insights were developed by adversary works such as Robert Dahl's *Who Governs?*,[5] students of the field gradually came to appreciate the fact that what separated the schools was less a matter of substance[6] than of methodology and ideology.[7] Following on that recognition, a series of comparative case studies based on a multi-method approach began to appear. Even more recently we have seen large-scale comparative studies[8] and the beginnings of some theoretical thinking about the structural bases and political consequences of various arrangements of power.[9]

Although this shift to a "comparative" perspective has been accomplished mainly within the continental limits of the United States, there are also examples of cross-national work.[10] Some of the first non-United States cities to receive the attentions of these researchers were the accessible Mexican border towns.[11] Steadily these investigations spread to other cities in Mexico, Central America, Venezuela, Colombia, Peru, and Argentina, numbering, in a recent count, more than twenty. Not unexpectedly, the evolution of research strategies abroad paralleled the earlier sequence.

In the case study tradition, Klapp and Padgett applied Hunter's method to Tijuana, Mexico, discovering that there was no power structure in this city, merely an "amorphous" collection of important individuals.[12] Graham's analysis of "Saragosa," Mexico, similarly found no durable power structure, but several cliques in business, the professions, and politics.[13] Hoskin's report on San Cristóbal, Venezuela, goes even further, describing six clusters of power in government, the political parties, the professions, society, and so forth, that make up a competitive elite.[14]

Other approaches have combined case study methods for the identification of elites with surveys of community residents. Drake's investigation of Manizales, Colombia, reasoned from such evidence that a small and inaccessible oligarchy controlled the city to the detriment of the general welfare.[15] In a related vein, Fagen and Tuohy show that the people of Jalapa, Mexico, are generally cynical about politics and distrustful of the economic-political leadership coalition.[16]

As we have noted, some of the first comparative studies using Latin American cities focused on border towns. D'Antonio and Form compared El Paso, Texas, and Ciudad Juárez, Mexico, in a longitudinal design that showed the latter to be developing a more competitive political system.[17] And in the first comparative study within Latin America, Miller contrasted Córdoba, Argentina, and Lima, Peru.[18]

We provide this partial listing of power studies in Latin American cities in order to indicate both the variety of results they obtain and their lack of systematic comparative methods. While single case studies have obvious limitations in generalization, few of these even cite strategic reasons for the selection of the particular town. Useful as they are, comparative studies focused on such unlikely pairs as El Paso–Ciudad Juárez or Córdoba-Lima contend with an array of conditions vitiating meaningful comparison, such as size, economic or political specialization, and national context. And we may add to all this the fact that the research methods employed in the separate studies are widely varied and probably sensitive to different characteristics of political organization.

Small wonder that the results of these inquiries are so disparate. Drake and Ocampo[19] report on the existence of tightly-knit oligarchies. Next along a continuum, Fagen and Tuohy acknowledge several elite groups that, nevertheless, unite in a fairly stable coalition. Less cohesive are the factional arrangements found by Graham, D'Antonio and Form, and Torres-Trueba.[20] And approaching the pluralistic ideal are the competitive systems described by Miller, Hoskin, Ebel,[21] and Ugalde.[22] We do not wish to suggest that such diversity is impossible or even unlikely. Indeed, we should anticipate important variation in the organization of political power across a set of cities that represent such diverse conditions. But the point is that without systematic comparative studies that attempt controlled comparisons and employ similar research procedures, it is impossible to determine whether the observed variation in results is factual, stemming from specifiable influences on the political system, or false, stemming from methodological discontinuities.

This problem was anticipated in the present study and has been addressed in two ways. First, we have selected for comparison four urban regions that are "stratified" or paired in ways that control for several factors that are likely to influence the political system (e.g., size, industrialization, national context). To state it conversely, we have tried to reduce some of the more obvious sources of unsystematic fluctuation. Second, we have applied a more or less standard method for identifying elites and characterizing the decision-making process. In addition to the features of this method presented in chapter 1, several comments are warranted on the subject of how we have attempted to eliminate some difficulties that have characterized studies of power executed in the United States, Latin America, and elsewhere.

One such difficulty is that all conventional techniques for studying power at the local level suffer from exclusive attention to the individual as the unit of analysis. So called "reputational" methods inquire of a set of knowledgeable community actors who the most important people are "when it comes to getting things done." Consensual nominations constitute the elite or power structure. Curiously, the critics of this method who advance a "decisional" strategy also focus on individuals, the difference being that their criterion for influence is not the person's reputation but actual participation in a set of reconstructed issues or decisions. The same observation applies to "positional," case study, participant observation, and more recent comparative techniques. A review of this literature will indicate that, whichever of these methods is employed, the dominant, almost exclusive, observational unit is the individual actor rather than the group, association, organization, or institution. The salient question is always *who* is most influential, *who* participates, *who* wins. To be sure, studies often indicate the occupational background and group affiliation of these individuals. But it is thus only indirectly that one gets a suggestion of the social organizational context of power, and even that suggestion rests on the questionable assumption that individuals are acting in the interests of their organizational constituencies. Seldom in this literature do we find observations based on groups or organizations as a unit of analysis. As a consequence, most studies of community power seriously neglect social structure.

A second problem is that all of these techniques tend to be ahistorical. When they do attempt to incorporate a longitudinal dimension it usually takes the form of a very brief historical sketch or a superficial classification of the occupations and ethnicity of earlier public officials. The result is historical naïveté in trend statements and future projections. Notable among these in the literature on North American cities is the general failure to recognize and analyze the increasing interdependence between the local community and institutions of the larger carrying society.

In this study we hope to avoid many of the problems mentioned. The historical baseline for an analysis of contemporary power structure has already been established. The methods employed here and in the next two chapters capitalize on all of the conventional techniques but go further in an effort to identify the organizational bases of power and the linkages between individual power-holders and organizations. In a broader sense, the methods and results presented here are not ends in themselves but contributions to the general framework of analysis that links social structure and economic development through the intervening processes of power and decision-making.

Finally, a problem encountered in analyses of *power* at the local and national levels is the fact that this key concept is seldom defined. Competing interpretations of the structure of power may often rest on differences among observers as to whether power is a "latent" or "manifest" property, whether it includes subtle processes of "influence" or should be confined to the exercise of "force." Accordingly, we shall indicate how the concept is understood here before turning to its empirical description.

A NOTE ON THE CONCEPT OF POWER

Power is one of those multi-purpose words that serve us equally in ordinary discourse and scholarly writing. Although a great deal of debate and confusion surrounds the definitional question, problems scarcely end there.[23] Scholars are sharply divided over the fundamental utility of the concept. Some have suggested that power is the basic datum of sociology and political science, analogous to force in physics,[24] while others have maintained that its explanatory potential may be insignificant outside of very restrictive prediction models.[25] The subtlety and complexity of power phenomena make their measurement a perennial problem, so that observers of roughly the same class of empirical events are able to reach diametrically opposed interpretations of their meaning.[26] Despite these differences, there persists a conviction that power relations are an inescapable fact of social organization and that, somehow, they must be measured and understood.

When we speak of "power" in ordinary language, a variety of images come to mind. Power implies strength, force, coercion, and the ability to dominate despite opposition. Yet, on further reflection, it becomes apparent that the dynamics of power may work in more subtle ways. Force need not be exercised if the threat of it is sufficient to gain compliance; this suggests the notion of "potential" power. Much of the power or ability to command held by individuals and institutions rests on authority rather than on power in the sense of force; compliance is proffered because it is thought to be right. Compliance may also serve the self-interest of the one who complies with the power-holder. Are such phenomena illustrations of power and, if so, is force central in the definition of the term? Moreover, must an actor always succeed in gaining compliance with his wishes in order for us to determine whether he has actual or potential power, or would we want to temper occasional successes with the idea of "influence" rather than power? Questions like these have produced a number of critical discussions of the concept of power that are incorporated in the definition proposed here.[27]

Max Weber defined power as "the chance (or probability) of a man or a number of men to realize their own will in a communal action even against the resistance of others who are participating in the action."[28] The definition offered here parallels Weber, adding only a specification of the means by which one's own will is realized and a clarification of certain entailed aspects of the term.

Power refers to the capacity to mobilize resources for the accomplishment of intended effects with recourse to some type of sanction(s) to encourage compliance. The greater this capacity, the higher the probability of "realizing one's own will even against resistance." This capacity is the generic term and is to be distinguished from the diverse sources upon which it may rest. Recourse to the application of sanctions distinguishes power from *influence*, which involves only the ability to mobilize resources. The notion of capacity also suggests that the attribution of power does not depend on its overt exercise but also includes *potential* or *latent ability*. Moreover, the attribution of power does not depend on success in the accomplishment of intended effects; one may lose a contest and still be said to have power (this, of course, is what the term probability in Weber's definition refers to, though it is often overlooked by those who prefer to read Weber as stressing only the ability to prevail over others). Finally, the definition specifies *intention* as distinguishing power from unintentional control.

It is also essential that we distinguish between the *bases* (or sources) of power and its *dimensions*. Concerning the bases, Weber allowed that power may derive from many sources. Of particular interest to him were "constellations of interest" and "established authority," though he was also well aware of the role of coercion.[29] Similar tripartite breakdowns are encountered in recent works under the heading "types of power." Etzioni speaks of coercive, normative, and remunerative power.[30] Mills discusses authority, manipulation, and coercion as "the three types [that] must constantly be sorted out when we think about the nature of power."[31] Lehman deals with the sociological consequences of power deriving from utilitarian, coercive, and normative resources.[32]

For the present, there seems to be no need to claim that these bases are exhaustive, but simply that they are essential to any analysis of power. We shall employ these three bases of power, defined as follows: *Authority* refers to voluntary compliance based on a belief in "the right to command and the duty to obey"[33] (authority here is equivalent to the term normative used by other authors). *Utility* refers to voluntary compliance based on self-interest rather than right (constellations of interest, remuneration, and manipulation are equivalent terms). *Coercion*, of course, is involuntary compliance based on force or the threat of force.

In addition to the foregoing bases of power, it will be useful to specify several *dimensions*. Much of the research literature in this field has been concerned with a single question about power, namely, how broadly or narrowly it is distributed. What this emphasis has obscured is that distributions are at least two-dimensional; they may be broad or narrow and at the same time may also be flat (rectangular) or peaked. Substantively, power may be distributed among many actors or a few (i.e., broad or narrow), and those actors may be more or less equal in their power. These two dimensions will be called, respectively, the *distribution of power* and the *inequality of power*.

A third dimension, the *coordination of power*, will be used to refer to the extent to which actors having power interact with one another, that is, how cohesive they are. Lehman has offered some insightful thoughts on how we may conceptualize the coordination of power in more detail. Of particular relevance in the present context is his differentiation between *intermember* and *systemic* power. "In its intermember form, the study of power relations focuses primarily on the competition over the allocation of scarce resources. In its systemic form, power refers to the capacity of some unit acting as an agent of the system to overcome resistance of system members in setting, pursuing and implementing collective goals."[34] Stated more simply, coordination of power or the lack thereof may be assessed in terms of whether individuals compete among themselves for power or whether power is lodged in organizations capable of pursuing collective interests. Since, as Lehman suggests, the latter alternative may be more often associated with successful attainment of goals, these two models may assume decisive explanatory utility.

Empirically, there is no necessary connection between the bases and dimensions of power. It may be, for example, that power based principally on authority and/or coercion takes the form of narrow distribution, inequality, and close (systemic) coordination, while power based on utility has the opposite social dimensions. This is an empirical issue to be decided in comparative studies.

In this chapter attention focuses primarily on analyzing the dimensions of power and, particularly, its distribution. Chapters 4 and 5 elaborate on the inequality and coordination of power and provide the principal materials for our judgments about its bases. In his "Marx as a Power Theorist," Olsen suggests several avenues for the development of a power theory of social organization. "Three directions in which theoretical extensions might be made are in the types of power considered, the resource bases available for generating power, and the possible patterns of actual power wielding."[35] Generally the objectives of this and the next two chapters correspond to that suggestion.

COMPARATIVE STRUCTURES OF POWER

The opening move in this analysis of power was to question people who, because of their positions in the social structure, can be presumed to have this type of knowledge. Research comparing perceptions of leadership by these "positional" samples with the perceptions of general or inexpert samples and "actual" leaders (as determined by additional criteria) tends to indicate that the positional and leader groups show high interagreement and low agreement with the general sample.[36] Obviously a number of problems arise, such as collective ignorance and misperception, the relationship between perceived and actual power, prestige as opposed to power, and so forth. While the procedure is far from self-sufficient, it does provide a good starting point for a series of complementary techniques.

Table 16 indicates some of the general results obtained in the initial steps of the procedure, which questioned positional samples in all four regions, plus influential groups in two of the four, concerning the most important persons in the political economy of the region.[37] These results suggest distinctive and contrasting structures of power in each of the four regions.

Guadalajara's influentials[38] predominantly represent two institutional sectors, industry and government. Between these two there is little overlap or multiple position-holding. Politicians are career professionals drawn from the ranks of the official party, whereas industrialists are occupationally committed to their own firms and seldom aspire to public office. Similarly, within the private sector there is little positional overlap. Although several of the industrialists participate in joint investments, each is financially and occupationally dependent on his own relatively autonomous firm. Some of these firms are family enterprises, but there are no cartels or industrial groups that control several major industries; that is, ownership of even the major firms is relatively well distributed. At the head of the influential group is the governor of the state, and three of his top lieutenants in the public sector also appear on the list. One banker and one local businessman represent the commercial sector and round out the list.

Monterrey's influential group is substantially different in character. Industrialists predominate and these come from a relatively limited range of manufacturing activities.[39] This impression is heightened by the fact that many of the top industrial firms are owned by a single extended family (i.e., beer, glass, synthetic fibers, and one of the two steel mills) and the list of nineteen influentials includes ten representatives of this family group. In addition to this dynasty there are a few of the new industrialists and several financiers who run investment firms that were capitalized by profits from industry. Like the financiers, the lawyers named are closely connected to these industries, reinvesting their profits and representing them in legal actions. Notably, only one political figure is mentioned, the governor of Nuevo León, who at one time was also an attorney in the employ of the industrial group. The results suggest that power resides in a single, close-knit group of industrialists with multiple interests in manufacturing and finance.

Cali's top influentials occupy a variety of positions and, not uncommon-

TABLE 16

INFLUENTIALS BY OCCUPATION AND NUMBER AND SOURCE OF NOMINATIONS RECEIVED IN FOUR REGIONS

Occupation	Nominations Received From			Total Nominations
	Private Sector	Public Sector	Other Influentials	
Guadalajara				
1. Governor of state	12	12	7	31
2. Industrialist, shoes	11	4	6	21
3. Banker	8	5	6	19
4. Industrialist, metal products	10	1	7	18
5. Director, state department of economy	7	7	3	17
6. Industrialist, food products	10	1	5	16
7. Industrialist, beverages	6	3	5	14
8. Treasurer of state	4	4	6	14
9. Industrialist, food products	5	2	6	13
10. Industrialist, textiles	1	3	4	8
11. Industrialist, construction	3	2	2	7
12. Industrialist, construction	3	1	3	7
13. Industrialist, metal products	4	0	3	7
14. Industrialist, chemicals	3	1	3	7
15. Mayor of Guadalajara	3	2	1	6
16. Industrialist, food products	3	1	1	5
17. Industrialist, construction	3	1	1	5
18. Director, regional planning agency	3	1	1	5
19. Businessman	2	2	1	5
Monterrey				
1. Industrialist, beer	11	6		17
2. Industrialist, steel	12	5		17
3. Governor of state	3	10		13
4. Financier	7	5		12
5. Industrialist, beer	7	4		11
6. Industrialist, steel	8	2		10
7. Industrialist, steel	8	1		9
8. Industrialist, glass	6	3		9
9. Industrialist, glass	6	2		8
10. Industrialist, synthetic fibers	6	2		8

Occupation		Nominations Received From			Total Nomina-tions
		Private Sector	Public Sector	Other Influentials	
11.	Industrialist, synthetic fibers	6	1		7
12.	Industrialist, steel	3	3		6
13.	Industrialist, construction materials	5	1		6
14.	Industrialist, steel	5	1		6
15.	Industrialist, textiles	4	1		5
16.	Financier	4	1		5
17.	Industrialist, textiles	5	0		5
18.	Lawyer	4	1		5
19.	Lawyer	4	1		5

Cali

		Private Sector	Public Sector	Other Influentials	Total
1.	Industrialist, paper products	27	12	13	52
2.	Director, regional development corporation	19	10	7	36
3.	Mayor, financier	11	12	7	30
4.	Senator, industrialist, newspaper owner	12	4	6	22
5.	Financier	14	2	6	22
6.	Rector, state university	9	7	5	21
7.	Governor of department	6	11	1	18
8.	Federal minister	7	5	5	17
9.	Director, sugar producers' association	7	1	3	13
10.	Industrialist, metal products	3	3	6	12
11.	Director, civic association	7	1	3	11
12.	Financier	5	3	1	9
13.	Industrialist, construction	5	1	3	9
14.	Industrialist, sugar	5	1	3	9
15.	Industrialist, newspaper owner	4	2	2	8
16.	Banker	6	1	0	7
17.	Industrialist, construction	3	2	2	7
18.	Businessman, politician	3	3	0	6
19.	Director, municipal services corporation	2	4	0	6
20.	Director, federal education service	4	1	1	6
21.	Director, industrial association	3	1	1	5

| Occupation | Nominations Received From | | | Total |
	Private Sector	Public Sector	Other Influentials	Nominations

Medellín

1.	Industrialist, textiles	13	8		21
2.	Financier	10	5		15
3.	Governor of department	5	8		13
4.	Mayor of Medellín	3	10		13
5.	Director, industrialists' association	9	3		12
6.	Director, development corporation	4	4		8
7.	Federal minister	3	5		8
8.	Banker	5	3		8
9.	Financier	6	2		8
10.	Financier	4	2		6
11.	Financier	3	3		6
12.	Industrialist, construction	3	3		6
13.	Financier	4	2		6
14.	Financier	2	2		4
15.	Industrialist, paints	3	1		4
16.	Director, municipal services corporation	1	3		4
17.	Industrialist, tobacco	2	2		4
18.	Industrialist, textiles	3	1		4

ly, two or more simultaneously. Of the twenty-one, eight are active in public positions, seven in industry (with some overlap), three in investment firms, two in educational institutions, and three in private interest groups. The initial impression given by the data is one of diversity in the constituency of the influential group. To some extent this is true, but at least two considerations must be introduced as qualifiers. First, multiple occupations imply a greater concentration of influence. For example, the two largest local industry-owning families also own the two principal newspapers; at least one-third of the influentials own large agricultural properties or are the sons of landowners with large holdings. Second, there is much circulation of these people among top positions. For example, three of the influentials are former mayors; several of the public leaders have returned to high posts in private industry since the survey; among the organizational roles on the list at least three were formerly held by others in the group of twenty-one. The traffic of influentials between public and private positions results from the fact that public office at the regional level in Colombia is often an amateur's game in which prominent private-sector people contribute a year or two as a public service.[40] The results indicate that power is held by an alliance of prominent individuals who move among key positions in the public and private sectors; leadership roles are undifferentiated. Within the private sector many of the top industrialists acquired their fortunes in agriculture before expanding into industry; landed and industrial elites overlap substantially. All of this results in frequent splits between factions of the public sector (especially at the federal level) and the private sector.

Finally, Medellín reflects the kind of diversity found in Guadalajara. Industrialists and financiers are most frequently named, although several political leaders also appear. The industrialists represent a fairly broad range of ownership and economic activity. Although political leaders do not predominate, they are important and work closely with the private sector. A summary impression is that we have here a coalition led by industrial and financial interests and including top representatives of the public sector.

The first conclusion to be reached from these data is that power and positions of influence are more narrowly distributed in Cali and Monterrey than in Medellín and Guadalajara. In the two former cases a close-knit elite dominates top positions, while in the second two the leadership group is coalitional and accessible to a wider range of participants, including public officials who are not simultaneously economic dominants.

Equally or perhaps more important in the analysis of structured power relations is the organizational context. Table 17 indicates those development-related organizations that positional leaders and influentials considered most important.

Guadalajara's development-related organizations are numerous and represent a variety of differentiated associational interests. They are numerous in the sense that several appearing on the list are composite organizations. There are, for example, some fifteen different industry-specific industrial chambers. The official party embodies separate organizations for workers, farmers, and public employees. Their variety is reflected in the inclusion of both economic interest groups and public-sector agencies. Further, the effective specialization of these groups is enhanced by the fact that their activities are coordinated through the public-sector Department of Economy and the private Coordinating Junta. Finally, the scope and scale of this set of organizations is broad; public and party agencies have extensive legal powers, and private-sector organizations, required by law, embrace practically all forms of economic activity.

Monterrey's organizational complex has less variety, with only two pub-

TABLE 17

INFLUENTIAL ORGANIZATIONS BY NUMBER AND
SOURCE OF NOMINATIONS RECEIVED IN FOUR REGIONS

Organization	Nominations Received From			Total Nomina-tions
	Private Sector	Public Sector	Other Influentials	
Guadalajara				
1. Chamber of Commerce	15	20	9	44
2. Industrial Chambers	12	19	8	39
3. Institute of Promotion and Economic Studies	4	16	3	23
4. Bankers' Association	10	4	3	17
5. Coordinating Junta of Private Initiative	4	8	5	17
6. Employers' Association	4	8	3	15
7. State Department of Economy	5	6	1	12
8. Official Political Party (PRI)	7	3	0	10
9. Labor Union (CROC)	8	2	0	10
10. Labor Union (CTM)	7	2	0	9
11. Urbanization and Planning Department of State Government	3	2	2	7
12. State Government	2	3	0	5
13. Municipal Works Council	0	2	3	5
14. Opposition Party (PAN)	1	3	0	4
15. Service Clubs	2	1	0	3
16. Productivity Education Institute	1	2	0	3
17. American Chamber of Commerce	2	1	0	3
18. Cattlemen's Association	0	3	0	3
Cali				
1. State University	23	17	12	52
2. Regional Development Corporation	14	15	10	39
3. Civic Action Association (UAV)	17	14	7	38
4. Industrialists' Association (ANDI)	17	11	8	36
5. Financial Corporation	15	2	7	24
6. State Government	9	8	3	20

| Organization | Nominations Received From | | | Total |
	Private Sector	Public Sector	Other Influentials	Nomination
7. Merchants' Association (FENALCO)	9	8	2	19
8. Municipal Services Corporation (EMCALI)	5	8	6	19
9. Municipal Government	7	8	2	17
10. Administrative Education Institute (INCOLDA)	7	3	7	17
11. Chamber of Commerce	6	2	2	10
12. National Educational Service (SENA)	3	2	5	10
13. Small Industrialists' Association	5	3	1	9
14. Local Bank	6	1	1	8
15. Sugar Producers' Association	5	2	1	8
16. Agriculturalists' and Cattlemen's Association (SAG)	3	3	1	7
17. Federal Agricultural Credit Agency	2	3	1	6
18. Paper Industry Corporation	4	1	0	5

| Occupation | Nominations Received From | | Total |
	Private Sector	Public Sector	Nomination
Monterrey			
1. Chamber of Commerce	16	11	27
2. Industrial Chambers	12	11	23
3. Public Development Planning Agency (COFIDE)	14	4	18
4. Employers' Association	4	9	13
5. Beer Industry	5	7	12
6. Private University	3	6	9
7. Bankers' Association	5	3	8
8. Realtors' Association	3	5	8
9. Service Clubs	4	4	8
10. Municipal and State Services Commissions	6	2	8
11. Steel Industry	4	4	8
12. Glass Industry	3	4	7
13. State Government	4	2	6
14. Private Educational Center	4	2	6
15. Steel Industry	1	4	5

| Occupation | Nominations Received From | | Total |
	Private Sector	Public Sector	Nominations

Medellín

1.	Industrialists' Association	13	9	22
2.	Public Development Corporation (IDEA)	8	8	16
3.	Municipal Services Corporation	3	10	13
4.	Textile Industry	5	5	10
5.	Financial Corporation	4	6	10
6.	Merchants' Association	8	1	9
7.	Textile Industry	4	4	8
8.	Private Development Corporation	4	4	8
9.	Cattlemen's Association	6	2	8
10.	Coffee Growers' Association	5	0	5
11.	Land Reform Agency	1	4	5
12.	Textile Industry	4	1	5
13.	Steel Industry	3	2	5
14.	Agricultural Bank	2	3	5
15.	Department Planning Agency	1	4	5

lic agencies included and the bulk of the list closely allied with industrial concerns. Nevertheless, there is a reasonable amount of differentiation, given the nature of the local economy, e.g., the university and commercial and realty groups are included. For similar reasons there is less, though not inconsequential, specialization; no overarching organizations formally co-ordinate separate interests, although this is done informally by the "industrial group" through the Industrial Chambers and the Employers' Association. In terms of scope and scale these organizations are at least on a par with Guadalajara's, although the pervasive role of government and the private sector are reversed. Large-scale industrial organizations are closely related and assume great responsibility for development planning, including welfare benefits for workers; the public sector assumes a secondary and supportive role.

The organizational picture in Cali is differentiated, with a variety of public and private interests represented. Specialization, however, suffers from a lack of coordinating bodies and, consequently, a good deal of duplication of effort exists. Among the several groups pursuing parallel yet seldom intersecting projects are the state government, the Industrialists' Association, the university, and the government-sponsored educational institutions. The two top institutions, the state university and the Regional Development Corporation (CVC), owe much of their success to the fact that they are relatively independent of the local community in financial and administrative matters. Given this lack of effective cooperation and the fragile character of governmental institutions under the present political system, the scope and scale of organizational activity is severely restricted.

Among Medellín's top organizations only two represent the public sector, but these are high on the list alongside the financial and industrial groups with which they share importance, making this case distinct from that of Monterrey. The other groups on the list indicate a variety of differentiated interests with specialized and coordinated functions. Although these organizations operate under the same legal mandate as those of Cali, their scope and scale are much more extensive. Because of the long history of regional autonomy, local government has developed in harmony with industry, fulfilling a wide range of supportive functions. The industrial organizations themselves are large in scale and comprehensive in their range of development activity. Medellín is the national headquarters of the Industrialists' Association, and under its aegis public and private development corporations have been organized in cooperation with the public sector.

An extremely effective, if little explored, technique for assessing the concentration of power in any locality is to compare the linkages between top persons and top organizations. The assumption is, of course, that power is more concentrated to the extent that there is a higher correspondence, or denser set of linkages, between these individuals and the organizational bases of power. In order to explore this question, lists of the administrative officers and boards of directors of the top organizations in each region were assembled and cross-referenced with influential persons.

Table 18 reflects some impressive results that are quite consistent with the interpretations of power structure patterns presented thus far. In Guadalajara the linkages are minimal. Six of nineteen influentials (less than one-third) are chief administrative officers of top organizations; the number of board member–officer linkages is thirteen, varying from zero to three per influential and averaging about .7, or 1.0 for all (nineteen) types of linkages per person. This implies that there are other important people heading the organizations listed as influential and other organizations headed by the people listed as influential; or, in short, a broader distribution of power.

Monterrey reflects the most concentrated structure of power. Eight chief administrative officers among nineteen influentials (42 percent) is not an especially high ratio, but some forty-five board member–officer linkages is

TABLE 18

LINKAGES AMONG INFLUENTIAL PERSONS AND ORGANIZATIONS IN FOUR REGIONS

GUADALAJARA

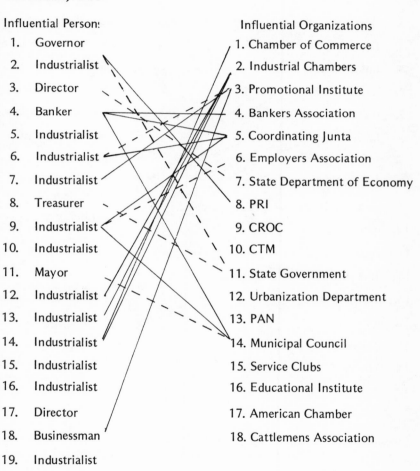

Influential Person:	Influential Organizations
1. Governor	1. Chamber of Commerce
2. Industrialist	2. Industrial Chambers
3. Director	3. Promotional Institute
4. Banker	4. Bankers Association
5. Industrialist	5. Coordinating Junta
6. Industrialist	6. Employers Association
7. Industrialist	7. State Department of Economy
8. Treasurer	8. PRI
9. Industrialist	9. CROC
10. Industrialist	10. CTM
11. Mayor	11. State Government
12. Industrialist	12. Urbanization Department
13. Industrialist	13. PAN
14. Industrialist	14. Municipal Council
15. Industrialist	15. Service Clubs
16. Industrialist	16. Educational Institute
17. Director	17. American Chamber
18. Businessman	18. Cattlemens Association
19. Industrialist	

Legend: — — 6   Chief Administrative Officer
—————13   Member of Board of Directors or Key Officer
     19   Total

MONTERREY

Influential Persons   Influential Organizations

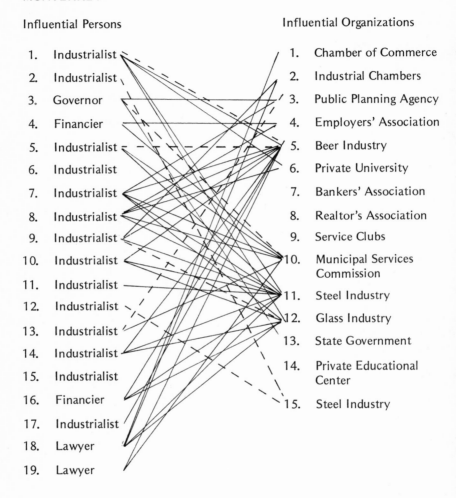

1. Industrialist	1. Chamber of Commerce
2. Industrialist	2. Industrial Chambers
3. Governor	3. Public Planning Agency
4. Financier	4. Employers' Association
5. Industrialist	5. Beer Industry
6. Industrialist	6. Private University
7. Industrialist	7. Bankers' Association
8. Industrialist	8. Realtor's Association
9. Industrialist	9. Service Clubs
10. Industrialist	10. Municipal Services Commission
11. Industrialist	11. Steel Industry
12. Industrialist	12. Glass Industry
13. Industrialist	13. State Government
14. Industrialist	14. Private Educational Center
15. Industrialist	15. Steel Industry
16. Financier	
17. Industrialist	
18. Lawyer	
19. Lawyer	

Legend: _ _ 8   Chief Administrative Officer
         —— 45   Member of Board of Directors or Key Officer
            53   Total

CALI

Influential Persons

Influential Organizations

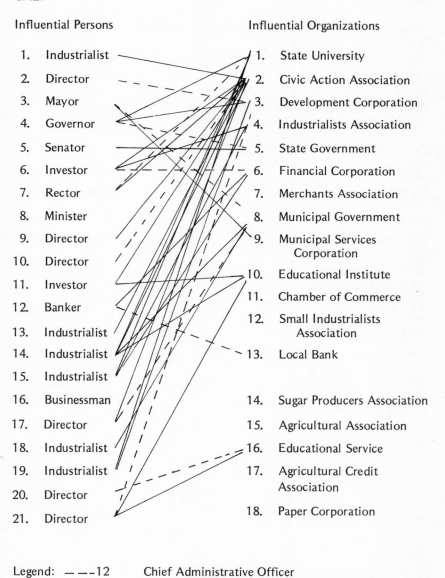

1. Industrialist
2. Director
3. Mayor
4. Governor
5. Senator
6. Investor
7. Rector
8. Minister
9. Director
10. Director
11. Investor
12. Banker
13. Industrialist
14. Industrialist
15. Industrialist
16. Businessman
17. Director
18. Industrialist
19. Industrialist
20. Director
21. Director

1. State University
2. Civic Action Association
3. Development Corporation
4. Industrialists Association
5. State Government
6. Financial Corporation
7. Merchants Association
8. Municipal Government
9. Municipal Services Corporation
10. Educational Institute
11. Chamber of Commerce
12. Small Industrialists Association
13. Local Bank
14. Sugar Producers Association
15. Agricultural Association
16. Educational Service
17. Agricultural Credit Association
18. Paper Corporation

Legend: ‒ ‒ ‒12   Chief Administrative Officer
          ——— 31   Member of Board of Directors or Key Officer
             43   Total

MEDELLIN

Influential Persons

1.   Industrialist
2.   Financier
3.   Governor
4.   Mayor
5.   Director
6.   Director
7.   Minister
8.   Banker
9.   Financier
10. Financier
11. Financier
12. Industrialist
13. Financier
14. Financier
15. Industrialist
16. Director
17. Industrialist
18. Industrialist

Influential Organizations

1.   Industrialists' Association
2.   Public Development Corporation
3.   Municipal Services Corporation
4.   Textile Industry
5.   Financial Corporation
6.   Merchants' Association
7.   Textile Industry
8.   Private Development Corporation
9.   Cattlemen's Association
10. Coffee Growers' Association
11. Land Reform Agency
12. Textile Industry
13. Steel Industry
14. Agricultural Bank
15. Department Planning Agency

Legend: — — —7   Chief Administrative Officer
         ———17   Member of Board of Directors or Key Officer
             24   Total

noteworthy, varying from zero to six and averaging 2.4 per person, or 2.8 for all (fifty-three) linkages. Cali is close to the more concentrated end of the continuum, with twelve of twenty-one influentials (over half) in chief administrative posts and some thirty other linkages varying from one to four and averaging 1.5 per person, or 2.0 for all (forty-three) linkages. Finally, Medellín is quite similar to Guadalajara; seven of eighteen influentials (39 percent) are chief administrators. Seventeen other linkages vary from zero to three per person, averaging .9, or 1.3 for all (twenty-four) linkages.

Further, in the more intensive studies of Guadalajara and Cali the influentials interviewed were asked sociometric questions relating to which of the other influentials they knew well and worked with in development projects. Guadalajara influentials were closely tied to an average of nine other people on the list while the figure was fifteen others in Cali.[41]

THE BROADER OUTLINES OF POWER AND CLASS

It should be emphasized once more that these results are not to be understood as an exhaustive treatment of the organization of power. What we have considered thus far are the historical foundations of elite structure (chapter 2) and a first approximation of contemporary patterns based on four measures: influential persons, influential organizations, individual-organizational linkages, and sociometric interlocks based on participation. More evidence is to follow on the ideological and attitudinal cohesiveness of leaders (chapter 4) and the process of decision-making (chapter 5). Nevertheless, at this point we may begin to fashion some tentative conclusions based on the first two approaches.

Table 19 is offered as a notational summary of the results of this chapter. The "types of power structures" are purely descriptive at this point, since we have yet to present all of the evidence that will elaborate the conceptual scheme. Yet, as the summary suggests, the four cases can be located on a continuum representing the distribution (concentration) of power as operationalized by influential-organizational linkages. Guadalajara falls at the more competitive end and Monterrey at the more monopolistic, with the four cases assuming something of a bimodal pattern.

From the data we may also draw some conclusions about the inequality of power. Notably, the four cases differ markedly in the roles of the public and private sectors. In Guadalajara, public-sector leadership is most decisive but operates on a coalitional basis with separate and coordinated private-sector organizations. In Medellín these sectoral leadership roles are reversed, but the coalitional arrangement is still much in evidence. Cali's most influential persons and organizations favor private-sector inter-

TABLE 19

TYPES OF POWER STRUCTURES
AND EMPIRICAL INDICATORS

	Concentration of Power			
	Low			High
	Guadalajara	Medellin	Cali	Monterrey
Total Linkages	19	24	43	53
Mean No. Linkages	1.0	1.3	2.0	2.4
Mean No. Joint Participants in Projects	9	---	15	---
Type of Power Structure	Publicly Directed Coalition	Privately Directed Coalition	Privately Dominated Factions	Privately Dominated Pyramid

ests and these are often in conflict with the public sector. Further, within both the public and private sectors there are internal factions (e.g., local versus federal government or progressive versus traditional economic interests such as the CVC and the landowners). In Monterrey, factions are relatively unknown; the industrial group and its allies in finance, commerce, education, and government constitute a relatively well defined pyramid of power. Certainly this is not to suggest that a few industrial leaders make all the decisions or monopolize all the positions of influence. For the moment it simply suggests that, in comparison with those of the other three cities, Monterrey's power structure is the most concentrated and well defined.

Recalling the general descriptions of social stratification from chapter 2, we are now in a position to analyze the class bases of power in the four regions. In the most general terms the four cases show wide variation in the extent to which power is distributed among classes. Taking the cases in reverse order, the influential persons and organizations in Monterrey are almost exclusively representatives of industrial ownership interests of the upper class. The only exceptions to this pattern of upper-class dominance are several organizations such as the Chamber of Commerce, public planning and services agencies, the university, and the state government, all of which are closely tied to the industrial group but also include middle-class economic groups.

In Cali, upper-class industrialists and financiers make up the modal category of influentials but representatives of government and education are also present. Although many of the latter set of individuals have upper-class origins, top organizations are more representative of such middle-class groupings as students, bureaucrats, merchants, small industrialists, and even the small agricultural stratum.

From the standpoint of influential individuals, Medellín is similar to Cali in terms of important organizations. However, we note here the first appearance of groups representing the lower classes (e.g., the land reform agency) and more groups with middle-class constituencies (e.g., the Public Development Corporation, the Municipal Services Corporation, the Merchants' Association, the Coffee Growers' Association, the agricultural bank, and the departmental planning bureaucracy).

Once again Guadalajara falls at the most open and representative end of the continuum. In contrast to the other cases, several influentials, particularly those of the public sector, have middle-class origins and constituencies. From the organizational standpoint we find for the first time labor groups and political parties nominally representative of the rural peasantry and urban working class. Only three or four of the organizations (the Industrial Chambers, the Bankers' Association, the Employers' Association, and the American Chamber) are predominantly upper-class organs. Most represent the middle sectors of the industrial, commercial, and service economy, and, indeed, the powerful public sector attempts to coopt a wide variety of groups.

These observations suggest that there is a close correspondence between the distributive structures of class and power. For example, in chapter 2 we noted the more and less egalitarian class structures of the paired cities Guadalajara-Medellín and Monterrey-Cali respectively. Here we find that the concentration of power tends to follow the same general pattern. And this is to be expected, given the fact that class-related resources (e.g., ownership and control of the means of production or position in the market place) are fundamental determinants of social power. But we must place equal stress on the fact that class and power are not isomorphic; position in the hierarchy of social classes is not an unerring indicator of position in the structure of power. For example, reasoning strictly from a social stratification perspective one might anticipate a more cohesive power elite in Cali and, possibly, be surprised by the pervasiveness of Monterrey's industrial group. In short, historically-conditioned patterns of class structure represent some of the most decisive influences on social power, but not the only ones. Other influences intervene and must be considered for a more complete understanding of the structure of power. Among these we would count ideology and politics, discussions of which follow.

4. Leaders and Leadership Ideologies

In the literature on development a great deal of emphasis has been properly placed on the role of ideas in social change. Nevertheless, theories of development that incorporate the ideological factor differ widely in their evaluation of its causal status. For some theorists, ideas and values lie at the root of the change process. Development is effected to the extent that individuals adopt an "achievement orientation" or "entrepreneurial spirit," and societies replace authoritarian and particularistic norms with ones based on creativity and universalism. At bottom, the obstacles to development are in the minds of men, and thus are capable of eradication through education and the diffusion of new ideas. Conversely, other theorists stress the epiphenomenal character of ideas. Ideologies may have determinant influences on social action, but they in turn derive from social structural conditions and assume importance as intervening variables rather than root causes.

If these positions are regarded as ideal typical formulations, then we would expect that most theories posit a more subtle relationship between ideas and social structure. Max Weber's *The Protestant Ethic and the Spirit of Capitalism*[1] is perhaps the classic work on this question. Writing in the wake of Marx and other historical materialists, Weber endeavored, not to refute their interpretation, but to balance it with a historical assessment of the independent role of ideas. Bendix puts it well when he observes:

> It is apparent from this review of Weber's earliest social and economic investigations that he asserted the importance of ideas and of the individual against the collectivism of the Marxists and the social evolutionists, but that he also emphasized the social foundations of individual action much as Marxism had done. . . . This relative independence of ideas could be recognized, in his judgment, without either denying or neglecting the influence of political and economic interests on the development of ideas.

99

(Bendix then quotes Weber's own comment on the analytic strategy he followed in *The Protestant Ethic.*)

> It is, of course, not my aim to substitute for a one-sided materialistic an equally one-sided spiritualistic causal interpretation of culture and of history. Each is equally possible, but each, if it does not serve as the preparation, but as the conclusion of an investigation, accomplishes little in the interest of historical truth.[2]

In this way Weber argued for the possibility of multiple or complex causal sequences and, most important, as his last sentence indicates, for an open-minded spirit of inquiry in which initial assumptions (preparation) guide the analysis rather than represent its conclusions.

In the discussion that follows, we adopt the Weberian position concerning the influence of leadership ideologies on the development process. That is, we shall examine the ways in which the perceptions and evaluations of elite groups are conditioned by social structural influences that vary across the four regions. But we shall also suggest that these ideologies have emergent properties deriving from unique congeries of historical and circumstantial influences that impart to them a certain autonomy in the developmental process.

Moreover, reciprocity between ideology and development arises from the fact that what a society may aspire to and define as "development" is itself an ideological judgment arrived at in the competitive exchange of political interests. Horowitz states the matter as follows: "The question of what constitutes development has itself become part of the general ideological struggle. Facts and figures on everything from consumer production to rates of capital reinvestment now serve as 'evidence' for the superiority of capitalism over socialism or socialism over capitalism."[3] Gusfield makes a similar point concerning the context of political action.

> Men refer to aspects of the past as tradition in grounding their present actions in some legitimating principle. In this fashion, tradition becomes an ideology, a program of action in which it functions as a goal or as a justificatory base. . . . In similar fashion to be 'modern' appears in many new nations as an aspiration toward which certain groups seek to move the society. 'Modern' becomes a perceived state of things functioning as a criterion against which to judge specific actions and a program of actions to guide policy.[4]

This perspective suggests at least one important source of the independent role of ideas, namely, the political struggle in which competition arises over the adoption and implementation of various ideological positions and their programmatic implications.

In order to address each of these aspects of the ideological question, we shall first describe the leadership groups with respect to their social characteristics. Next, a variety of indicators are provided to characterize the content of leadership ideologies across the four cases. Third, we endeavor to explain ideological differences in terms of the social characteristics of both leaders and regions. Finally, the patterned differences between ideological perspectives in the four regions are interpreted contextually in a way that will provide a background for the analysis of decision-making in chapter 5.

SOCIAL CHARACTERISTICS OF LEADERS

The initial task of this analysis is to indicate something about the leadership strata in the four regions. Here we shall deal with the entire leadership sample in each region, that is, people from public- and private-sector organizational posts as well as influentials in the two cities where they were interviewed. There is no difficulty in describing all of these respondents as leaders. Although some are demonstrably more important than others, all occupy key positions in economic and political organizations that set them apart from the general public. Further, they constitute a nearly exhaustive universe of the directors of important agencies and interest groups in the development process, so that their representativeness is not at issue.[5] Table 20 indicates the distribution of leaders interviewed by position.

Table 21 reports data on the distribution of leadership groups according to nine selected social characteristics. Comparisons based on these data must take into account the fact that the sampling procedure differed in Guadalajara and Cali (the more intensively studied) from that employed in Monterrey and Medellín (the less intensively studied). In the two former regions, larger samples of subleaders were drawn and influentials were included. For that reason, interpretation of the table should follow two-by-two comparisons of similarly generated samples when the total columns are being analyzed. Public- and private-sector samples were similar in all cases and can be compared across all four.

The age variable is of no great moment, although a few points are worth noting. For the most part, public-sector leaders tend to be younger than those of the private sector, reflecting, perhaps, the lower status of government work in that it seems to require less experience. Interestingly, the data for Guadalajara provide an exception to the pattern, with more nearly equivalent age distributions in the two sectors, and this would follow from the earlier discussion of the uniquely important role of government in this region. Understandably, the influentials of Guadalajara and Cali tend

TABLE 20

INTERVIEWEES BY REGION AND POSITION

	Guadalajara	Cali$_a$	Monterrey	Medellín	Total
Public Sector	31	31	22	19	103
Private Sector	34	39	20	21	114
Influentials	18	17	(4)$_b$	(4)$_b$	35
Total	83	35	42	40	252

a) The tables in this chapter will present data on the four regions in
this order since the more and less intensive methodology suggests
that on some items (e.g., SES) direct comparisons are meaningful
only across the Guadalajara-Cali and Monterrey-Medellín pairs,
not across all four.

b) Included in the public or private sector were interviewees nominated
with sufficient frequency to quality as influentials.

to be somewhat older than the organizational leaders. Another interesting
point that corroborates local perceptions in Cali is the relative youthful-
ness of the leaders; over 60 percent are under forty-five, which contrasts
noticeably with Guadalajara. The same is true of the Monterrey-Medellín
comparison, the latter city having a more youthful corps of organizational
leaders (though the numbers are small, 75 percent are under forty-five).

With respect to educational attainment, the data are impressively consistent and leave no doubt that these respondents represent an elite group
in Latin America. Across all ten subdivisions of the leadership samples
(with the one exception of Monterrey's private sector, where numbers are
small), over half of the leaders are university educated. In two-by-two
comparisons, more leaders in Cali had received university and postgradu-
ate training than in Guadalajara (88.2 percent versus 74.7 percent).
Though it is not reported in this table, a larger proportion of Cali leaders
than of those in Guadalajara received their education in private and foreign universities (32.2 percent versus 14.5 percent), an item of some significance. Similarly, the educational level of leaders in Medellín is higher
than in Monterrey. These global cross-national differences may be due to
historical circumstances, since widespread higher education is more recent
in Mexico than in Colombia.

In the structured interviews, leaders were asked to reconstruct their career histories leading up to their present positions. One of the ways in which this material can be used is in the measurement of professional experience. That is, the number of years devoted to the present position as well as related earlier positions (variable 3) provides a rough index of professionalization. Clearly this variable is correlated with age, but the correlation is far from perfect and varies across cases, suggesting that other, situational factors are at work.[6] Here the general pattern supports our previous speculation concerning the higher status and professionalization of the private sector over the public across all cases except Guadalajara, for reasons already noted. In paired comparisons, differences between Guadalajara and Cali are large, the latter having a higher proportion of leaders with little professional experience and very few with twenty years or more (a category containing nearly a quarter of the Guadalajara leaders). This fact also seems to support observations concerning the high turnover of personnel, lack of continuity, and amateurish character of local leadership in Cali. The data for Monterrey and Medellín are quite similar, with the former having an advantage in the more experienced categories.

A second and possibly more compelling measure of professionalization is the relationship between a person's educational background and present position (variable 4). A fairly common phenomenon in Latin America is the existence of university graduates (notably lawyers and engineers) who do not practice their professions. There are undoubtedly many reasons for this situation, among which the conventional explanation of upper-class indolence is probably far less important than structural restrictions on opportunity, as the "brain drain" problem would suggest. Whatever its manifold causes, the extent to which educated professionals do in fact practice their skills is an excellent measure of professionalization. Across all cases, public-sector leaders are found to be engaged in occupations more closely related to their educational backgrounds. This fact runs counter to the foregoing interpretations of age and professional experience and leads to the conclusion that, although public organizational leaders are generally younger and less experienced, they are professional in the sense of applying their training to their present occupations. When that is taken into consideration, some familiar patterns reappear. Leadership in Guadalajara and Monterrey is more professionalized than in each of their counterpart cities in terms of the proportion of leaders engaged in occupations closely related to their educational specializations. Again the Monterrey-Medellín differences are not as substantial.

Another variable, the fifth, having to do with professionalization and mobility, is the method by which leaders attained their present position. Here the results are rather strikingly in unison. Generally, over half of the

TABLE 21

SELECTED SOCIAL CHARACTERISTICS OF LEADERS BY REGION (In Percent and (N))

| Variable | GUADALAJARA | | | | CALI | | | |
	Public Sector	Private Sector	Influential	Total	Public Sector	Private Sector	Influential	Total
Age								
25-34	19.4	26.4	16.7	21.7	41.9	23.1	11.8	27.
	(6)	(9)	(3)	(18)	(13)	(9)	(2)	(24
35-44	26.1	17.7	16.7	20.5	38.8	28.2	35.3	33.
	(8)	(6)	(3)	(17)	(12)	(11)	(6)	(29
45-54	35.5	26.4	27.8	30.2	9.7	38.5	35.3	27.
	(11)	(9)	(5)	(25)	(3)	(15)	(6)	(24
55-64	16.1	17.7	22.2	18.0	3.2	7.7	17.6	8.
	(5)	(6)	(4)	(15)	(1)	(3)	(3)	(7)
65+	3.2	11.7	16.7	9.6	6.4	2.6	0	3.
	(1)	(4)	(3)	(8)	(2)	(1)		(3)
Total	100.0	100.0	100.0	100.0	100.0	100.0	100.0	100.
	(31)	(34)	(18)	(83)	(31)	(39)	(17)	(87
Educational Attainment								
Primary	6.5	2.9	5.6	4.8	3.2	7.7	5.9	5.
	(2)	(1)	(1)	(4)	(1)	(3)	(1)	(5)
Secondary	3.2	11.8	11.1	8.4	6.4	15.4	0	9.
	(1)	(4)	(2)	(7)	(2)	(6)		(8)
Secondary and Specialization	3.2	23.5	5.6	12.0	3.2	12.8	5.9	8.
	(1)	(8)	(1)	(10)	(1)	(5)	(1)	(7)
University	80.6	52.9	77.8	68.7	61.3	51.3	52.9	55.
	(25)	(18)	(14)	(57)	(19)	(20)	(9)	(48
Post Graduate	6.5	8.8	0	6.0	25.8	12.8	35.3	21.
	(2)	(3)		(5)	(8)	(5)	(6)	(19
Total	100.0	100.0	100.0	100.0	100.0	100.0	100.0	100.
	(31)	(34)	(18)	(83)	(31)	(39)	(17)	(87

MONTERREY			MEDELLIN		
Public Sector	Private Sector	Total	Public Sector	Private Sector	Total
27.3	5.0	16.6	52.7	28.6	40.0
(6)	(1)	(7)	(10)	(6)	(16)
40.9	25.0	33.3	36.8	33.3	35.0
(9)	(5)	(14)	(7)	(7)	(14)
18.2	40.8	28.5	5.3	19.0	12.5
(4)	(8)	(12)	(1)	(4)	(5)
13.6	20.0	16.7	0	9.6	5.0
(3)	(4)	(7)		(2)	(2)
0	10.0	4.8	5.3	9.6	7.5
	(2)	(2)	(1)	(2)	(3)
100.0	100.0	100.0	100.0	100.0	100.0
(22)	(20)	(42)	(19)	(21)	(40)

Public Sector	Private Sector	Total	Public Sector	Private Sector	Total
0	5.0	2.4	0	4.8	2.5
	(1)	(1)		(1)	(1)
4.5	20.0	11.9	0	9.5	5.0
(1)	(4)	(5)		(2)	(2)
9.1	25.0	16.7	0	0	0
(2)	(5)	(7)			
63.6	35.0	150.0	100.0	81.0	90.0
(14)	(7)	(21)	(19)	(17)	(36)
22.7	15.0	19.0	0	4.8	2.5
(5)	(3)	(8)		(1)	(1)
100.0	100.0	100.0	100.0	100.0	100.0
(22)	(20)	(42)	(19)	(21)	(40)

Variable	GUADALAJARA Public Sector	Private Sector	Influential	Total	CALI Public Sector	Private Sector	Influential	Tota
Professional Experience								
0-4 yrs.	38.7 (12)	38.2 (13)	0	30.1 (25)	51.6 (16)	43.6 (17)	17.6 (3)	41 (3(
5-9	25.8 (8)	23.5 (8)	16.7 (3)	22.9 (19)	29.0 (9)	17.9 (7)	17.6 (3)	21 (1!
10-14	6.5 (2)	14.7 (5)	11.1 (2)	10.8 (9)	6.5 (2)	10.3 (4)	23.5 (4)	11 (1(
15-19	9.7 (3)	5.9 (2)	22.2 (4)	10.8 (9)	9.7 (3)	17.9 (7)	17.6 (3)	14 (1:
20+	19.4 (6)	14.7 (5)	50.0 (9)	24.1 (20)	0	7.7 (3)	11.8 (2)	5 (5
NA (not ascertained)	0	2.9 (1)	0	1.2 (1)	3.2 (1)	2.6 (1)	11.8 (2)	4 (4
Total	100.0 (31)	100.0 (34)	100.0 (18)	100.0 (83)	100.0 (31)	100.0 (39)	100.0 (17)	100 (8
Education and Present Occupation								
Unrelated	12.9 (4)	29.4 (10)	27.8 (5)	22.9 (19)	3.2 (1)	43.6 (17)	47.1 (8)	2! (2
Somewhat related	25.8 (8)	23.5 (8)	11.1 (2)	21.7 (18)	32.3 (10)	20.5 (8)	11.8 (2)	2: (2
Closely related	61.3 (19)	47.0 (16)	61.1 (11)	55.4 (46)	64.5 (20)	35.9 (14)	41.2 (7)	4: (4
Total	100.0 (31)	100.0 (34)	100.0 (18)	100.0 (83)	100.0 (31)	100.0 (39)	100.0 (17)	100 (8

MONTERREY			MEDELLIN		
Public Sector	Private Sector	Total	Public Sector	Private Sector	Total
31.8	20.0	26.2	36.8	14.3	25.0
(7)	(4)	(11)	(7)	(3)	(10)
31.8	40.0	35.7	36.8	38.1	37.5
(7)	(8)	(15)	(7)	(8)	(15)
22.7	5.0	14.3	15.8	28.6	22.5
(5)	(1)	(6)	(3)	(6)	(9)
9.1	10.0	9.5	10.5	9.5	10.4
(2)	(2)	(4)	(2)	(2)	(4)
4.5	25.0	14.3	0	9.5	5.0
(1)	(5)	(6)		(2)	(2)
0	0	0	0	0	0
100.0	100.0	100.0	100.0	100.0	100.0
(22)	(20)	(42)	(19)	(21)	(40)
9.1	40.0	23.8	0	28.6	15.0
(2)	(8)	(10)		(6)	(6)
9.1	20.0	14.3	31.6	28.6	30.0
(2)	(4)	(6)	(6)	(6)	(12)
81.8	40.0	61.9	68.4	42.8	55.0
(18)	(8)	(26)	(13)	(9)	(22)
100.0	100.0	100.0	100.0	100.0	100.0
(22)	(20)	(42)	(19)	(21)	(40)

Variable	GUADALAJARA				CALI			
	Public Sector	Private Sector	Influ-ential	Total	Public Sector	Private Sector	Influ-ential	Total
Method of Obtaining Present Position								
Family, personal connections	3.2 (1)	11.8 (4)	16.7 (3)	9.6 (8)	3.2 (1)	7.7 (3)	5.9 (1)	5.7 (5)
Appointed with-out experience or education	6.5 (2)	0	0	2.4 (2)	12.9 (4)	17.9 (7)	23.5 (4)	17.2 (15)
Appointed with experience or education	48.4 (15)	73.5 (25)	16.7 (3)	51.8 (43)	54.8 (17)	61.5 (24)	41.2 (7)	55.2 (48)
Promoted from within	38.7 (12)	2.9 (1)	11.1 (2)	18.11 (15)	29.0 (9)	7.7 (3)	0	13.8 (12)
Founder	3.1 (1)	11.8 (4)	55.6 (10)	18.1 (15)	0	5.1 (2)	29.4 (5)	8.0 (7)
Total	100.0 (31)	100.0 (34)	100.0 (18)	100.0 (83)	100.0 (31)	100.0 (39)	100.0 (17)	100.0 (87)
Organizational Memberships								
0-1	12.9 (4)	32.4 (11)	0	18.0 (15)	25.8 (8)	29.7 (12)	11.8 (2)	25.2 (22)
1-3	45.2 (14)	44.2 (15)	11.2 (2)	37.4 (31)	45.1 (14)	35.9 (14)	11.8 (2)	34.5 (30)
4-5	16.2 (5)	14.7 (5)	27.8 (5)	18.0 (15)	22.6 (7)	20.5 (8)	35.2 (6)	24.1 (21)
6 or more	6.4 (2)	2.9 (1)	33.4 (6)	10.8 (9)	3.2 (1)	7.7 (3)	41.2 (7)	12.6 (11)
NA	19.4 (6)	5.9 (2)	27.8 (5)	15.7 (13)	3.2 (1)	5.1 (2)	0	3.4 (3)
Total	100.0 (31)	100.0 (34)	100.0 (18)	100.0 (83)	100.0 (31)	100.0 (39)	100.0 (17)	100.0 (87)

MONTERREY			MEDELLIN		
Public Sector	Private Sector	Total	Public Sector	Private Sector	Total
9.1	25.0	16.7	10.5	4.8	7.5
(2)	(5)	(7)	(2)	(1)	(3)
9.1	5.0	7.1	5.3	9.5	7.5
(2)	(1)	(3)	(1)	(2)	(3)
68.2	50.0	59.5	57.9	52.4	55.0
(15)	(10)	(25)	(11)	(11)	(22)
13.6	5.0	9.5	26.3	19.0	22.5
(3)	(1)	(4)	(5)	(4)	(9)
0	15.0	7.1	0	14.3	7.5
	(3)	(3)		(3)	(3)
100.0	100.0	100.0	100.0	100.0	100.0
(22)	(20)	(42)	(19)	(21)	(40)
13.6	20.0	16.7	36.9	19.0	27.5
(3)	(4)	(7)	(7)	(4)	(11)
45.4	20.0	33.4	31.6	23.8	27.5
(10)	(4)	(14)	(6)	(5)	(11)
13.6	15.0	14.2	21.1	33.4	27.5
(3)	(3)	(6)	(4)	(7)	(11)
18.2	40.0	28.6	10.6	14.3	12.5
(4)	(8)	(12)	(2)	(3)	(5)
9.1	5.0	7.1	0	9.5	5.0
(2)	(1)	(3)		(2)	(2)
100.0	100.0	100.0	100.0	100.0	100.0
(22)	(20)	(42)	(19)	(21)	(40)

Prestige Club	GUADALAJARA				CALI			
Variable	Public Sector	Private Sector	Influ-ential	Total	Public Sector	Private Sector	Influ-ential	To
Prestige Club Membership								
No	71.0	64.7	5.6	54.2	67.7	48.7	5.9	4
	(22)	(22)	(1)	(45)	(21)	(19)	(1)	(4
Yes	12.9	29.4	83.3	34.9	29.0	46.2	88.2	4
	(4)	(10)	(15)	(29)	(9)	(18)	(15)	(4
NA	16.1	5.9	11.1	10.8	3.2	5.1	5.9	
	(5)	(2)	(2)	(9)	(1)	(2)	(1)	(4
Total	100.0	100.0	100.0	100.0	100.0	100.0	100.0	10
	(31)	(34)	(18)	(83)	(31)	(39)	(17)	(2
Socioeconomic Status (SES)								
Low	9.7	8.8	0	7.2	3.2	17.9	0	
	(3)	(3)		(6)	(1)	(7)		(8
Medium	80.6	79.4	55.6	74.7	70.9	59.0	41.2	5
	(25)	(27)	(10)	(62)	(22)	(23)	(7)	(5
High	9.7	11.8	44.4	18.1	25.8	23.1	58.8	31
	(3)	(4)	(8)	(15)	(8)	(9)	(10)	(2
Total	100.0	100.0	100.0	100.0	100.0	100.0	100.0	10
	(31)	(34)	(18)	(83)	(31)	(39)	(17)	(8
Social Mobility								
Downward	0	5.9	0	2.4	9.7	7.7	0	6
		(2)		(2)	(3)	(3)		(6
Stationary	29.0	32.4	44.4	33.7	54.8	51.3	52.9	52
	(9)	(11)	(8)	(28)	(17)	(20)	(9)	(4
Upward	71.0	61.7	55.6	63.9	35.5	41.0	47.1	40
	(22)	(21)	(10)	(53)	(11)	(16)	(8)	(3
Total	100.0	100.0	100.0	100.0	100.0	100.0	100.0	10
	(31)	(34)	(18)	(83)	(31)	(39)	(17)	(8

MONTERREY			MEDELLIN		
Public Sector	Private Sector	Total	Public Sector	Private Sector	Total
72.7	45.0	59.5	89.5	42.9	65.0
(16)	(9)	(25)	(17)	(9)	(26)
18.2	50.0	33.3	10.5	47.6	30.0
(4)	(10)	(15)	(2)	(10)	(12)
9.1	5.0	7.1	0	9.5	5.0
(2)	(1)	(3)		(2)	(2)
100.0	100.0	100.0	100.0	100.0	100.0
(20)	(42)		(19)	(21)	(40)
0	15.0	7.1	0	9.5	5.0
	(3)	(3)		(2)	(2)
63.6	70.0	66.7	94.7	81.0	87.5
(14)	(14)	(28)	(18)	(17)	(35)
36.4	15.0	26.2	5.3	9.5	7.5
(8)	(3)	(11)	(1)	(2)	(3)
100.0	100.0	100.0	100.0	100.0	100.0
(22)	(20)	(42)	(19)	(21)	(40)
0	0	0	10.5	9.5	10.0
			(2)	(2)	(4)
27.3	35.0	31.0	15.8	42.9	30.0
(6)	(7)	(13)	(3)	(9)	(12)
72.7	65.0	69.0	73.7	47.6	60.0
(16)	(13)	(29)	(14)	(10)	(24)
100.0	100.0	100.0	100.0	100.0	100.0
(22)	(20)	(42)	(19)	(21)	(40)

leaders across cases have worked their way up, being appointed to their posts as a result of education and experience. Pairwise, it is noted with consistency that many more Cali leaders were appointed without requisite experience or education than was the case in Guadalajara. In Monterrey, in contrast to Medellín, more than twice as many attained their positions through personal and family ties. To state it differently, these data support in part the interpretations of Cali's less professionalized leadership and Monterrey's close-knit industrial group. But these differences are less significant than the modal trend of advancement based on achievement. In that vein Guadalajara and Medellín reflect greater mobility than their counterparts, since larger proportions of leaders are promoted from within their organizations or found new agencies and enterprises.

Organizational membership is a particularly useful measure of political participation and leadership style. These data are not to be confused with the evidence on interorganizational linkages or interlocking directorates presented in the previous chapter. The sixth variable in table 21 is based on membership in voluntary, professional, and social or civic organizations, rather than on holding remunerative occupational posts. The distributions for Guadalajara and Cali are generally similar, although a regrettably large number of not-ascertained responses in the former case makes interpretation difficult. In both, the influentials are, understandably, more active participants. The differences between Monterrey and Medellín are more striking: the number of Monterrey leaders participating in six or more organizations is more than twice the figure for Medellín. When one compares just public- and private-sector leaders across all four cases, Monterrey and Medellín both reflect more active organizational participation than do Guadalajara and Cali. As we shall see, this fact supports a common complaint in the two less-industrialized cities to the effect that local leaders lack a "spirit of association."

The organizational-membership variable was further broken down in an effort to operationalize prestige. In each of the four cities there were two high-status social clubs, the country club and a downtown businessmen's club. Since membership in each of these was costly, required highly-placed sponsorship, and seemed to embody most of the city's social elite, belonging to one or both was taken as an indicator of high prestige status. Perhaps the most interesting facet of these data is the fact that organizational leadership is not closely associated with social prestige. The number of public and private leaders belonging to these clubs is consistently less than a majority and falls as low as 10 to 12 percent. As would be expected, some 80 percent of the Guadalajara and Cali influentials belong to these clubs, but from the larger picture we could conclude that the pattern in these four cities is similar to Floyd Hunter's characterization of

Atlanta, Georgia: "Society prestige and deference to wealth are not among the primary criteria for admission to the upper ranks of the decision makers."[7] Paired comparisons indicate that a relatively large proportion of Cali leaders belong to the high-status clubs, while the proportion is about a third in the other cities. This is a good indicator of the closer connection between upper-class status and leadership in the more insular case of Cali.

A more inclusive measure of socioeconomic status (SES) was constructed from a combination of the variables on education and occupational level.[8] In a general sense all of these leaders are high-status people by virtue of their university education and the occupational position that led to their inclusion in the sample. In order to investigate internal SES differences within these samples, a somewhat "telescoped" index was used here to highlight differences. Interestingly, public- and private-sector distributions are relatively similar across cases. Here, clearly, the intermediate SES position is the modal category across cases, but large differences exist in the paired comparisons. The characteristic differences that appear indicate a larger proportion of high-SES leaders in Cali and Monterrey, the two regions with more concentrated structures of power. Although the differences are not great, they reinforce our conclusions regarding the convergence of status and power derived by separate methods.

An implication that might be drawn from these figures is that the more egalitarian distribution of SES in Guadalajara and Medellín reflects a more open society and greater social mobility. The last variable in table 21 deals with social mobility, summarizing the differences between the occupational level of respondents and their fathers. The results are consistent with the foregoing interpretation except in one case. Guadalajara and Medellín reflect a good deal of openness or upward mobility, whereas leaders in Cali tend to be more stationary. The exception is Monterrey, where, despite its concentrated structure of power, upward mobility is quite high.

Because of the fundamental importance attached to mobility, a more detailed presentation of the respondents' occupational levels by those of their fathers is provided in table 22.[9] Note here that we may contrast all four regions jointly, since the data are based on standardized comparisons of the respondents with themselves (i.e., their parental backgrounds). Guadalajara, Monterrey, and Medellín each reflect a good deal of occupational mobility; the data are so similar as to be indistinguishable in view of the small samples. In the same order of regions the modal category is the fourth (professional) level, with figures of 71 percent, 74 percent, and 90 percent respectively. When the fourth and fifth levels are combined, the distribution of respondents is 91 percent, 93 percent, and 95 percent respectively. Each of these may be compared with the combined percentages

TABLE 22

SOCIAL MOBILITY TABLES – FATHER'S OCCUPATIONAL LEVEL BY RESPONDENT'S OCCUPATIONAL LEVEL IN FOUR REGIONS

GUADALAJARA

Father's Occupational Level	Respondent's Occupational Level						
	1	2	3	4	5	Total	Column %
1	0	2	0	1	1	4	4.8
2	0	0	2	10	0	12	14.5
3	0	0	2	27	4	33	39.8
4	0	0	0	20	5	25	30.1
5	0	0	1	1	7	9	10.8
Total	0	2	5	59	17	83	—
Row %	0	2.4	6.0	71.1	20.5	—	100.0

MONTERREY

Father's Occupational Level	Respondent's Occupational Level						
	1	2	3	4	5	Total	Column %
1	0	0	0	3	0	3	7.1
2	0	0	1	3	0	4	9.5
3	0	0	2	15	3	20	47.6
4	0	0	0	9	3	12	28.6
5	0	0	0	0	2	2	4.8
Total	0	0	3	31	8	42	—
Row %	0	0	7.1	73.8	19.0	—	100.0

CALI
Respondent's Occupational Level

Father's Occupational Level	1	2	3	4	5	Total	Column %
1	0	0	2	0	0	2	2.3
2	0	0	0	2	1	3	3.4
3	0	0	7	18	2	27	31.0
4	0	1	4	31	9	45	51.7
5	0	0	1	2	7	10	11.5
Total	0	1	14	52	19	87	—
Row %	0	1.1	16.1	59.8	21.8	—	100.0

MEDELLIN
Respondent's Occupational Level

Father's Occupational Level	1	2	3	4	5	Total	Column %
1	0	0	2	0	0	2	5.0
2	0	0	0	6	1	7	17.5
3	0	0	0	14	1	15	37.5
4	0	0	0	12	0	12	30.0
5	0	0	0	4	0	4	10.0
Total	0	0	2	36	2	40	—
Row %	0	0	5.0	90.0	5.0	—	100.0

Legend: Occupational levels: 1) Unskilled and agricultural workers; 2) semiskilled and skilled workers, craftsmen, artisans; 3) small business proprietors, sales and clerical workers, public employees; 4) managers, lawyers, engineers, supervisors; 5) top corporate executives, top political offices, owners of large industrial and commercial enterprises.

Cases on the diagonal line indicate no mobility. Cases above the diagonal line indicate upward mobility and those below the line indicate downward mobility.

of fathers occupying a lower level (i.e., 3, 2, or 1), which are 59 percent, 64 percent, and 60 percent. In short, for these three cases about 60 percent of the respondents' fathers were employed in the lower three occupational ranks, while about 90 percent of the respondents were employed in the upper two. The situation is different in Cali; here the modal category for fathers and sons is the fourth (professional), and the two (i.e., father-column and son-row) distributions are a good deal more similar than in the other three cases. The evidence rather strongly suggests that Cali's leadership group is relatively more closed and rigid in comparison to the openness and mobility in the other three regions.

This depiction of the social characteristics of the leadership groups provides a key to understanding the ways in which they will perceive and act on developmental problems.

PERCEPTIONS OF THE DEVELOPMENTAL PROBLEM

Following Karl Mannheim, we shall conceive of ideologies as partial, group-determined perspectives on the experiential world. It was Mannheim's thesis "that there are modes of thought which cannot be adequately understood as long as their social origins are obscured."[10] Having dealt with the social origins of the leadership groups, we turn now to the content of their ideas, notably their development ideologies.

A useful starting point for determining how the leaders perceive the developmental problems confronting their regions was to ask them what they regarded as the principal advantages and disadvantages for economic progress. Tables 23 and 24 tabulate responses to these open-ended questions according to the frequency with which certain items were mentioned.[11]

In Guadalajara, the most common perceived advantages have to do with natural resources (1, 2, 7). These are followed by physical infrastructure works (3, 5) such as roads, the airport, electricity, and gas installations. Human resources come next in importance, with qualified, artisan trained labor (4), political leadership, the "quality of the people," and the educational system. As we have learned from Guadalajara's history, these perceptions are "correct" in regard to material-locational resource endowments and the emphasis put on political and educational development. Monterrey provides an interesting contrast in that the importance of human and material factors are reversed; individual initiative (1) and educational opportunities (2) rank ahead of infrastructure (3), and this is an interesting comment on the strength of the regional ethos and its self-fulfilling function.

Leaders in Cali, as in Guadalajara, predominantly stress the importance of natural resources (1, 2, 4, 6). The "quality of the people" (3) is relatively high on the list but it is intended here to refer to their aspirations for improvement rather than their accomplishments. Next come infrastructure works, particularly in transportation (5, 9). Future potential for agricultural and industrial development (7) represents another aspirational advantage, while the presence of other large cities (markets) in the region (8) is closely related to location. As in the Mexican cases, Medellín provides a basic contrast to Cali, with leaders citing overwhelmingly the importance of human resources and the Antioqueño personality (1, 4). This factor is followed at some distance by infrastructure resources (2, 5), and untapped agricultural opportunities (3). The data suggest an interesting, if tentative, generalization.

It would appear that transitional areas coping with developmental problems are more apt to see their advantages in hard physical terms (natural resources and infrastructure), whereas industrially developed areas can afford the structurally myopic luxury of self-congratulation. An interesting illustration of this insensitivity to structural factors is the mention, in both industrialized regions, of their agricultural difficulties when, in fact, the natural immunity to self-sufficient agriculture and the hacienda system seems to be one important key to their successful development.

Turning to perceived regional disadvantages, we see that Guadalajara leaders place heavy emphasis on the "egoistic," individualistic character of the population that militates against economic cooperation, joint investment, true corporate enterprises, and, generally, a "spirit of association" (1). It would be difficult to overestimate the prevalence of this theme in local circles. Interestingly, local confidence is reflected in the second most common response, to the effect that the region has no developmental disadvantages (2). These responses are followed distantly by complaints about the excessive concentration of decision-making power and tax revenues in Mexico City (3), the need for more educational facilities (4), and the heavy urban migration with its attendant pressure on urban services. In Monterrey, when it comes to disadvantages we see a curious reversal of the previous tendency. Leaders now emphasize physical problems, generally the poverty of the region's natural resources (1, 2, 3, 4). Urban migration and urban problems (5) follow.

Perceptions of disadvantages in Cali closely resemble those in Guadalajara, particularly in the overwhelming importance of individualism or the lack of a spirit of association (1). Urban migration is second and the prideful comment that no disadvantages exist (3) is also prominent. And the same complaints about government centralization and inefficiency are heard (4). Next come deficits in infrastructure services (5, 6, 7). Only Cali leaders mention problems of labor relations (8) and the difficulties posed

TABLE 23

LEADERS' PERCEPTIONS OF ADVANTAGES OF THE REGION

GUADALAJARA

Advantage	Freq. of Mention
1. Natural resources (water, soil)	32
2. Climate	28
3. Communications (highways, airport)	25
4. Qualified labor and good labor relations	24
5. Infrastructure services (electricity, gas)	23
6. Political leadership and stability	19
7. Location (markets)	18
8. Quality of the people (responsibility)	15
9. Educational system	11

MONTERREY

Advantage	Freq. of Mention
1. Quality of the people (initiative)	17
2. Educational system (universities)	11
3. Infrastructure services (electricity, gas)	10
4. Industrial potential	9
5. Qualified labor	8

CALI

Advantage	Freq. of Mention
1. Agricultural production (soil)	47
2. Location (rivers, markets)	31
3. Quality of the people (aspirations)	23
4. Climate	22
5. Communications (port, roads, air)	22
6. Natural resources generally	20
7. Potential for more agricultural and industrial production	15
8. Other big cities in department	11
9. Infrastructure services (electricity)	11

MEDELLIN

Advantage	Freq. of Mention
1. Quality of the people (ethnicity, initiative)	30
2. Water, electricity	12
3. Potential for agriculture	6
4. Geographical hardships promoting achievement spirit	5
5. Infrastructure generally	4

TABLE 24

LEADERS' PERCEPTIONS OF DISADVANTAGES OF THE REGION

GUADALAJARA

Disadvantage	Freq. of Mention
1. People lack entrepreneurial, associational spirit	28
2. None	15
3. Centralization of federal government	8
4. Lack of education	8
5. Population growth (migration)	6

MONTERREY

Disadvantage	Freq. of Mention
1. Lack of primary materials	14
2. Lack of water	14
3. Difficulties of agricultural development	8
4. Lack of energy (electricity, gas)	7
5. Population growth (migration)	5

CALI

Disadvantage	Freq. of Mention
1. People lack entrepreneurial, associational spirit	32
2. Population growth (migration)	17
3. None	11
4. Political inefficiency and centralization	10
5. Poor communications	9
6. Lack of infrastructure services (electricity, flood control)	8
7. Lack of educational facilities	7
8. Labor problems (unions)	6
9. Monopolies (foreign investment)	5

MEDELLIN

Disadvantage	Freq. of Mention
1. Lack of communications (isolation)	20
2. Difficulties of agricultural development	18
3. Low incomes of many (rural poverty)	10
4. Lack of natural resources	6

by such a large contingent of important nonlocal firms in the area (9). In Medellín, as in Monterrey, there is strong agreement on physical and infrastructure deficiencies (1, 2, 4), and here, for the first time, some mention is made of the plight of the poor (3).

We may now hazard the converse of the foregoing generalization: in their perceptions of disadvantages, leaders in transitional areas tend to lay their problems to human failings, whereas those in successfully industrialized regions admit only to the constraints of the environment. This is far from paradoxical: it would seem reasonable (or "logical") for those who credit their success to their own initiative to view their limitations as to some extent naturally imposed. Conversely, those who are striving to succeed understandably see their potential existing "out there," as yet unfulfilled due only to human factors that can be changed. Clearly there are elements of reality in each of these perspectives. But it is also true that the transitional cases have "quality people" and that the industrialized regions had unique resource advantages. In view of this, the observed patterned differences in perceptions are best understood as ideologies in the sense in which we have defined the term.

The next set of interview questions addressed respondents' perceptions of the principal problems facing the region's further development and their judgment as to the most effective means of solving these problems. The earlier question on disadvantages was posed at a general level, referring to "given" constraints or the environment within which development policy operates. Here the question was more specific (though there is some overlap or duplication) and sought to identify more immediate issues of practical policy deserving high-priority consideration.

One notable feature of table 25 is the overall frequency with which social welfare problems of the general population are mentioned as pressing problems. In Guadalajara the plight of the rural peasantry (1, 5, 7) and the lack of mass education (2) dominate the list. The low rate of investment (3, 10) emphasizes again "traditional" individualism. From a more technical economic standpoint, leaders are aware of the trade imbalances produced by the region's rather exclusive concentration on manufacturing of food products and the nonlocal control of new industry (4). Next, political centralization is mentioned (6), followed by the related, and "realistically" implausible, complaint of a lack of infrastructure services (9). Interestingly, urban migration (8) is relatively low on the list, representing less of a "problem" than in Monterrey, where it was the most frequently cited item, despite the fact that Guadalajara's population has been increasing more rapidly over the last twenty years. It would seem that this problem acquires its greater importance in Monterrey because urban services are less adequate to the task of accommodating its growing numbers, as is indicated by the frequent mention of deficient urban services (4, 5). Indeed, when the need to decentralize industry (6) is interpreted as a means of deflecting urban migration and overcrowding, the "urban problem" is the dominant theme in Monterrey (1, 3, 4, 5, 6). Also important are concern over the capacity of existing infrastructure services (water, electricity, gas) to sustain further industrial expansion (2) and the perennial preoccupation with education (3).

Cali's perceived problems are very similar to those of Guadalajara. Educational needs (1) and rural-urban poverty (2, 6) head the list, which includes such parallel items as trade difficulties (3), political problems (4), lack of credit (5), and population growth (7). Leaders of the two regions mention seven closely comparable problems in roughly the same order of importance. Medellín, like Monterrey, reflects a dominant theme that could be described as a distributional or welfare problem. Educational needs (1), rural underdevelopment (2), unemployment (4), and poverty (5) all reflect concern for the less privileged segments of the population.

If ideologies are defined as group-determined partial perspectives fashioned in the competitive political struggle, then an equally important feature of any ideology is that it entails a program of action, a way of relating to and acting on the perceived reality. In that sense the most explicitly ideological questions posed at this stage of the inquiry concerned the leaders' judgments as to the most effective solutions to the problems confronting the region.

Generally, leaders put great stock in the value of education as a remedy for developmental problems: education headed the list of solutions in three of the four areas and was prominently mentioned in the fourth (table 26). In Guadalajara the next three items were devoted to methods of solving the "rural problem." The fifth and sixth solutions address the issue of individualism by suggesting, rather vaguely, that people act in closer association. The last two items deal with more technical economic changes. Solutions offered by Monterrey leaders are less nebulous and focus mainly on "physical" works such as locating new industry outside the city to reduce problems of overcrowding (1) and constructing new industrial (2) and urban (3) infrastructures. In Cali the "agricultural problem" follows education, but, in contrast to Guadalajara, here the emphasis is on raising productivity within the present structure of land tenure rather than on promoting reforms. This, of course, is consistent with the interests of Cali's high-status, rigid, propertied elite. It is interesting to note that local leaders mention with approval the helping role of foreign aid and investment (3). As in Guadalajara, measures to promote a spirit of association and

TABLE 25

LEADERS' PERCEPTIONS OF KEY DEVELOPMENTAL PROBLEMS OF THE REGION

GUADALAJARA

Problem	Freq. of Mention
1. Rural underdevelopment (low incomes, lack of credit)	38
2. Lack of education	34
3. Low rate of investment	17
4. Trade difficulties (lack of exports, foreign ownership, terms of trade)	14
5. Lack of land tenure security	13
6. Politics (centralization, dishonesty)	12
7. Lack of credit (industrial, rural)	12
8. Population growth (migration)	11
9. Lack of infrastructure	11
10. Lack of new industry	11

MONTERREY

Problem	Freq. of Mention
1. Population growth (migration)	15
2. Lack of infrastructure services (water, electricity, gas)	14
3. Lack of education	10
4. Housing	8
5. Lack of urban services (streets, water, sanitation)	7
6. Need to decentralize industry	6

CALI

Problem	Freq. of Mention
1. Lack of education	45
2. Unemployment (poverty, income distribution)	32
3. Trade difficulties (balance of payments, one crop economy)	15
4. Lack of leadership (in public administration and entrepreneurial groups)	15
5. Lack of credit (public and private)	14
6. Rural-agricultural underdevelopment	13
7. Population growth (migration)	9
8. Health	9
9. Lack of urban services	8

MEDELLIN

Problem	Freq. of Mention
1. Lack of education	13
2. Rural-agricultural underdevelopment	13
3. Lack of financing for new projects	12
4. Unemployment	10
5. Poverty and maldistribution of income	9

TABLE 26

LEADERS' PERCEPTIONS OF EFFECTIVE SOLUTIONS TO DEVELOPMENTAL PROBLEMS

GUADALAJARA

Solution	Freq. of Mention
1. Education	39
2. Higher productivity in rural areas	33
3. More extensive credit	30
4. Security of land tenure	21
5. More industrial investment	17
6. Better coordination of public and private sectors	15
7. Expanded markets (exports)	13
8. Planning and technical assistance	13

MONTERREY

Solution	Freq. of Mention
1. Industrial decentralization	14
2. Infrastructure works (water, electricity)	12
3. Education	10
4. Urban works	6

CALI

Solution	Freq. of Mention
1. Education	41
2. Agricultural developing (marketing, technical assistance)	17
3. International aid and foreign investment	16
4. Promote organizational coordination (planning, civic action)	16
5. Better terms of trade	14
6. Tax reforms	13
7. More private investment (association, incentives)	12

MEDELLIN

Solution	Freq. of Mention
1. Education	14
2. Tax reform	10
3. Expanded employment	9
4. Develop organizations (planning, education)	9
5. Improve communications (esp. in rural areas)	9

joint investment are cited as vague solutions to the perennial problem of individualism (4, 7). Practical economic proposals are represented by the items on trade (5) and tax reform (6).

At the time of the study, tax reform was a prominent issue in Colombia, as reflected in the emphasis Medellín leaders place on this item. Characteristic of regional attitudes was the view that the federal tax system unfairly penalized the ambitious entrepreneur and should be reformed to provide greater incentives to those who are willing and able to establish new enterprises. Broader employment opportunities (3), as opposed to income redistribution or welfare measures, are uncritically recommended as a solution to the thematic general welfare problem. Similarly, better communications with rural areas (5) would appear to be the answer to rural underdevelopment. Organizational planning is mentioned as the mechanism for instrumenting these solutions (4).

Viewed as developmental ideologies, these proposed solutions are perhaps most noteworthy for their tone of moderation and status-quo leaning. In every case, more education is regarded as a Rosetta stone for deciphering the problems of development. The uncritical faith in this measure is reflected by a general absence of any mention of the type of education recommended (university or primary, professional or vocational), the distributional reforms needed, or the occupational opportunities (or lack thereof) available to better-educated persons. The value of education is taken as self-evident, capable, in some unspecified way, of producing people who may then solve many of the remaining problems despite the fact that present problems exist through no lack of recognition or understanding.

Collectively, the solutions offered seem to span an ideological continuum ranging from conservative status-quo orientations to proposals for moderate reform. Within that truncated range the leaders of Guadalajara are the most clearly reformist, which is understandable given the greater impact of revolutionary change in that region. Their reformist orientation is most evident in the proposals for redressing the rural inequities and overcoming traditional styles of individualism and self-sufficiency born of their agrarian past. Although ranking the regions ideologically with these data is necessarily impressionistic, Medellín would seem to qualify as the next most reformist. Expanded employment opportunities and rural infrastructure works (communications) are mentioned, indicating some concern for the general welfare. Yet all of the suggestions assume the continued success of time-honored methods. In different ways Monterrey and Cali are nonreformist. The Monterrey leaders' solutions entail technical and physical manipulations that will have the effect of re-equilibrating the system and providing higher levels of services to keep it going. In Cali nearly all of the suggested solutions may be interpreted as reinforcing the present distribution of interests. Agricultural development, for example, is offered, not as a way of improving the lot of the peasantry, but as a method of augmenting the productivity of the present system.

To summarize this section, developmental ideologies, as measured by leadership perceptions of problems and solutions for regional growth, represent a relatively narrow spectrum bounded by moderate reformism and status-quo conservatism. Interestingly, the contents of these ideologies are noticeably psychologistic. The call for better-educated individuals more capable of association and cooperation is a remedial article of faith, with only the more industrialized regions placing equal emphasis on technical solutions. These patterned emphases and differences are not surprising. Historical actors understandably think chiefly in personalistic terms— sometimes with great success, as the self-fulfilling prophecies of regional character in Monterrey and Medellín indicate. Concerning the nonradical character of leadership ideologies, this too is to be expected, since the leaders are leaders of the present system. Radical proposals seldom come from such groups, though they may be differentially predisposed to enact extensive changes. That question is next on the agenda as we take up some specific ideological items and the factors accounting for different orientations.

CORRELATES OF DEVELOPMENTAL IDEOLOGIES

In the structured interviews several manifestly ideological questions were put to local leaders. One that seems to go to the heart of political and economic perspectives concerns the appropriate scope of governmental activities vis-à-vis the private sector.[12] Specifically, leaders were asked, "What do you consider to be the role of the public and private sectors in the promotion of development?" Responses were coded in three categories, the first strongly supportive of a private enterprise system with minimal government intervention, the second based on active government regulation of the economy but excluding public ownership of enterprises, and the third involving a mixed system of public and private ownership. Since the question was open-ended, there were no restraints on more leftist responses such as emphasis on a socialist economy. In fact, however, no such responses were obtained; the trichotomy exhaustively handled the answers.

The first item in table 27 indicates some interesting and, by now, predictable patterns. Private-sector leaders understandably are more enthusiastic partisans of a strictly free-enterprise system. But more impressive is the fact that the modal response in all four regions favors some measure of government intervention in the economy. It should be noted parentheti-

TABLE 27

LEADERSHIP IDEOLOGIES BY REGION (In Percent and (N))

Variable	GUADALAJARA				CALI			
	Public Sector	Private Sector	Influ- ential	Total	Public Sector	Private Sector	Influ- ential	Tot.
Scope of Government								
Minimal (Private Enterprise)	6.5 (2)	41.2 (14)	0	19.3 (16)	9.7 (3)	25.6 (10)	23.5 (11)	19 (1`
Government Regulation	12.9 (4)	17.6 (6)	27.8 (5)	18.1 (15)	67.7 (21)	51.3 (20)	47.1 (8)	56. (4$
Mixed System	74.2 (23)	35.3 (12)	61.1 (11)	55.4 (46)	19.4 (6)	20.5 (8)	29.4 (5)	21 (1$
N.A.	6.5 (2)	5.9 (2)	11.2 (2)	7.2 (6)	3.2 (1)	2.6 (1)	0	2. (2)
Total	100.0 (31)	100.0 (34)	100.0 (18)	100.0 (83)	100.0 (31)	100.0 (39)	100.0 (17)	100. (8`
Changes Necessary								
No	38.7 (12)	23.5 (8)	55.6 (10)	36.1 (30)	6.5 (2)	5.1 (2)	17.6 (3)	8. (7)
Yes	48.4 (15)	61.8 (21)	33.3 (6)	50.6 (42)	87.1 (27)	87.2 (34)	76.5 (13)	85. (74
N.A.	12.9 (4)	14.7 (5)	11.1 (2)	13.3 (11)	6.5 (2)	7.7 (3)	5.9 (1)	6. (6)
Total	100.0 (31)	100.0 (34)	100.0 (18)	100.0 (83)	100.0 (31)	100.0 (39)	100.0 (17)	100. (87
Directions of Change								
Government Reform	6.5 (2)	26.5 (9)	11.1 (2)	15.7 (13)	9.7 (3)	41.0 (16)	35.3 (6)	28. (25
More Cooperation	29.0 (9)	35.3 (12)	11.1 (2)	27.7 (23)	51.6 (16)	35.9 (14)	29.4 (5)	40. (35
Private Responsibility	12.9 (4)	0	11.1 (2)	7.2 (6)	25.8 (8)	7.7 (3)	11.8 (2)	14. (13
N.A./Inappro- priate	51.6 (16)	38.2 (13)	66.7 (12)	49.4 (41)	12.9 (4)	15.4 (6)	23.5 (4)	16. (14
Total	100.0 (31)	100.0 (34)	100.0 (18)	100.0 (83)	100.0 (31)	100.0 (39)	100.0 (17)	100. (87

	MONTERREY			MEDELLIN		
	Public Sector	Private Sector	Total	Public Sector	Private Sector	Total
	22.7 (5)	30.0 (6)	26.2 (11)	10.5 (2)	42.9 (9)	27.5 (11)
	4.5 (1)	45.0 (9)	23.8 (10)	47.4 (9)	42.9 (9)	45.0 (18)
	68.2 (15)	25.0 (5)	47.6 (20)	42.1 (8)	14.3 (3)	27.5 (11)
	4.5 (1)	0	2.4 (1)	0	0	0
	100.0 (22)	100.0 (20)	100.0 (42)	100.0 (19)	100.0 (21)	100.0 (40)
	54.5 (12)	50.0 (10)	52.3 (22)	5.3 (1)	19.0 (4)	12.5 (5)
	40.9 (9)	50.0 (10)	45.2 (19)	89.5 (17)	71.4 (15)	80.0 (32)
	4.5 (1)	0	2.4 (1)	5.3 (10	9.5 (2)	7.5 (3)
	100.0 (22)	100.0 (20)	100.0 (42)	100.0 (19)	100.0 (21)	100.0 (40)
	4.5 (1)	35.0 (7)	19.0 (8)	15.8 (3)	33.3 (7)	25.0 (10)
	18.2 (4)	5.0 (1)	11.9 (5)	57.9 (11)	33.3 (7)	45.0 (18)
	18.2 (4)	10.0 (2)	14.3 (6)	15.8 (3)	4.8 (1)	10.0 (4)
	59.1 (13)	50.0 (10)	54.8 (23)	10.5 (2)	28.6 (6)	20.0 (8)
	100.0 (22)	100.0 (20)	100.0 (42)	100.0 (19)	100.0 (21)	100.0 (40)

Variable	GUADALAJARA Public Sector	Private Sector	Influ- ential	Total	CALI Public Sector	Private Sector	Influ- ential	Total
Foreign Investment								
Beneficial/ Necessary	19.4 (6)	35.3 (12)	11.1 (2)	24.1 (20)	35.5 (11)	28.2 (11)	41.2 (7)	33.3 (29)
Beneficial if Regulated	51.6 (16)	38.2 (13)	55.6 (10)	47.1 (39)	41.9 (13)	51.3 (20)	41.2 (7)	46.0 (40)
Mixed Blessing	9.7 (3)	20.6 (7)	11.1 (2)	14.5 (12)	19.4 (6)	12.8 (5)	17.6 (3)	16.1 (14)
Disadvantageous	6.5 (2)	2.9 (1)	5.6 (1)	4.8 (4)	0	2.6 (1)	0	1.1 (1)
N.A.	12.9 (4)	2.9 (1)	16.7 (3)	9.6 (8)	3.2 (1)	5.1 (2)	0	3.4 (3)
Total	100.0 (31)	100.0 (34)	100.0 (18)	100.0 (83)	100.0 (31)	100.0 (39)	100.0 (17)	100.0 (87)
Party Identifi- cation (Mexico)								
Opposition	6.5 (2)	11.8 (4)	0	7.2 (6)				
Apolitical	9.7 (3)	41.2 (14)	16.7 (3)	24.1 (20)				
P.R.I.	64.5 (20)	29.4 (10)	55.6 (10)	48.2 (40)				
N.A.	19.4 (6)	17.6 (6)	27.8 (5)	20.5 (17)				
Total	100.0 (31)	100.0 (34)	100.0 (18)	100.0 (83)				
Party Identifi- cation (Colombia)								
Conservative					48.4 (15)	33.3 (13)	52.9 (9)	42.5 (37)
None					3.2 (1)	10.3 (4)	5.9 (1)	6.9 (6)
Liberal					45.2 (14)	51.3 (20)	41.2 (7)	47.1 (41)
N.A.					3.2 (1)	5.1 (2)	0	3.4 (3)
Total					100.0 (31)	100.0 (39)	100.0 (17)	100.0 (87)

MONTERREY			MEDELLIN		
Public Sector	Private Sector	Total	Public Sector	Private Sector	Total
18.2 (4)	20.0 (4)	19.0 (18)	0	33.3 (7)	17.5 (7)
40.9 (9)	50.0 (10)	45.2 (19)	78.9 (15)	33.3 (7)	55.0 (22)
18.2 (4)	15.0 (3)	16.7 (7)	10.5 (2)	14.3 (3)	12.5 (5)
4.5 (1)	10.0 (2)	7.1 (3)	5.3 (1)	19.0 (4)	12.5 (5)
18.2 (4)	5.0 (1)	11.9 (5)	5.3 (1)	0	2.5 (1)
100.0 (22)	100.0 (20)	100.0 (42)	100.0 (19)	100.0 (21)	100.0 (40)

0	30.0 (6)	14.3 (6)
9.1 (2)	50.0 (10)	28.6 (12)
86.4 (19)	15.0 (3)	52.4 (22)
4.5 (1)	5.0 (1)	4.8 (2)
100.0 (22)	100.0 (20)	100.0 (42)

36.8 (7)	28.6 (6)	32.5 (13)
10.5 (2)	19.0 (4)	15.0 (6)
52.6 (10)	52.4 (11)	52.5 (21)
0	0	0
100.0 (19)	100.0 (21)	100.0 (40)

Variable	GUADALAJARA				CALI			
	Public Sector	Private Sector	Influ- ential	Total	Public Sector	Private Sector	Influ- ential	Tot
Objectives of Development								
Economic	9.7	32.4	5.6	18.1	25.8	38.5	23.5	31
	(3)	(11)	(1)	(15)	(8)	(15)	(4)	(2
Institutional	9.7	8.8	5.6	8.4	32.3	7.7	11.8	17
	(3)	(3)	(1)	(7)	(10)	(3)	(2)	(1
Economic and Reformist	29.0	29.4	22.2	27.7	25.8	41.0	35.3	34
	(9)	(10)	(4)	(23)	(8)	(16)	(6)	(3
Reformist	16.1	14.7	11.1	14.5	9.7	2.6	5.9	5
	(5)	(5)	(2)	(12)	(3)	(1)	(1)	(5
N.A.	35.5	14.7	55.6	31.3	6.5	10.3	23.5	11
	(11)	(5)	(10)	(26)	(2)	(4)	(4)	(1
Total	100.0	100.0	100.0	100.0	100.0	100.0	100.0	10C
	(31)	(34)	(18)	(83)	(31)	(39)	(17)	(8

Ideological
Index (Scope of Government and Foreign Investment)

	Public Sector	Private Sector	Influ- ential	Total	Public Sector	Private Sector	Influ- ential	Tot
0 (Conservative)	3.2	11.8	0	6.0	3.0	10.3	20.0	1(
	(1)	(4)		(5)	(1)	(4)	(3)	(9
1	3.2	35.3	0	15.7	24.3	20.5	13.3	21
	(1)	(12)		(13)	(8)	(8)	(2)	(1
2	19.4	11.8	22.4	16.9	36.4	38.5	33.3	39
	(6)	(4)	(4)	(14)	(12)	(15)	(5)	(3
3	45.2	23.5	55.6	38.6	18.2	23.1	6.7	18
	(14)	(8)	(10)	(32)	(6)	(9)	(1)	(1
4 (Liberal)	12.9	11.8	5.6	10.6	9.1	2.6	13.3	6
	(4)	(4)	(1)	(9)	(3)	(1)	(2)	(6
N.A.	16.1	5.9	16.7	12.0	3.0	5.1	13.3	3
	(5)	(2)	(3)	(10)	(1)	(2)	(2)	(3
Total	100.0	100.0	100.0	100.0	100.0	100.0	100.0	10(
	(31)	(34)	(18)	(83)	(31)	(39)	(17)	(8

	MONTERREY			MEDELLIN		
	Public Sector	Private Sector	Total	Public Sector	Private Sector	Total
	13.6 (3)	10.0 (2)	11.9 (5)	10.5 (2)	14.3 (3)	12.5 (5)
	13.6 (3)	20.0 (4)	16.7 (7)	5.3 (1)	4.8 (1)	5.0 (2)
	22.7 (5)	40.0 (8)	30.9 (13)	36.9 (7)	47.6 (10)	42.5 (17)
	22.7 (5)	20.0 (4)	21.4 (9)	31.6 (6)	14.3 (3)	22.5 (9)
	27.3 (6)	10.0 (2)	19.0 (8)	15.8 (3)	19.0 (4)	17.5 (7)
	100.0 (22)	100.0 (20)	100.0 (42)	100.0 (19)	100.0 (21)	100.0 (40)
	14.3 (3)	10.0 (2)	11.9 (5)	5.3 (1)	14.3 (3)	17.5 (7)
	4.8 (1)	20.0 (4)	11.9 (5)	10.5 (2)	14.3 (3)	5.0 (2)
	9.5 (2)	40.0 (8)	23.8 (10)	15.8 (3)	28.6 (6)	22.5 (9)
	33.3 (7)	10.0 (2)	21.4 (9)	26.5 (5)	19.0 (4)	22.5 (9)
	19.1 (4)	20.0 (4)	19.1 (8)	31.6 (6)	14.3 (3)	22.5 (9)
	23.8 (5)	0	11.9 (5)	10.5 (2)	9.5 (2)	10.0 (4)
	100.0 (22)	100.0 (20)	100.0 (42)	100.0 (19)	100.0 (21)	100.0 (40)

cally that here we will compare more freely all four regions, rather than restricting the analysis to pairwise contrasts, since the different sampling procedures do not seriously bias these ideological items.[13] The modal response in the Colombian cities favors active government regulation of the economy and in the Mexican cities a mixed system of public and private ownership. This item may justifiably be regarded as constituting a right-to-left ideological continuum, with the Mexican cases more to the left than the Colombian. Taken separately, the most liberal responses are in Guadalajara, followed by Monterrey, Medellín, and Cali. Clearly the national context strongly influences this pattern. Public ownership of basic industry is an accomplished fact in Mexico and, therefore, understandably approved. What is perhaps more interesting is the set of intranational patterned differences that dovetail neatly with earlier evidence on power, SES, and mobility. Here the leadership of Guadalajara is more liberal than that of Monterrey, and that of Medellín more so than that of Cali. Finally, there is evidence to suggest that comparable samples of United States leaders would reflect a decidedly more conservative orientation,[14] and this implies that in the larger picture Third World leadership ideologies are more leftist than those of the advanced Western nations or, at least, of the United States.[15]

The second item in table 27 deals with opinion on whether or not basic changes are necessary in the relationships between the public and private sectors. Of interest is the fact that Colombian leaders exhibit greater dissatisfaction with the present system. This item was essentially contentless, but was followed by a question concerning the kinds of changes suggested by those who believed change was necessary. Although the most common response here was an even-handed suggestion that more cooperation be promoted, it is noteworthy that Colombian leaders tend to place more blame on government for existing problems and to suggest government reforms as the next most desirable change.

Attitudes toward foreign investment are another key indicator of political-economic ideology that has particular salience in developing countries.[16] Generally speaking, the data here reflect a somewhat surprisingly tolerant attitude. The modal response in all four regions is one that favors foreign investment provided it is regulated within guidelines of national welfare. This fact deserves emphasis because of its contrast to widely-held beliefs concerning the rabidly nationalistic orientations of Latin American leaders. The question of whether or not these leaders should be hostile to foreign investment quite aside, it turns out that they are in the main approving. When we take the regions separately, two interesting points emerge. In Cali, where foreign investment is most extensive, attitudes are most favorable, and in the more industrially developed regions of Monterrey and Medellín attitudes are least favorable. This makes sense in terms of foreign investment, which tends to concentrate in industrial enterprises, thus representing more of a threat to already industrialized regions. Paradoxically, however, more critical attitudes are present in those regions where current levels of foreign investment are less of a "problem."

Political party systems are so vastly different in Mexico and Colombia that cross-national comparisons are meaningless. Intranational comparisons, however, provide some characteristic contrasts. In Mexico, of course, the official party, Partido Revolucionario Institucional (PRI), dominates political life, and about half of the two samples of leaders identify with the party. Obviously this is especially true of public-sector leaders whose positions depend on party loyalty. In Mexico a common and completely unanticipated response to the question "What political party do you identify with?" was "I am apolitical" or "I am a *técnico*, not a *político*." About one-fourth of the leaders offered this alternative, indicating, it would seem, that to be "political" carries the connotation of having ambitions for a public office at the disposal of PRI, while being apolitical implies a more professional career interest. The system itself is not generally a debated matter, many respondents observing that the government and PRI are doing a good job of running the country, which is, after all, their business. The non-PRI responses are noticeably higher in Monterrey, a city well known for its independence and its opposition to the federal system.

Conservative and Liberal party labels have had no great significance in Colombia since the advent of the National Front government. The data suggest that Medellín leaders tend toward Liberal Party support more than those in Cali, but although this may be true it is of minimal substantive importance in contrast to other items.

It was suggested earlier that conceptions of what constitutes development are themselves imbued with ideological significance. In order to get at that question, leaders were asked what they felt should be the goals of the developmental process. Responses to this open-ended question proved somewhat difficult to code, which accounts for the relatively small differences and the large proportion of not ascertained (N.A.) responses. Nevertheless, some suggestive patterns do emerge. Responses were grouped into four categories ranging from rather narrowly economic goals (e.g., a higher gross product) to reformist ambitions (e.g., elimination of inequities in class privilege or of poverty). Between these two poles were institutional objectives (e.g., better government and education) and responses that combined economic and reformist goals. In general, economic and reformist objectives provided the modal response across cases. When the last two categories are combined, Medellín exhibits the highest proportion of "pro-gressive" responses, followed by Monterrey, Guadalajara (with a very large number of N.A.s), and Cali. Of note is the fact that Cali registered the smallest proportion of strictly reformist statements. A tentative inter-pretation of these data is that the more industrialized regions are better able to afford the luxury of looking beyond the more immediate problems of development, an observation that complements earlier generalizations regarding perceived problems and solutions.

In order to provide a somewhat more differentiating "ideological in-dex," the two key items concerning the scope of government and foreign investment were combined.[17] This final item in table 27 indicates again that Guadalajara leaders are the most liberal, followed by those of Mon-terrey, Medellín, and Cali. If the first three categories are combined as the percent conservative, the figures are 38.6, 45.2, 52.5, and 72.3 respectively.

A final problem that requires some discussion concerns the determinants of these ideological orientations. It would be possible, though somewhat cumbersome, to cross-tabulate all of the social characteristics of leaders by the ideological items for each region. Alternatively, a more succinct over-view may be obtained by combining all four samples and evaluating sever-al key determinants of ideology. Although this procedure obscures internal differentiation within the four samples, it is particularly useful in provid-ing a summary outline of the data.

Three key hypotheses that might be advanced concerning an explana-tion of the observed patterned differences in ideological orientations are: (1) they are a result of the positions of leaders (public, private, influential); (2) they are a result of the particular characteristics of the regions, includ-ing the influence of national economic-political practices; (3) they are a result of the socioeconomic status positions of the leaders themselves.

Table 28 addresses the three hypotheses and provides a summary mea-sure of association that may be used to evaluate the relative importance of each.[18] Assuming that the positions of leaders can be ranked in a rough order of importance from the public sector to influentials, it turns out that position is a poor predictor of ideology, refuting the first hypothesis. When the four regions are placed in rank order from the most conservative to the most liberal, this variable proves to be a somewhat better predictor of ideology, suggesting mild support for the second hypothesis. Although SES is not a strong predictor of ideology, it is the best of the three, suggesting that the third hypothesis enjoys the most support. More generally, we may conclude that region and SES (not themselves significantly correlated) interact and jointly provide the best explanation of ideological orientation. To state it differently, we may conclude that there is moderate support for an explanation that embraces both the second and third hypotheses.

TABLE 28

LEADERSHIP IDEOLOGIES BY POSITION, REGION, AND SOCIOECONOMIC STATUS (SES) IN ABSOLUTE NUMBERS

| | | IDEOLOGICAL INDEX | | | | | |
| | | Conservative | | | | Liberal | |
	0	1	2	3	4	N.A.	Total
Position Public	9	18	28	29	12	7	103
Private	10	21	31	31	12	9	114
Influential	3	6	9	10	4	3	35
Total	22	45	68	70	28	19	252

gamma = +.09

Region Cali	9	19	35	15	6	3	87
Medellín	3	8	10	14	4	10	40
Monterrey	5	5	9	9	9	5	42
Guadalajara	5	13	14	32	9	10	83
Total	22	45	68	70	28	19	252

gamma = +.20

SES Low	4	0	8	3	1	3	19
Medium	14	38	43	53	18	10	176
High	4	7	17	14	9	6	57
Total	22	45	68	70	28	19	252

gamma = +.31

SUMMARY

We began this chapter with several objectives, including, first, a description of the content of leadership ideology and the extent to which it varied across the four cases. The results clearly indicate that significant variation does obtain. Despite their common locations in developing societies and their similar social backgrounds (e.g., age, education, organizational leadership position), the leaders reflect a series of patterned differences in ideological orientation, differences that cut across levels of development (i.e., transitional-industrialized) and national context and that separate each of the four cases. This brings us to another objective cited earlier, namely, the causal influence of structural factors on the one hand and autonomous circumstances on the other.

It will be recalled that two separate indicators were presented in operationalizing the liberal-conservative ideological continuum. The first was based on the reformist versus status-quo character of perceived solutions to developmental problems. Here Guadalajara ranked as the most liberal (reformist) and Cali as the most conservative, with Medellín tending toward the liberal pole and Monterrey toward the conservative. The second indicator was more explicit, based on a combination of questionnaire items dealing with the scope of government and foreign investment. Here the continuum locations were similar, with Guadalajara representing the liberal pole and Cali the conservative, although the order of the intermediate cases was reversed. Given the imprecise character of the underlying variable, this "triangulation" is sufficiently in agreement to suggest confidence in the substantive significance of the continuum, with the single proviso that the relative locations of the intermediate cases are somewhat indeterminate.

With these differences in mind we may now return to some of the structural explanations of regional differences in leadership ideology. It will be recalled that the distribution of socioeconomic status was more egalitarian in Guadalajara and Medellín, intermediate in Monterrey, and most concentrated in Cali. Upward social mobility was common in all cases except Cali. The social prestige of leaders (as measured by membership in exclusive clubs) was substantially greater in Cali than in the other regions, which were quite similar on this variable. The professionalization of leadership groups was highest in Guadalajara, followed by Monterrey, Medellín, and Cali. Table 29 provides a rough summary of these characteristics and is to be understood only as a notational device, not as the more detailed results themselves. What this summary presentation shows is the consistent patterning of structural variables associated with ideological orientations. The more the leadership is socioeconomically egalitarian, mobile, and professionalized, and the less it is exclusive (or prestigious), the more liberal or progressive is its development ideology. Conversely, the more it is restricted in its socioeconomic base, nonmobile, unprofessionalized, and prestigious, the more conservative or status quo–oriented is its development ideology.

Although this generalization fits the summary pattern, several important qualifications temper its uniformity. First, with respect to a number of the discrete items presented earlier (e.g., perceptions of advantages and disadvantages, foreign investment, objectives of development) it was demonstrated that the level of industrialization was a better predictor than

TABLE 29

APPROXIMATE RANK ORDER OF LEADERSHIP GROUP CHARACTERISTICS

	Liberalism	Egalitarian Distribution of SES	Upward Mobility	Leadership Prestige	Profession-alization
Guadalajara	1	1	1	4	1
Monterrey	2	3	2	3	2
Medellín	3	2	3	2	3
Cali	4	4	4	1	4

those social characteristics; patterned differences occurred across the Monterrey-Medellín and Guadalajara-Cali cases. Second, on other items the principal dimension of differences was cross-national. Third, as was demonstrated in the foregoing evaluations of three hypotheses concerning ideological differences, social and regional variables interact in their influences. Finally, that discussion indicated that the predictive power of separate variables was not especially great, suggesting that a number of other explanatory factors are probably involved. Although we have no empirical basis for determining what these additional factors may be that account for the variance left unexplained by the structural variables included here, the regional histories suggest a number of unique and autonomous influences that go beyond an exclusively structuralist causal interpretation.

Many of these explanations unique to separate regions derive from the special features of the regions' historical development. Guadalajara's more progressive ideological orientation is obviously a product of the great impact of the Mexican Revolution in this region, a fact, in turn, explained by prerevolutionary economic organization. Cali's conservative orientation is closely linked to its agrarian structure and concentrated, high-status elite. Nevertheless, in each region there appear to be ideological influences less intimately connected with social and economic structure and acting in a more independent and autonomous fashion. In this category we would include the articulate regional ethos in Monterrey and Medellín that is a source of self-confidence and of pragmatic assessments of developmental problems. In these same cities, regional separatism and trade proximity with other nations (including the United States) have promoted the diffusion of developmental ideologies from the more advanced countries. In Cali the diffusion of ideas is evident in the important state university, the popularity of progressive management ideologies, and the T.V.A.-style regional development corporation. Although these ideas have yet to alter the conservative mood of the majority of leaders, they do appear to contribute to an ideological split between the old guard and a few progressive elements. In both Guadalajara and Medellín a strong religious tradition and spirit of civic pride have been inherited from colonial times, influencing, no doubt, contemporary ideologies related to social welfare.

In summary, the structural explanations for ideological differences in the four regions are many and, taken together, account for a substantial portion of the observed patterns. Although this seems true for the majority of the data presented in this chapter, it does not exhaust the question. Some of the ideological variance remains to be explained and, though the problem goes beyond a straightforward quantitative solution, it is more than likely that some of the answers lie in unique or independent historical factors. Finally, there are a number of new influences affecting ideological orientations. In order to assess these and satisfy another objective mentioned earlier in this chapter, the impact of ideology on action, we turn next to an analysis of the actual process of development decision-making.

5. Decisions for Development

Ultimately, the accomplishment or failure of development must be located in the activities of people and organizations. This fact requires that we turn attention to the actual process in which power is exercised and decisions affecting change are made. Previous chapters dealing with regional histories, power structures, and leadership ideologies in a sense merely set the stage and provide the actors for the drama in which developmental policy takes shape. Analysis of the decision-making process addresses directly Harold Lasswell's formula for defining politics: "Who gets what, when and how."[1] The process in which matters of policy are defined, allotted priorities, and acted upon provides the operative link between social structure, power, and their consequences for more and less development. The question of policy-making is so fundamental that many treatments of development, including the perceptive and influential writings of Albert O. Hirschman, focus exclusively on this nexus of the larger process.[2]

Moreover, the analysis of decision-making is crucial from a methodological standpoint. First, it provides an independent check on the judgments of leaders regarding influential actors. Second, in conjunction with the historical record and the data on power structures it provides another method of determining who wields power, through what organizational mechanisms, for what ends.

Here, as before, we anticipate that autonomous or emergent influences may arise from the political process. The stories of developmental projects are full of surprises; accidental and unintended events are as common as individuals struggling successfully against the social structural odds. Indeed, development projects often entail attempts to alter the constraining features of the social structure, thereby adding a new source of variation to the developmental process.

A DECISIONAL FRAMEWORK

Those projects or issues that represent important decision-making foci across regions are likely to vary considerably in their scope, duration, and consequences. In order to treat a variety of events within a common orientation we need an analytic framework that will allow for meaningful comparison. A first step in that direction is to clarify the term "decision," which serves as a masthead for this analysis. The term is chosen advisedly, since it connotes the behavior of actors making certain choices within a larger process shaped both by those choices and by the determinate contributions of history and social structure that specify a limited set of alternatives. To put it differently, it expresses the idea that actions affecting development are neither freely elected nor completely determined, but arise out of the interaction between people and circumstances. Too frequently in studies of decision-making the term is reified to imply the literal notion that at a given point in time a specified actor or group of actors receives an identifiable set of "inputs" and "makes a decision" that gives rise to certain "outputs." Although sometimes convenient methodologically, this imagery is unrealistic and particularly ill-suited to the analysis of broad policy questions. In contrast, we shall define decision-making as *the incremental and continuous process in which actors make choices about their environment within certain varied yet structurally determined alternatives.* Decisions are not isolated events but actions in a seamless web of past history and the anticipated future; they may be more and less constrained, more and less conscious. In all events, they are *patterned* activities and it is this patterning that becomes the focus of analysis.

Thus defined, the decision-making process may be analyzed with respect to three points:

1) *The actors.* Individuals and organizations that have decisive influence on the process; their numbers, backgrounds, constituencies, and concentration.

2) *Consensus, conflict, and cooperation.* The manner in which decision-making participants interact; whether they share objectives, have irreconcilable or antagonistic goals, or manage to cooperate despite different policy objectives.[3]

3) *Priorities.* The empirical content of policy objectives; whom they cost and/or whom they benefit.

While these analytic points do not exhaust the questions that could be raised about decision-making processes, they are sufficiently inclusive to address the major outlines within a manageable format.

TABLE 30

DEVELOPMENTAL PROJECTS IN FOUR REGIONS (NOMINATIONS)

Guadalajara

Economic Planning (35)
Infrastructure Works (30)
  (Gas, Airport)
Urban Development (28)
Industrial Promotion (21)
Agricultural Development (14)

Cali

The C.V.C. (45)
Agricultural Development (23)
University Programs (19)
Pan American Games (12)
Industrial Promotion (10)

Monterrey

Industrial Promotion (21)
Urban Development (19)

Medellín

Public Services Corp. (19)
Development Promotion (12)

DEVELOPMENTAL PROJECTS

Any analysis of the decision-making process must first identify which events are to be studied. Typically, this is left to the discretion of the investigator and is decided on the basis of availability of information, access, scope, manageability, or, generally, considerations of convenience that may bear little relationship to the importance of the events. In an effort to identify those projects having the greatest significance in the four regions, organizational leaders were asked to specify "the principal projects or activities that have affected the development of the region." These spontaneous suggestions were then grouped in substantively common categories and ranked according to their frequency of mention. The results appear in table 30. For practical reasons and for conformity with the research design, five projects in Guadalajara and Cali and two in Monterrey and Medellín were subjected to a case study analysis. The unanticipated similarity of these projects is evident and may suggest a more general agenda for future research on policy-making in Latin America.

Several methods were employed in the case study analyses of these projects. Initial interviewees were asked to tell what they knew of the activities they mentioned and to identify principal participants. Subsequently, many of the prominently-mentioned participants were also interviewed concerning the activity and asked to name other persons involved. In this fashion a pool of participants in each project area was identified (see table 1). In addition to these interviews a variety of official documents, reports, research studies, promotional literature, and newspaper accounts were assembled to provide a general background and chronology of events in the project area.

In each of the regions, developmental projects were closely intertwined, representing distinguishable thrusts within a general strategy. As we shall see, decision-making seemed to be predicated on a "master theme" shaped by ideological orientations and practical opportunities, with the specific projects reflecting some facet of that theme. In order to convey a sense of this interrelatedness, the following descriptions will not take up the projects in serial fashion but will attempt to weave them together in unified and distinctively-patterned portraits.

GUADALAJARA

Laying the Foundation: Inveterate Planners and Local Boosters

In the higher circles of policy-making in Guadalajara one finds a notable preoccupation with the notion of economic "planning." Not only was this most frequently cited among important activities in the promotion of development, its assumed efficiency took on the status of a cherished belief. For these leaders the perceived objectives of economic development were within reach if only the essential data could be assembled and a rational plan could be developed to eradicate evident obstacles through coordinated action. Conversely, contemporary failings were laid to an inadequate understanding of the basic facts, irrationality, and, most important, lack of coordination. As a result, efforts to improve the planning function were abundant, particularly in the creation of new bureaucracies and liaison committees whose work would be orchestrated by consensual and rational ends.

For example, when our respondents spoke of economic planning activities they made explicit reference to the coordinated endeavors of three agencies, the State Department of Economy, the private-sector Jalisco Institute of Promotion and Economic Studies, and Plan Lerma, a federally-sponsored regional development agency. Each of these was of recent creation, and, in the eyes of local leaders, together they represent the most salient and effective innovations for promoting change. Consequently, it will be useful to describe briefly the origins and activities of these organizations.

The State Department of Economy was established by Governor Francisco Medina Ascencio, who began his six-year term of office in 1964. Under previous administrations the parent agency had been a two-man operation devoted mainly to public relations work. After 1964 the department quickly became the most important state agency, headed by a nationally-known economist and employing a staff of more than one hundred. The basic functions of the department are several. It is, first of all, a research and accounting operation engaged in measuring all branches of economic productivity in the state and identifying areas of deficiency or opportunity. It also serves an important liaison function with the private sector, maintaining close ties with local industrialists and negotiating concessions to new firms interested in locating in the region. A third major activity of the department is arranging seminars and conventions designed to stimulate interest in local investment. Important seminar round-tables were held in August of 1965 and June of 1967 that produced volumes of contributed papers that analyzed the economic problems and prospects of the state. From a promotional standpoint, Guadalajara is a favorite convention site for national groups (e.g., of bankers, industrialists, engineers, hotel owners), and these assemblies are hosted by the department, whose director typically addresses the group concerning local investment opportunities. From a planning standpoint, the department's principal concern in recent years has been the problem of economic decentralization. For planning purposes the state has been divided into five regions, and elaborate studies have been conducted regarding the economic potential of each. Although these efforts have met with little success, it is the continuing ambition of planners to have new industries locate in some of the less populated areas of the state.

The Jalisco Institute for Promotion and Economic Studies was established in 1963 on the initiative of a small group within the industrial chambers, notably people in the construction industry. Initially the organization employed only four people and concentrated mainly on data collection. In 1966 it was expanded with the appointment of a topflight economist-director and the reorganization of activities into four departments, market studies, public relations, feasibility studies, and industrial engineering. The institute is financed, in roughly equal proportions, by the Chambers of Commerce and Industry, local firms, and contract research. Some of this research is done for the Department of Economy—for example, a "Guide for Investors" dealing with economic opportunities in 144 towns within the state. Another key feature of the institute is the fact that private-sector leaders saw its creation as a way of strengthening their position vis-à-vis government planning activities. Prior to its creation, private-sector leaders felt they lacked the hard data and planning expertise necessary to influence public policy. Despite its recent origins, the institute is now regarded as the third most influential local organization, and much of this reputation derives from its highly professional approach to economic problems. In the last few years it has also become the fulcrum of private-sector coordinating activities, working intimately with the separate chambers and interest groups (associations of bankers, employers, et cetera) and, in turn, influencing government.

The third planning agency is more regional in character and is concerned with agricultural development. Plan Lerma is involved with the agricultural productivity of the Lerma and Santiago river basin, a vast area including portions of nine central states. Initially part of the State Hydraulic Resources Department, the agency became independent in 1963 as a result of the efforts of its dedicated founder and multi-million-dollar grants from the federal government and the Inter-American Development Bank. Like Cali's C.V.C., the organization was conceived along the lines of the T.V.A. Its tasks are three-fold: basic investigation (aerial photography, classification of soils, climatological studies, et cetera), planning (economic studies), and project implementation (electrification, dams, veterinary clinics, et cetera).[4] For the most part, only the first and second of these tasks have been addressed so far. Plan Lerma is by far the largest of the three planning organizations in terms of scope, personnel, and funding. Nevertheless, its regional orientation and autonomous funding somewhat dilute its impact on Guadalajara and immediate surroundings. But the agency's technical expertise and nonpolitical ambitions make it widely respected locally, and there is a fair amount of cooperation between Plan Lerma and the other planning agencies.

Clearly the most impressive feature of these planning efforts is the fact that three such distinct and relatively professionalized organizations should exist in Guadalajara. It is also worth noting that they work in some degree of unison, particularly in the case of the department and the institute. In the other three regions we find no parallel to Guadalajara's planning effort, despite the fact that the efficacy of this approach is widely accepted. Yet, on reflection, one may question the practical accomplishments of these organizations. Although their reports and analyses are a delight to the data-hungry social scientist and professional planner, one wonders more generally, "For whom all the planning?" Where are the intrepid entrepreneurs or state enterprises that might act on these revealed rational opportunities? And if these are lacking, does not the planning process become a fetish? Obviously these questions occur to the planners, whose response is, typically, that in the absence of an aggressive investment mentality their strategy is to show the way and provide foundations for those few, often foreign, enterprises that will set an example.

This strategy is best illustrated by turning to the related area of infrastructure works. Guadalajara's one-time isolation has been successfully surmounted through the creation of most of the infrastructure necessary for industrial expansion. Indeed, the supply of electricity, roads, dams, water, and gas have all outrun demand in an imbalance of what Hirschman calls the social overhead capital (SOC)/direct productive activities (DPA) ratio.[5] This is due, no doubt, to the strength of the public sector and to "most favored" treatment by a federal government interested in investing public revenues in those regions that combine political loyalty and potential developmental dividends.

The two specific infrastructure projects that leaders regarded as most important to the region's growth were the provision of natural gas and the expansion of the airport. In the early 1960s, Guadalajara's lack of natural gas as a cheap source of industrial energy was rumored to have been the reason why several interested firms decided ultimately not to locate in the city. The initiative for the project was provided by the private sector, which financed and undertook a cost-benefit study of an extension of the gas viaduct then terminating in Salamanca, some 150 miles away. This show of interest in the private sector caught the attention of Governor Juan Gil Preciado, who, with the support of local industrialists, approached the nationalized petroleum company (PEMEX). At the time, however, PEMEX was having financial difficulties and declined this new 200-million-peso expenditure.   When the new governor, Francisco Medina Ascensio, took office in 1964, the gas project was revived as one of his principal priorities. The governor and a delegation from the private sector went to Mexico City to argue their case, exercising, according to one observer, a good deal of "political force" in the process. Perhaps a more convincing explanation for their success on this occasion was the improved financial status of PEMEX. The construction of a natural gas viaduct got under way in 1965 and was completed two and a half years later, though not without incident. A study by the Jalisco institute indicated that the projected price of natural gas delivered in Guadalajara was going to be higher than in other cities, thus placing the region in a non-competitive position. Private-sector revelations on this point produced a rift with the governor, who had worked hard for the project and objected to this ungrateful haggling over price. However, the dispute was soon quelled when PEMEX agreed with the arguments of the institute and reduced the price of gas to competitive levels. The characteristic bottom line to this story was that once gas was available, promising to reduce industrial costs, local firms were reluctant to adopt the innovation. Here, as elsewhere, the efforts of planners and decision-makers outran the effective demand of local industry and thus failed to animate development in Hirschman's sense of the appropriate mix of social overhead and direct productive activities.

The expansion of Guadalajara's international airport followed a similar course, although here the initiative came from the public sector. In the early 1960s it became evident to state officials that modernized airport facilities were necessary so as to capitalize on two opportunities. First, a lucrative tourist trade was increasingly being attracted to the city on trips to Jalisco's beach resort town of Puerto Vallarta. Second, by accommodating direct flights of the jumbo jets from the United States, a cost incentive would be provided for the location of light manufacturing and assembly plants that shipped their products by air. In 1964 the governor convened a group of private-sector leaders, suggesting that government and local business each put up 10 percent of the estimated cost as a way of impressing the federal government with their commitment to the project. Again private-sector leaders implemented this fund-raising drive, through the Chambers of Commerce and Industry, which shortly elicited the funds necessary to attract federal approval of the additional 80 percent. Today Guadalajara's airport is elegant, boasting the longest runway in Latin America and direct flights to several Southwestern United States cities.

In both of these projects several important characteristics of the decision-making process are illustrated. First, things get done: both of the projects were successfully realized within a few years. Second, whether the initiative comes from the public or the private sector, the first step is to obtain the support and cooperation of the other. Institutions and individuals in the two sectors coordinate and work in relative harmony on these major undertakings, if not on all. Third, it is ultimately the federal government that is responsible for the greatest share of regional projects. Guadalajara's principal resource is local harmony and commitment, which give it important leverage on the federal budget. Finally, the projects themselves aim not so much at spurring the development of indigenous enterprise as at laying a foundation that will attract external investment.

That series of projects referred to by respondents under the general rubric of urban development represents a more locally oriented activity. As we noted in chapter 2, concern for the quality of Guadalajara's urban environment dates from the colonial era, owing to the city's early importance as a cultural, administrative, and ecclesiastical center. Beginning in 1941, a series of "urbanization laws" were enacted by the state of Jalisco for the purpose of establishing local planning commissions and Councils of Municipal Collaboration. In Guadalajara the Council for Municipal Collaboration is composed of fourteen members, five from the public sector (the mayor, director of public works, a representative of the state urban planning agency, et cetera) and nine from the private sector (Chamber of Commerce, service clubs, Engineers' Association, Bankers' Association, et cetera). Traditionally this has been a high-level organization; many of the influentials have served on the council and several have been its president. The principal function of the council is to identify, on the advice of its members, public agencies, and citizen groups, those neighborhoods of the city in need of urban works such as paving, street lighting, water, drainage, and electricity. Once that determination is made, registered property owners in the affected area must approve the project and are subsequently taxed in proportion to the extent their property benefits from the improvement.[6]

The bare essentials of this arrangement are mentioned here in order to emphasize the fact that from an early date Guadalajara has developed organizational procedures for meeting the demand for urban services, and these procedures entail public-private cooperation, engendering a good deal of confidence in the system. Among our four cities this form of municipal collaboration is unique (although Medellín has a more recently established analog) and certainly helps account for the relative absence of slums and decaying neighborhoods in Guadalajara.

Another key aspect in the explanation of urban development is the powerful role of the public sector coupled with the incentives of national politics. State governors, not surprisingly, seek to make a name for themselves, often in the hope of rising to some federal post at the end of their administration. The most obvious way of doing this is by playing to local strengths, further enhancing the city through some dramatic new work. Most renowned in this area was Jesús González Gallo, who, between 1946 and 1952, created many monuments to himself, including the cross-shaped central plaza, the wide avenues, a bus terminal, and recreational parks. Subsequent governors have followed suit, leaving the legacy of a large central market, a produce market, a modern railway center, more parks and avenues, a state library, a center of artisan crafts, a convention center, and much more. Parenthetically, most of these governors also succeeded in obtaining federal cabinet posts on the strength of their reputations.

The question that arises here is, how—in addition to creating an attractive and highly livable city—do these activities affect economic development. The answer, of course, varies. Some of these projects were costly white elephants. The state library, for example, was constructed in such a way that its interior is too humid to store books without damage and it stands empty. The new convention center is too far from downtown hotels to attract much use. Yet the majority of these undertakings have had more encouraging effects. Transportation and the distribution of goods is less costly, the public markets maintain a busy petty commerce, and well-served urban neighborhoods support a lively construction industry. In a more general vein, an attractive, well-planned city provides many developmental lures that can be tangibly summarized by the desire of people to live there.

Indeed, the charms of the city, along with the availability of infrastructure services and locational advantages vis-à-vis regional markets, are major planks in that campaign to attract new investment that respondents refer to as industrial promotion. Consistent with earlier themes in the decision-making process, local leaders construe the aim of industrial promotion primarily in terms of attracting new productive investment from outside the region and, more specifically, from the United States. Organizations of both public and private sectors engage in these endeavors, often collaboratively.

Here it will be useful to comment briefly on national and local policy regarding foreign investment, since the matter is widely misunderstood. There is a widespread myth that no enterprise in Mexico can have more than 49 percent foreign capital. Although no such law or practice exists, the fiction is good politics in that it reinforces Mexican nationalism while promoting investor confidence through the idea of association with "Yankee know-how." In actual fact, policy in this area is highly variable and ruled, for the most part, by expediency. Several types of enterprises, such as petrochemicals, are clearly barred to foreign investment. The "Mexicanization" laws of 1945 sought to restrain foreign controlling interests in the fields of broadcasting, film making, airlines, publishing, "basic" chemicals, merchant shipping, fishing, soft drinks, rubber, fertilizer and insecticides, and several others.[7] Apart from these areas—some of which are not in conformity with law—foreign enterprises are subject only to the same rules governing national ones and require no official approval prior to their establishment. An "exception" that is routinely circumvented has to do with the prohibition of foreign property ownership within 100 kilometers of the border or within 50 kilometers of the coast. Government leverage with foreign firms comes, not from the power to give or deny permission to enter the country in most lines of activity, but from control over the granting of permits and import licenses. For this reason, foreign companies typically negotiate with the federal Secretary of Industry and Commerce prior to location. The government usually tries to obtain the best possible terms with respect to national interests on questions of public stock issues, local management personnel, number of jobs, and location in areas that will best promote regional growth. Nevertheless, the great concentration of these firms in Mexico City and its surroundings testifies to the fact that the government is not generally successful. A new firm may represent enough advantages on enough of the important criteria for the government to relent on others. There are no known cases, in Guadalajara at least, of firms that were denied operating necessities at the conclusion of the negotiation process. In Guadalajara, where investor mentality tends to be quite conservative and short-sighted, public policy actively solicits foreign investment and is more than flexible in the concessions it asks of new industry.

The state government utilizes several strategies for attracting outside investment. The principal monetary incentives under its control are tax concessions, including the suspension of state taxes for a ten- or fifteen-year period and assistance in obtaining concessions on federal taxes and import duties. Beyond that, the Department of Economy is active in the sponsorship of conventions and trade delegations that draw potential investors. The department has sponsored studies and published reports on new economic opportunities in the state that are routinely distributed to these visiting delegations.[8] Further, in many specific ways local government has shown a marked willingness to provide for the needs of new firms; "To help snag the Kodak plant, for example, the city agreed to lay in an extra water supply."[9]

Private-sector promotional activity is typified by the regular exchange of industrial and commercial delegations with United States cities. In 1968 a group of prominent local figures and resident American managers made trips to Houston, San Antonio, and San Diego for the purpose of talking up investment opportunities and opening lines of trade. Closely associated with these promotional tours are optimistic publicity releases, such as a piece carried in the "Business Abroad" section of *Business Week* for January 13, 1968, claiming in its title "Business Shakes up a Lotus Land," or articles in the English-language *Mexican-American Review* that characterize Jalisco as "Mexico's Awakening Giant,"[10] "Mexico's Golden West,"[11] and a center for "Executive Living."[12] During the visit of a delegation from San Diego, California, the hometown paper reported (dateline, Guadalajara):

> A group of San Diegans on a goodwill tour yesterday got a startling briefing on the business, industrial and investment climate in this booming second city of Mexico.
>
> At a breakfast sponsored at the American Chamber of Commerce here and again at a luncheon hosted by the traveling San Diego Chamber of Commerce members, this was made clear time and again: Mexico in general and Guadalajara in particular extends a hand of welcome to U.S. investors.[13]

One local investment firm devotes its energies to selling Mexican securities to United States investors. In 1967 the firm did more than twenty million dollars' worth of business, and its executives note that local banks could do much more to stimulate investments if they adopted a more aggressive and competitive policy of seeking out opportunities. As it is, they point out, local banks have trouble handling the incoming investment from their company alone, another indicator that the conservative business mentality, rather than any true shortage of capital, is a factor restricting growth. Reluctant local wealth prefers the security of real estate and fixed rentals, leaving the industrial sector open to foreigners. Influential policy-makers in government, industry, and commerce, in turn, actively solicit and aid nonlocal investors.

In order to assess the impact of these promotional activities, case study analyses were made of the location decisions of three important new firms, Kodak, Burroughs, and Phillip Morris. Executives of these corporations claimed that local blandishments were welcome but of relatively minor consequence in the decision. Local leaders in alternative city sites were similarly hospitable. Rather, they attached crucial importance to such physical advantages as the availability of water, proximity to markets and producers, the relative absence of earthquakes (in the case of film making), and the fact that Mexico City was so saturated with industry that necessary services were in short supply. Following these practical considerations, it was also noted that Guadalajara provided a pleasant urban environment, but that fact weighed little in the initial decision. This, of course, contrasts sharply with the perception of local leaders, who would give considerably more credit to their boosterism in "landing" these firms.

Generally speaking, the overindustrialization of Mexico City and Guadalajara's physical and infrastructure advantages, combined with an open arms policy, have all resulted in a rapid increase in nonlocal investment (principally from the United States but including Mexico City and Monterrey interests).

> With new people has come new capital. In 1962, for example, only 1.5 million dollars of new money was generated. In 1963, the figure rocketed to 13 millions. In 1964, 24 million dollars flowed into the city; and, in 1965 new capital totalled more than 67 million U.S. dollars. No small part of this increase has come from major U.S. firms, or their Mexican affiliates, who have established plants in or adjacent to Guadalajara.[14]

Foreign investment is often justified as a developmental expedient on the grounds that it attracts new capital and technology, provides economies of scale for the exploitation of new and complementary lines of productivity, and creates new sources of employment. We would emphasize that a growing body of recent research repudiates each of these claims and argues, on the contrary, that foreign investment promotes dependency and underdevelopment.[15] Yet, assuming that decision-makers in Guadalajara may be unaware of this recent research, they certainly recognize other liabilities involved in foreign investment, such as oligopoly and repatriation of profits. Why, then, the open-arms policy and the predominant tendency to attract nonlocal or foreign capital? Why the policy of courting firms that fail to meet even the conventional justifications, i.e., firms that create few new jobs and often compete with local enterprise? Once again the explanation is found in the peculiar characteristics of the political system. Taking their cues from national goals, local administrations attempt to run up impressive gains in capital investment, industrialization, and gross product. Those "accomplishments," in turn, tend to be rewarded by career advancement and preferential treatment for the state by the federal government. Private-sector decision-makers subscribe to these policies for related reasons. Some operate industries that have already entered into partnership arrangements with United States firms; others feel that their particular business will stand to gain, irrespective of the source of economic growth. Public and private leaders alike were either unaware of or unconcerned with potentially deleterious effects of foreign investment. And this is understandable. In the first place, they simply mirrored attitudes of the national administration during this period. In the second, they made up an elite having the most to gain in the short run from this policy.

A fitting contrast to industrial promotion is found in the final area of policy-making. Agricultural development is a topic in which it is possible to trace more directly some of the consequences of elite policy for the larger population. Paradoxically, the problem of agricultural productivity and rural standards of living simultaneously embraces some of Jalisco's greatest successes and failures. In 1959 the state administration headed by Juan Gil Preciado, with the aid of Plan Lerma, initiated a new program of agricultural development called Plan Jalisco. Plan Jalisco was not one integrated design but a variety of programs including studies of climate and soil, improvement of seeds and fertilizers, technical assistance, new irrigation and transportation services, a new slaughterhouse and produce market in Guadalajara, and plans for the expansion of food-processing industries in rural areas.[16] In reality, everything that was done in agriculture was included as a part of this "plan" and every gain in agricultural productivity was attributed to its influence. For these reasons, the real significance of Plan Jalisco was a renewed emphasis on the rural sector by an administration that followed a long tradition of emphasis on urban works. Indeed, Governor Gil Preciado earned such a reputation from Plan Jalisco that at the end of his administration in 1964 he, a former school teacher, was appointed federal Minister of Agriculture. This, in turn, played no small role in the continuation of Plan Jalisco in a second stage after 1964.

In the ten-year period ending in 1968 the effects of this program, direct and indirect, were evident. The value of agricultural productivity experienced a four-fold increase and its gross product was increasing at a faster rate (9 percent) than the total state gross product (7.7 percent). The largest gains were in corn production, which tripled, vaulting Jalisco into first place among the corn-growing states of the republic.[17] In milk production the state rose to second place nationally, and important gains were made in beans, sugar cane, and cattle.

Given these impressive gains, it might seem incidental to observe that dire poverty still exists in the countryside, the assumption being that this unfortunate legacy is on the decline as productivity increases are enjoyed by an ever larger segment of the peasantry. In fact, however, that assumption is mistaken; for the most part, these gains have been accomplished at the expense of the peasantry, whose general welfare has increased not at all. The point is fundamental and requires careful documentation.

In the first place, income differences between the rural and urban sectors are vast and on the increase.[18] In the rural areas Mexico's developmental miracle is belied by notably high rates (for Latin America) of infant mortality, illiteracy, and malnutrition and by low per capita income.[19] On a regional basis Jalisco ranks near the middle of a composite scale of rural poverty.[20] Acknowledging the facts of rural underdevelopment, we have still to answer the question of whether this is due to historical legacies now in the process of amelioration or a result of deliberately discriminatory policies. The evidence from this case study analysis supports the second, exploitation hypothesis.

Discriminatory policies reinforcing rural underdevelopment vary subtly. Among the more clearly exploitive are instances of the expropriation of *ejido* lands standing in the path of urban development in Puerto Vallarta. Less blatant but more extensive is the practice of failing to provide unambiguous legal title to reformed lands. Since PRI is the bargaining agent and court of appeal for most land title disputes, the insecurity of land tenure provides party officials with a useful source of patronage and control over potential rural unrest. Selective allocations of loans through the public Ejido Bank serve similar political control functions.[21] Yet by far the most important and subtle forms of institutional discrimination are agricultural credit policies. As we have seen, available investment capital in Jalisco is scarce, meaning that private banks have very little interest in risky, low-yield agricultural investment. Understanding that fact, the federal government between 1924 and 1965 has set up three public agricultural banks and a fund for channeling more private investment into the primary sector. Nevertheless, these institutions are underfinanced in comparison with credit needs, inefficient in their operation, and widely perceived as corrupt.[22] Further, it is the stated policy of these banks to allot their limited funds among "good subjects of credit," meaning private property holders and the more successful *ejidatarios*. Several local informants estimated that 80 percent of Jalisco's rural population cannot qualify for credit. One study in the Guadalajara area indicated that only 13 out of 105 farmers in a poor *ejido* received bank credit and that the percentage was not much higher in a more prosperous one.[23] Moreover, those who do get credit often have bad experiences with the banks, including demands for kickbacks and the untimely arrival of seed and fertilizer, which may result in crop failures from inopportune planting and fertilizing. (Typically, the loan is only 20 percent in cash and 80 percent in kind, though repayment is 100 percent in cash.) As a result, many poor farmers indicate that they prefer dealing with local loan sharks, who charge a minimum of 24 percent per season and up to 50 or 60 percent (compared to the official 9 to 12 percent through the banks), because these loans are in cash and are free of bureaucratic red tape. Others admit to leaving their lands idle or (illegally) renting them to large operators and hiring themselves out as laborers.[24]

Of course, practical arguments are advanced for these policies, based on capital shortages and the need to intensify and modernize agriculture. Underlying these arguments is the assumption that land reform and small communal holdings are less productive than large-scale operations. In fact, however, the accumulating evidence indicates that, given time to get under way, the *ejidos* are equally or more productive, even within the discriminatory credit policies.[25] This suggests that arguments in support of agricultural credit policies based on productivity serve as an ideological justification for systemic inequalities. Clearly, productivity gains have been made under these policies, but they are gains enjoyed by only a small proportion of private owners who have always been prosperous commercial farmers. Public policy has effected no redistribution of productivity and income in favor of the peasantry. On the contrary, private commercial farmers have enjoyed the far greater part of the increase, leaving the peasantry in a relatively worsened condition, their potential power coopted by the political system. Here, as elsewhere, it should be noted that agricultural credit policy is made at the federal level; the agricultural banks are federal institutions. In an effort to record substantial developmental accomplishments, state officials have merely implemented these inequality-producing practices with a flair.

Summary

Employing the decisional framework set out earlier, we may now draw some generalizations from these case studies of policy-making.

Actors in the decision-making process constitute a relatively large group that represents rather evenly the public- and private-sector organizational networks. Yet the distribution of power and authority is such that government is the more dominant party in a publicly-led coalition. The regional influence of the federal government is extensive, particularly in the areas of infrastructure and agricultural development, although a good measure of local autonomy is reflected in unique planning and urban development works. As a result of externally-oriented promotional activities, foreign corporations are becoming increasingly important.

Consensus and cooperation characterize the policy-making process. Local groups are in accord with federal goals and typically coordinate their initiatives in order to present a united front. Few instances of conflict within this elite were found.

Regional priorities reflect principally an emphasis on rapid industrial growth, and this, in turn, implies attracting large investors from outside the region rather than measures to gradually expand indigenous industry. Nearly equal in importance is the value placed on urban development and maintenance of the city's reputation. Implied in this are a series of activities that benefit the less privileged urban groups in petty commerce, services, and housing. Neglected and sometimes paying the price for these priorities are the peasantry and the small manufacturers adversely affected by nonlocal control of certain fields of production.

CALI

No Change from the Top: The Mystique of Progress and the Mechanics of Continuity

The policy-making process in Cali is dominated by two themes, the politics of agriculture and the pains of transition to an urban-industrial center. Indeed, these two themes frequently conflict with one another, their intersection giving rise to many of the distinctive features of regional politics. These factors figured prominently in the creation of Cali's regional development corporation (C.V.C.), a project that is both prototypical and overwhelmingly recognized by respondents as the most important event among recent developmental efforts (see table 30).

The C.V.C. (Corporación Autónoma Regional del Cauca) was formally established in 1954 as a self-governing authority for the generation of electrical power and such related works as irrigation, flood control, land reclamation, and agricultural services. (The initials C.V.C. referred originally to the three-department region the new corporation was intended to serve: Cauca, Valle, and Caldas. Although the other departments later dropped out, the initials were retained.) In some senses the C.V.C. was the dream of one man, José Castro Borrero, son of a wealthy land-owning family and former mayor but, nevertheless, a progressive in his role as head of the Industrialists' Association in the late 40s and early 50s. For at least twenty years various ideas for regional development had circulated but never taken root.[26] As early as 1948 Castro began his efforts to arouse the interest of local industrialists in the idea of an autonomous regional authority that would tackle, first, problems of electrification, flood control, and irrigation, with the longer-term ambition of integrating all of the resources of the valley to promote greater productivity. From the beginning, the belief was that these goals could not be accomplished through the existing organizational structure, which was viewed as overly centralized in the national capital, insensitive to regional problems, and generally inefficient. The first difficulty met by this plan was that no legal precedent existed for an autonomous regional authority, hence this organizational innovation would require an amendment to the centralist constitution.

But local leaders adopted a more incremental set of goals. In 1951 Castro became acquainted with Milo Perkins, a petroleum engineer with Standard Oil who informally advised on the project, indicating the kind of basic information needed in planning. In 1953 the federal government issued Decree Number 653, which provided a stimulus for the creation of private electrical power companies. Perceiving this as a useful entering wedge on the legal problem, Castro began active efforts to convince the Industrialists' Association and wrote to Perkins for suggestions on North American firms equipped to conduct a study of the region and draw up a plan along the lines of the T.V.A. Perkins then recommended his friend and former director of the T.V.A., David Lilienthal, suggesting at the same time that the Industrialists' Association invite Lilienthal for a fact-finding visit. At this point the Industrialists' Association began to show real enthusiasm and sent two of its prominent members to the federal Minister of Public Works to obtain support and to ask that the plan, still quite informal, be recommended to Rojas Pinilla, the military leader who had just seized control of the government.

Through discussions with Perkins, David Lilienthal became interested in the idea. After leaving the T.V.A. he had set up a private consulting firm devoted to international development, and the Cauca Valley was to be the first of his major regional development schemes, followed later by similar plans for Iran and Vietnam's Mekong delta.[27] After surveying the region in March of 1954, Lilienthal concluded that its size, topography, river system, and potential demand for electrical energy made it an ideal site.

Following his visit, Lilienthal set about obtaining a loan for the project from the World Bank. Meanwhile, Cali leaders, working through the Industrialists' Association, set up a committee, first headed by Castro and later by Bernardo Garcés Córdoba, that dedicated itself to getting the necessary enabling legislation passed by the National Congress. With the support of President Rojas a National Constitutional Assembly was called in 1954 that passed two important measures. One was an act empowering public corporations with territorial jurisdiction and access to national and international credit, the second a legislative decree of October 22, 1954, approving the Corporación Autónoma Regional del Cauca. The success of the project to this point was attributed to the organizational efforts of local leaders and the pressures they were able to exert on the president.

The first serious opposition to the C.V.C. came in 1955 when it became evident that the corporation's normal operation would require a land sur-tax of four mills per taxed peso on those proprietors whose holdings exceeded a value of 50,000 pesos. At this point a strong opposition campaign took root among large landowners, particularly the cattlemen. Organized by the Cattlemen's Association, the opposition argued that such efforts were needed not in the valley but in less developed regions, that electrical needs could be met by existing facilities, that the plan was a "foreign plague" imposed by groups unfamiliar with Colombian realities, that it infringed on the sacred rights of private initiative, that it violated the Constitution, and, generally, that it was a ruinous scheme of "Byzantines" and "academics."[28] Evidently the protracted efforts of the opposition landed elite were serious enough to cause President Rojas to reconsider his earlier support. Although we will never know, because a national plebiscite deposed Rojas in 1957, local observers felt that his continuation in office could have spelled the demise of the C.V.C.

In the long run, of course, the C.V.C. survived and contributed greatly to regional development. Available electrical energy was increased many-fold. Flood control and land reclamation brought under cultivation thousands of hectares of formerly useless land. Irrigation and technical assistance promised greater productivity for additional acreage. Yet the C.V.C. has not survived its opposition unscathed; landowners continue to oppose increases in the corporation's tax base and maintain a system of assessments in which large properties are underevaluated.[29] As a result, C.V.C. projects are continuously imperiled and depend on the uncertain financing of international loans or special appropriations from the federal government. Perhaps more important is the fact that the C.V.C. is forced to work outside the conflictual entanglements of local politics, thereby foregoing opportunities for interorganizational cooperation.

This mood of conflict between progressive developmentalists and landed elites also characterizes the policy area that respondents refer to as agricultural development. As we found in chapter 2, the Cauca Valley has labored historically under the problems of inequitable land tenure, low productivity, and extensive land use. Some evidence suggests that the threat of expropriation embodied in the Land Reform Act of 1961 has encouraged landowners to turn to more intensive cultivation.[30] If this is a trend, its effects on productivity are so far rather undramatic. In recent years a few crops such as corn and rice have registered substantially higher yields and livestock production is more intensive. Yet sugar cane continues to dominate production and its cultivation on the large estates has not increased in productivity, which probably has a lot to do with the fact that the total value of agricultural production has risen slowly. In this area Colombian exports are regulated by quotas established in the United States Sugar Act. But if only a certain amount of sugar can be profitably produced for internal markets and export, then the crux of the agricultural problem is the failure of the large landowners to diversify into foodstuffs the nation now imports. This judgment is supported by the strong positive correlation, earlier cited, between land quality, estate size, and extensive use.[31]

What explains the intransigence of the rural elite? In the first place, this is a historical pattern not easily reversed except through major coercive reforms. In the second place, those mild reforms that have been attempted are countered by a reactionary policy developed by the landowners and their representatives in the sugar cane and cattlemen's associations.

The issue of land reform seriously strains federal-regional relations and polarizes local groups themselves. The intensity of this conflict is ironic, for two reasons. First, the Colombian land reform law was arrived at in a gradual way,[32] and its 1961 version, regarded as mild by Latin American standards, is aimed principally at the confiscation of unused lands. [33] Second, despite its size and agricultural potential, Valle del Cauca ranked eleventh among fourteen departments in the amount of land expropriated by 1968.[34] To state it more directly, a mild law the impact of which has been minimal in Valle del Cauca has, nevertheless, aroused intense resentment. Clearly this testifies to the strength and solidarity of the landholding elite, which not only has managed to stave off serious reform in the region but has also kept its proponents on the defensive.

Obviously, land reform is a complex question allowing multiple points of view. With respect to the Cauca Valley, proponents of reform argue that land tenure is still highly unequal and that large holders continue inefficient land usage in the face of low productivity and extreme rural poverty. Indeed, they charge that landlords have intentionally subverted reforms in the defense of their own interests. Agricultural interest groups argue on the contrary that the only solution for rural prosperity is large-scale commercial farming and that their technical answers to current problems (e.g., better marketing facilities, credit, and technical assistance) are undercut by talk of confiscation that discourages the agriculturalist from making new investments on his land. As one observer suggested,

"You can't run commercial agriculture like a garden," and government pressure in that direction will only demoralize the farmer. There are probably elements of truth in both these positions, but the larger truth is that, while expropriation has been very limited in the region, the landowners themselves have not delivered on the promise of greater productivity and rural prosperity. Part of that failing may be due to factors beyond their control, but there are equally obvious courses they could take—including productivity increases, diversification, more jobs, better salaries, sale of unused lands, provision of credit to small farmers, et cetera—that they have not. Cooler heads have little sympathy for the landowners, feeling that expropriation of lands in use is a remote possibility and that all they have to fear is being reluctantly cajoled into more efficient practices. If this is true, as the evidence indicates, and if it is added to earlier observations concerning the concentration of landholding and wealth, the persistence of the hacienda system, and the solidarity of the elite against changes like the C.V.C., then the structure of power in this respect would have to be judged as little changed from its historic pattern.

Similar elitist tendencies are found in those university programs that respondents considered progressive stimulants to regional development. As we discovered in chapter 3, Universidad del Valle is regarded as the most influential institution in the region. Since its founding in 1945 the university has acquired a national and international reputation, owing principally to its excellent medical school. Unlike the century-old universities in other major cities that conform to the scholastic or tradition-bound "Latin university model," Universidad del Valle resembles more the North American pattern. And this is no accident, given the involvement of the Rockefeller Foundation in funding the university's growth.

When respondents spoke of university projects promoting development, they generally made specific reference to a management training program established within the School of Economics in 1964. The impetus for this program came from a group of young business leaders and sons of important families that began meeting informally early in 1963 to discuss local development problems. The purposes of the Tuesday Night Group, as it came to be called, were to get to the source of local developmental problems and to see if some of these might yield to the concerted efforts of a younger and better-educated generation. After a year of meetings and analysis, the group began looking for an institutional vehicle that might effect some of the solutions they envisaged. Reviewing local organizational structure, they soon ruled out the public sector, which lacked professionalism or policy continuity, and private interest groups like the Industrialists' Association, which they felt only represented special interests. The university was chosen as the appropriate vehicle and members of the Tuesday

Night Group began offering suggested changes in university policy. The responsiveness of the university was demonstrated at this point by its offer to the group of young leaders that one of its members take over management of the economics faculty. In this manner Reinaldo Scarpetta became dean of the Division of Social and Economic Sciences.

Scarpetta's plans involved, first, converting the school's theoretical-economics orientation to a practical business-school approach and, second, adding new subdivisions: a night school, a program in agricultural economics, and a special "masters program in industrial administration for high executives." Of these several programs it is clearly the latter that has received the most publicity and acclaim. Several factors account for the emphasis put on the "high executives" program. The Young Turks behind the program were convinced that direct, practical bearing on community economic institutions was the hallmark of effectiveness. Second, they were in a hurry: rather than wait for contemporary students to work their way up in the business world, they felt it more practical to go straight to the heads of local enterprise and bring them back into a part-time university program. Finally, as a result of their own training, mainly in United States business schools, they subscribed uncritically to a management ideology, the view that significant change must "come from the top." The elitist character of the program is clearly articulated by one of its promoters:

> The program must be aimed at the "movers" and "shapers." In any society or region there are a few men at the top of the "strategic human capital" pyramid who set the environmental stage. They are the individuals who, if they put their minds to it, can transform society from within and from the top down without tearing it apart through conflict. It is these men, and only these, who through their involvement and leadership, can root a development program in the local soil, create the climate in which it will flourish, and give it the kind of nourishment that will bring it long-range growth and vigor.[35]

This program, and presumably its assumptions about the sources of social change, appealed broadly to the members of Cali's power structure. From the time of the program's creation in 1964 until 1968 some 200 leading figures in the business community and government, including more than half of our sub-leaders and influentials, had enrolled in the eighteen-month masters curriculum.[36] The question arises, "What have been its effects?"

A supportive discussion of this "revolution from the top" notes rather meagerly that several enterprising executives used their training to conduct market surveys, indicating new product opportunities, while others improved the accounting procedures of their firms.[37] Such gains are not particularly impressive coming from carefully preselected business leaders with college degrees and experience. Reported achievements are mainly in efficiency, with no mention of such larger benefits as increases in jobs or incomes. One can scarcely underrate long-term influences and changes in attitudes, but these intangible benefits must be evaluated against the region's pressing inequalities of class and income. While educational priorities were being given to a program tailored to the interests of an elite, one that set "standards of admission and performance such that only the most highly qualified individuals could gain admission . . . [and in which] being a part of the program became a widely accepted symbol of prestige,"[38] broad segments of the university's student body were protesting the restricted channels of educational mobility and the clientist policies of the administration.[39]

It should be understood that this evaluation applies only to certain university programs cited as important by leaders. In medical education, public health, agricultural research, and community action studies some important work is under way. The role of the university in providing broader educational opportunities and creating a consciousness of social problems is evident in the very fact of student protest. Further, Universidad del Valle is unusually well administered for the provision of quality education. Perhaps the most serious problem it faces is financial. Like the C.V.C., it is perilously dependent on auxiliary sources of funding. Budgetary reprisals are said to follow the student protests originally inspired by allocative priorities. Obviously the university administration will continue having to contend with these conflicting pressures. The important question will be whether it will do so in the interests of the elite or the general welfare, and, so far, there are examples of both.

The same kind of developmental mystique surrounding the management training program was also found in the effort of local leaders to bring to Cali the Pan American Games of 1971. In concrete terms it was hoped that the event would attract new federal investment in badly needed urban infrastructure works (a new airport, roads, public housing, et cetera). In a more general sense they also believed that such an extravaganza would "put Cali on the map," giving it an inter-American reputation that in turn would be a source of local pride and outside investment.

The history of Cali's selection by the Pan American Games Committee is fairly simple. It was the idea of a single individual, Alberto Galindo, who died before its realization. Winning the interest of several local leaders and the important civic action association, U.A.V. (Unidad de Acción Vallecaucano), a "Pro Site Committee" was formed, including many of our influentials. Under U.A.V. auspices special promotional literature was prepared, selling the city and promising the construction of necessary facilities. Although Lima and Miami provided some stiff competition, the games committee chose Cali because, local observers feel, it was the sporting thing to do and reflected their aims for the broader promotion of athletics.

Following approval, a new U.A.V. committee was formed, again heavily interlarded with influentials, for planning the feat. At the time this study was conducted the games were still three years away, making it difficult to comment in detail on the planning process. Nevertheless, several things were clear in the early going. First, heavy public works expenditures were entailed for which there was no firm arrangement on funding. Second, it was evident that substantial costs would have to be borne by the federal government, and familiar conflicts were already developing with regard to the distribution of costs and the speed with which nationally-sponsored works would be initiated (especially a new airport). Third, local groups conducted no serious studies of the long-term costs and benefits of the scheme, evidently unaware of the fact that analyses conducted in Tokyo and Mexico City suggested the potentially damaging economic consequences of inflationary public works spending and of temporary price hikes that might persist long after the event. On the contrary, they seemed to see it as a way of commanding greater federal attention, financial and otherwise, to the city's needs, assuming that they only stood to gain in the bargain.

It is true that Cali's need for urban development is extreme. Most serious is the lack of adequate housing and urban services (water, electricity, sanitation) in the extensive squatter communities forming a semicircle around the city's eastern perimeter. Low-cost housing programs of the federal and city governments and a private foundation are very limited in scope and, typically, are not accessible to most of the needy population. And similar deficiencies affect the entire population; many sections of the city are subject to flooding, electrical service is irregular, an estimated two-thirds of the streets are unpaved or in disrepair, public transportation is minimal, and parks or recreational facilities are noticeably absent. In these areas of responsibility there is no dearth of public agencies, yet department and city authorities in public works and urban planning complain of inadequate funding. A system of beneficiary assessment for urban works is recent and has to contend with the fact that many potential beneficiaries have nothing to be assessed. Without confirming or placing responsibility for the allegation, it is significant that numerous respondents believe the city's various urban programs to be graft-ridden and predicated on payoffs between politicians and contractors. But that belief could have little substance without changing the explanation for these urban problems, which lies more directly at the door of organizational conflict and a leadership style that gives low priority to public welfare needs. Here again the C.V.C. and a parallel urban agency (EMCALI) with important joint achievements in the provision of aqueducts, telephones, and electricity are exceptions that prove the rule, since they operate as autonomous agencies less fettered by local leadership and political constraints.

To return to the Pan American Games project, it is difficult to see the connection between this spectacle and the very real urban problems, despite our respondents' easy assumption that the first would generate motivation to deal with the second. This, of course, implies that urban problems stem from a lack of motivation rather than from rapid migration, organizational inefficiency, class and income inequalities, and neglect—a rather unlikely proposition. Just as economic impact studies did not precede efforts to attract the games, neither did they follow the event. For present purposes it is sufficient to note that little serious attention was given to the costs of the project and how these related to the desired benefits. It was simply and mysteriously assumed that there would be some connection.

In the final policy-making area, industrial promotion in any planned or coordinated form is yet to be realized. For several years Cali leaders have talked about the wisdom of creating a local agency responsible for basic economic studies and the promotion of new industrial investment. Currently this kind of work is partially attended to by the C.V.C., the Industrialists' Association, the university, and local offices of the Colombian Institute of Administration (Instituto Colombiano de Administración, or INCOLDA). After the reported changes at the university it was generally agreed that the most likely organizational nucleus for such an agency would be the university-based Center of Investigations on Economic Development; or at least this was the ambition of the Tuesday Night Group. Initial steps in that direction were taken in 1964–1965, when the state government signed contracts with the center for a series of studies leading to a development plan for the department. The first of these studies, appearing in 1966, reflected both the technical competence of its authors and the disturbing fact that the regional economy was in a serious slump. Regrettably, the work was not continued. Illustrating the often-noted lack of policy continuity, a new administration in 1966 canceled the center's contracts, dashing hopes for a new agency arising from this quarter. Private-sector leaders, members of the Tuesday Night Group, and many influentials were bitterly disappointed by the action, taking it as another example of bad faith and concluding that future endeavor would not make the mistake of trying to work with government.

By late 1968 a new group of young leaders calling themselves "Grupo B" (as opposed to local influentials whom they explicitly referred to as

"Grupo A") were holding meetings organized through private interest groups (ANDI and INCOLDA) and discussing again some kind of research and promotional agency. In the meantime, very little effort was being devoted to this kind of work outside the C.V.C. and the university. In contrast to Guadalajara, where three large, professionalized, and coordinated agencies were engaged in research and promotion, the idea in Cali remained in the talking stages, evidently another victim of insular leadership and organizational conflict.

Summary

Actors in the decision-making process represent for the most part the private interests of the higher social strata. Although individuals and organizations of the public sector are encountered in these projects, the individuals tend to be prominent members of the business community filling short-term public posts, and important organizations deliberately operate separately from the local organizational network. Government occupies a secondary role in policy-making, often at odds with the *privately-led status elite monopoly*. To be sure, there are instances of progressive and youthful splinter groups within this monopoly. But they reflect similar class interests and their differences with the dominant elite center more on form than content, more on "modern" versus old-fashioned methods of promoting development than on the objectives and beneficiaries of that development. For the most part, individual and organizational actors reflect a narrow community of interests; decision-making participants are highly concentrated across projects.

Comparative evidence supports this conclusion. The interviews with influentials in Cali and Guadalajara included an item on their participation in the five policy-making areas. The average number of projects in which influentials participated was 2.5 in Cali and 2.0 in Guadalajara. The number of multiple-issue participants (i.e., influentials participating in three or more projects) was 11 of 21 in Cali and 4 of 19 in Guadalajara. A slightly different indicator is the average number of influentials participating in the projects (i.e., the total number of influential-project linkages divided by five, the number of projects): the figures were 11 for Cali and 7 for Guadalajara. In short, these quantitative comparisons bear out the finding that participation and influence are more narrowly distributed in Cali.

Due to fissures between regional groups and the federal government, as well as the heavy presence of foreign firms, the range of local control over decision-making is limited by nonlocal influences.

Though there are limited instances of *cooperation, conflict* pervades the decision-making process, frequently spelling the failure of project initiatives. *Regional priorities* heavily favor the status elite of businessmen, industrialists, and landowners, many of whom are the same people. In none of the policy areas did non-elite interests receive significant attention, the assumption being that you feed the sparrows by feeding horses. The rural sectors, the urban poor, and even the reduced middle class pay the price of the inattention to the general welfare that these projects reflect.

MONTERREY

Industry vs. the City: Coping with the Limits of Growth

In accordance with the research design, two policy-making areas were studied in Monterrey and Medellín. In the Monterrey case, industrial promotion and urban development were closely related issues receiving comparable mention and representing, in many senses, two sides of the same coin. The city's rapid industrialization and attendant population increase have created great strains on available urban services. Recent efforts to curb this growth through industrial decentralization and upgrading of the urban environment contend with the problem of reversing time-honored policies.

Monterrey leaders talk of industrial promotion in both a general and a specific sense. Generally they have in mind the continued expansion of large industrial firms into other regions of the republic. While local investment opportunities are far from exhausted, industrialists realize that continued growth at accustomed rates will entail looking to new markets in Mexico and abroad. As we have seen, the Monterrey Industrial Group has extended to Guadalajara its operations in banking, beer, and steel. Additional new investment has concentrated on Mexico City and the United States border towns. At the same time, the private-sector Association for the Promotion of Mexican Exports (AFEM) is actively seeking new international markets for locally-manufactured products.[40] But, in addition to these general and conventional business practices, "industrial promotion" in Monterrey has come to stand for the goal of decentralizing industry in the state of Nuevo León, channeling new plant investments into secondary towns.

Among the most influential organizations charged with this responsibility is Monterrey's Commission for Industrial Promotion and Economic Development (COFIDE). The enabling legislation of December 1964 defined COFIDE as a decentralized public organization set up for the purpose of "study, diffusion, promotion, and coordination of the industrial development of the state of Nuevo León."[41] Its specific charges are to maintain an inventory of state resources, conduct studies concerning industrial promotion, distribute information on the advantages of the state for new industry, participate in state infrastructure works, collaborate with the state planning commission, sponsor industrial, commercial and agricultural expositions, and assist other public and private agencies in the state. The law also stated that the commission would be presided over by an appointee of the governor and work with a board containing members selected by and representing the state government, the Chamber of Manufacturing Industries, the Chamber of Commerce, the Bankers' Association, and the various cities within the state.

Though charged with an elaborate set of duties, the commission had made some important strides by 1969. An industrial directory for the state published in 1968 lists names and addresses of 2,840 firms cross-classified by size and type of industry. A bimonthly bulletin deals with current developments in the regional economy and frequently discusses the problem of decentralization, giving descriptions of the advantages of industrial location in smaller towns. A typical issue indicates that "Metropolitan Monterrey, an urban-industrial area in rapid expansion, has consequently created for itself serious problems of housing, education and public services. In view of this, it is necessary to initiate industrial decentralization outside the area."[42]

Following this issue were others devoted to opportunities in the nearby towns of Linares, Cadereyta Jiménez, and Sabinas Hidalgo. COFIDE also researches and distributes material of a more explicitly promotional nature. One booklet entitled "Invest in Nuevo León," is published in English and represents an effort to attract foreign investment to meet the need for 315,000 new jobs in the next fifteen years. Yet COFIDE's promotional work is not confined to the United States; it has supplied material for articles on Monterrey to the national and international press, claiming that its message has reached Europe, Canada, Australia, Japan, and the countries of Latin America.

From all indications it appears that, although COFIDE is interested in industrial promotion and economic studies in a general sense, its most obvious ambition and raison d'être is to cope with the decentralization problem. High rates of immigration and natural population increase have put a severe strain on available natural resources (e.g., water), urban services, and jobs. Concern with this problem was one of the principal reasons for establishing COFIDE as early as 1964 for the purpose of trying to reverse population trends.

It seems fair to say that with respect to this goal the agency has met with little success. Monterrey's hinterland is not very attractive to industrial investment, and, even if a number of the more realistic opportunities were seized, their net effect on Monterrey's population increase would probably be very slight. The population of the three previously-mentioned towns proposed as sites for decentralized industry totals less than the annual increase in metropolitan Monterrey. Moreover, the decentralization policy appears predicated on several erroneous assumptions about those urban migrants who contribute to the city's overcrowding. That is, it is assumed that migrants constitute a homogeneous group of unskilled agricultural workers pulled to the city by the lure of industrial jobs. Under that assumption, new industry in secondary towns would seem an effective way of diverting migration from Monterrey. But a closer examination reveals that migrants are an occupationally heterogeneous group pushed from the rural areas by changes in agricultural production and seeking all manner of employment in the city, including industrial but more typically commercial and service. Further, these migrants tend to choose Monterrey for relocation because kin and friends already living in the city assist in the transition, sometimes arranging jobs before the migrant arrives.[43]

These facts about the migration process suggest that, whatever its other virtues, the industrial decentralization policy is not likely to succeed in stemming this source of urbanization. Nevertheless, failings in that endeavor can hardly be lodged with COFIDE, which has done all that could be expected of it in this area and has also competently addressed other problems, working in harmony with the aims of the industrial elite and local organizations. If a failing can be laid to any single source, it would have to be the decision of local leaders to attempt to stem the tide of urbanization rather than to accept it as a reality and cope with it through stronger public programs. Indeed, it was in the field of urban development that policy-making received its poorest marks. The seeming paradox that leaders mention this as a key developmental project is explained by the fact that only recently has the problem been recognized in the higher circles, and new initiatives to deal with it were current at the time of this study.

The historical record of efforts to initiate urban development programs in Monterrey is one of a long series of frustrations and failures. In 1926 a planning commission was established and a program for improving city streets was begun. From all indications these efforts were on the same scale as those made in Guadalajara twenty years earlier. In 1931 private-sector efforts were begun, particularly under the direction of the Chamber of Commerce, to create a comprehensive plan for development. The initiative failed because of a "lack of resources and collaboration from the government."[44] Similar attempts were made in 1933, 1942, and 1946 with the same result. The most apparent explanation for this inaction in the face of mounting problems was a persistent conflict between public officials and local industrialists and businessmen.

In 1950 the long awaited "Points for the Regulatory Plan of the City of Monterrey" finally appeared under the auspices of the privately-endowed Institute for Social Studies. The plan contained recommendations for needed streets and highways, channeling of the river that bisects the city, land usage, zoning, schools, recreational facilities, et cetera. Among these proposed works only one, channeling of the river, was realized in the ensuing years, and generally speaking this first serious effort at attacking urban problems fell on deaf ears.

Perhaps as a result of continuing local concern in some quarters, the state government in 1963 finally established, within the old planning commission, a new department charged with the task of producing an official, updated regulatory plan. Although the resources and support made available were minimal, this new group, under the direction of the architect Cortés Melo, initiated an elaborate study of Monterrey's urban needs that was some four years in the making. In addition to containing a good deal of basic information, the first report of this group made certain modest recommendations that, according to Cortés Melo, were "apparently considered but later ignored by local authorities."[45]

Fortunately for the new planners, a change in governors occurred in October of 1967, bringing in a man much more sympathetic to their ideas. In his inaugural address Eduardo Elizondo stated that the "general condition of the city is deplorable and without any parallel" among the problems to be attacked by the new administration. On his instructions new legislation was quickly passed and by December of 1967 the legal basis had been laid for municipal and state citizenship councils. Their primary task was to promote urban works through organizational methods quite similar to those employed in Guadalajara. It is, in fact, widely acknowledged that Monterrey (like many other Mexican cities) patterned its system after that which Guadalajara had initiated some twenty-six years earlier. By 1969 work had begun on the widening and rerouting of small stretches of several downtown streets. In a variety of other areas of needed urban services no new projects had been initiated locally, although the federal government is continuing work on water and electrical problems. Given this belated beginning, one has to wonder whether Monterrey will be able to meet even its most pressing urban needs in the foreseeable future.

As local observers unfailingly point out, the urban problem is, at bottom, political. A weak public sector and ever-present tension between government and the industrial group has forestalled action on projects that fail to meet the more immediate interests of the business community. The industrial group has acted effectively and unilaterally in the areas of education, industrial infrastructure, and company social services including low-cost housing. But beyond. that, in matters of public welfare, Monterrey's leadership has failed to exercise responsibility or to provide support to those who might.

Summary

Actors in the decision-making process include some public-sector organizations, yet government is weak and leadership resides overwhelmingly within an *industrial elite monopoly*. Key individuals and organizations reflect a narrow range of interests. Most of the influentials are intimately connected with the industrial group, and ten of the nineteen belong to the same extended family. Important organizations are either arms of the industrial group or public agencies created at its behest. Although Monterrey decision-makers are often in *conflict* with the federal government, *consensus*, primarily, and *cooperation* characterize local decisions, and industrial group control is accepted if not admired. The *priorities* of the power structure entail more of the same: industrial growth and expansion into other regions. Similarly, those projects that dovetail with the priorities of industrial expansion (education, infrastructure, pacification of company workers) are effectively executed. To the extent that social problems enter into the decision-making process, the emphasis is on trying to avoid them rather than solve them, though glimmers of change may be appearing in urban concerns.

MEDELLÍN

We Can Do More: Maintaining and Distributing the Largesse

Popular slogans reflect a good deal of that intangible commodity we call a "regional ethos." Characteristically, whitewashed walls in Guadalajara sport the banner of the official party (PRI) and pithy quotations from the current president. In Monterrey, the emblem of the rightist opposition party (PAN) is unusually common in public places, while the art of sloganeering in any cause is much reduced in Cali. Unavoidable on Medellín's thoroughfares are signs and stickers proclaiming *Los Antioqueños Podemos Hacer Más* (Antioquians, we can do more). This ambition to do more refers not only to industrialization and productivity but also to public services.

Medellín's urban environment boasts a number of remarkable achievements. The central city is well planned, containing broad avenues and modern highrise structures alongside quaint sections that preserve colonial charm in a city planner's dream of the intelligent blending of old and new. Historically, large industries have located in the smaller *municipios* adjacent to the central city's commercial and residential districts. Despite sustained, though not overwhelming, population growth, new settlements on the periphery have been woven into the fabric of this textile capital of Latin America. Extensive slums are unknown and, though an occasional cluster of shacks can be found, public housing programs have struggled to keep pace with immigration. Most neighborhoods are served by a complete set of urban services, and, where these may be deficient, new works are almost invariably under way. The intense regional pride of the Antioqueño is manifested in the comportment of his city as much as his person.

In chapter 2 it was demonstrated that civic-minded works have a long tradition in Antioquia. More recently, the provision of urban services has been given modern organizational form in the Public Enterprises of Medellín (EEPP). The historical antecedents of this organization are several. Originally, basic services such as water and power were developed by private companies sponsored by or serving the mines and nascent industry. In 1919 a public Municipal Enterprises was established that began absorbing privately-operated services in the interests of greater efficiency under a single authority. Nevertheless, this system was far from satisfactory because the growing needs of industry and the metropolitan area could not be met by municipal governments. What was required was an autonomous regional authority, and at the time there was no legal basis for that kind of organizational innovation.

Ironically, given Medellín's early developmental accomplishments, the solution was pioneered by advocates of the C.V.C. in Cali when they succeeded in persuading the National Constitutional Assembly of 1954 to enact changes allowing autonomous public corporations. At the same time in Medellín a prominent former executive of Municipal Enterprises, congressman, publisher, educator, and holder of many industrial posts, Diego Tobón Arbeláez, then vice president of the Industrialists' Association, began to promote the idea of a C.V.C.-like organization in Antioquia.[46] In 1954 Tobón went to Cali to observe developments on the C.V.C. and conferred with David Lilienthal on his idea for Medellín. At the same time, he discussed the possibilities of a loan with World Bank officials working with the C.V.C. Returning to Medellín after the October 22, 1954, founding of the C.V.C., Tobón began planning the new organization with the mayor of Medellín and former banker, Dario Londoño Villa, and a team of city officials and industrialists. Initially there was some debate over whether the planned authority should embrace a variety of services or confine itself to electrical power. Evidently this was motivated by a fear in some quarters of creating too powerful a public bureaucracy. On Lilienthal's advice, stemming from the T.V.A. experience and his own convictions, Tobón stuck to the concept of integrated services and prevailed.

On August 6, 1955, the legislation authorizing EEPP was passed without opposition. The act called for an autonomous public corporation, with its own financing, to take charge of electrical energy, telephones, water, and sanitation (sewer drainage) for Medellín and surrounding *municipios* in the valley. The organization is run by a director elected by a seven-member board composed of the mayor, who presides, two members of the City Council, and four members chosen by the mayor from lists provided by the National Bank, the Industrialists' Association, the Merchants' Association, the Chamber of Commerce, and commercial banks.[47] Thus, in its founding as well as its organizational structure EEPP reflects the cooperative participation of the public and private sectors.

Assisted by loans from the World Bank, the Inter-American Development Bank, and A.I.D., elaborate projects have been completed in each of the areas of chartered responsibility. Most impressive are three separate centers for generating electrical power, and a fourth under construction in 1968, that take advantage of uniquely advantageous topographical conditions (i.e., numerous rivers and mountain valley dam sites). The ratio of one telephone for every ten persons in Medellín is said to be the best in the country and additional lines are in progress. The water supply is more than adequate and includes treatment plants. Drainage and sewage facilities are admittedly inadequate "due to the incessant demographic and industrial expansion of the city, which has demonstrated the necessity of initiating a complete plan of modernization of the system."[48] New initiative is being taken on this problem. By 1968 EEPP was managing a budget of 700 million pesos within a work force of 3,000 people.

Recognizing the problems of rapid urbanization, EEPP formed a new Division of Housing Habilitation in 1964 for the expressed purpose of extending water, electricity, and sanitation services to new areas of urban settlement. By 1968 new investments totaling 22 million pesos had benefited 46 *barrios*, 11,000 dwelling units, and 80,000 residents. Projected plans for 1969 and 1970 included an additional 50 million pesos with a target of 12,000 dwelling units and benefits for 84,000 people.[49] With this kind of organizational anticipation of urban problems within a tradition of civic-minded public service,[50] it is little wonder that Medellín enjoys a reputation as one of Latin America's most progressive cities.

Similar attributes characterize the second area of decision-making. When mentioning development promotion as a key project area, Medellín respondents noted particularly the work of two groups, the public-private Institute for the Economic Development of Antioquia (IDEA) and the private-sector Development Corporation (*Codesarrollo*), both of which also ranked high among influential organizations.

IDEA was formed in 1964 and began operating in 1965 as a unique decentralized development bank lending public funds to private enterprises. The plan for IDEA was conceived by a former governor and his cabinet secretary and was later passed into law by the assembly of the department. Essentially, it involved setting up a development bank with the proceeds of the sale of the department-owned railroad to the federal government for 156 million pesos. Later this sum was supplemented by assigning to IDEA the stock owned by the department in a cattle-raising enterprise, bringing its total capital to about 200 million pesos.[51]

IDEA calls itself a development bank because it is designed to supplement other commercial and governmental banking operations by providing loans only to projects that are unable to get conventional financing. Other criteria employed in project selection include limitation to businesses that will operate in Antioquia, will serve the general interest, are well planned, and promise recuperation. In order to evaluate each of these questions, IDEA employs a technical staff that works jointly with the departmental planning agency in determining project selection and priorities. This same staff has offered free technical assistance to local firms. In order to keep its capital in rapid rotation, IDEA has so far limited its operations to "medium term" loans, that is, for a maximum of five years. Loans are administered by a financial division separate from the technical group.

IDEA also is concerned with promoting balanced regional growth by concentrating on areas with unexploited natural resources. For this purpose it has cooperated with the offices of national planning and departmental planning to identify distinct regions, determine their resource capabilities, and project a plan of "structural equilibrium in the development of the department."[52] By 1968 IDEA had invested in two important projects reflective of its interest in new kinds of activity, a tourism firm that also promotes artisan crafts and a lumbering company planning forestation and the production of paper products. Under examination were plans for a financial corporation and an industrial park development.

Codesarrollo was founded in 1962 by a group of prominent private-sector leaders, many of whom had also served in public posts and qualified as influentials. As a private, nonprofit institution, *Codesarrollo* had several purposes: it was predicated on the belief that better development planning required greater input from the private sector, it was hoped that this initiative would ameliorate public-private differences in outlook through greater cooperation, and, by focusing chiefly on welfare problems, it operationalized the belief that social responsibility was as much the concern of private enterprises as of government.

Codesarrollo is financed 70 percent by individual and corporate contributions (a list of donors includes most of the top firms in manufacturing and finance and several influentials) and 30 percent by contract services for technical studies. In 1967 its total annual budget was a somewhat modest 548,379 pesos. The corporation is divided into three branches of activity: research and planning, formation and training, and operations.[53] The annual report for 1967 lists current projects and accomplishments in each of these fields. Under research and planning, studies had been conducted on the feasibility of an industrial park in conjunction with IDEA and AID funding, an urban plan for the city of Rionegro, the problem of prostitution in Medellín,[54] and several smaller projects carried out by local students. Under formation and training are a variety of vocational education programs focusing on rural community development and cooperatives in conjunction with the land reform agency, shoemaking, rural housing, weaving, and farming. Finally, in the operations department specific works were being executed, including road-building in rural areas, school construction, recreational facilities, self-built housing, youth centers, development of Indian communities (including provision of land titles), agricultural credit, and several others.

Although its staff and budget are not large, the activities of *Codesarrollo* are impressive and unique in contrast to those in our other regions. Three characteristics seem to define their uniqueness. First, we have here a case of voluntary assumption of social responsibility by the private sector in a region where public sector services are already extensive. Second, the programs are specifically directed at poor and marginal rural groups with what appears to be a genuine and nonexploitative interest. Third, in various project areas *Codesarrollo* is working in effective collaboration with a variety of other organizations including IDEA, AID, EEPP, the offices of departmental and national planning, the National Education Service (SENA), the Colombian Institute of Land Reform (INCORA), several national credit agencies (IFI, *Caja Agrario*, ICT), and the Colombian Institute of Social Security (ICSS). In this respect it resembles IDEA, which is also tied in with other authorities, and, further, by providing a "backstop" source of investment credit IDEA follows in a tradition of extending the distribution of developmental benefits.

We should exercise some restraint in crediting these organizations with any far-reaching consequences. Although regarded as influential, they are relatively small and of recent creation. Certainly there are structural forms of social and economic inequality in the region that will not yield to these ameliorative projects. But for present purposes the larger point is that these groups follow a pattern documented in the case study of EEPP, a much larger operation, and in the history of Antioquia from colonial times. Moreover, in contrast to other regions, nowhere in this study do we encounter such a clear pattern of cooperative leadership emphasizing the distributional and qualitative side of economic development.

Summary

Actors in decision-making represent a cross-section of public and private groups and there is a fair amount of individual movement across these lines. Regional government is not so much a respected partner in the process as an extension of the broad interests of a *privately-led coalition*. Influential persons and organizations are inclusive of most regional interests, and project participation is broadly collaborative. Though *cooperation* is an apt phrase for Medellín, *consensus* is the watchword of decisional objectives, stemming not from the dominance of a single institutional sector, as in Monterrey, but from the incorporation of many into a policy-making process that enjoys extensive legitimacy. *Priorities* clearly include continued industrial growth, but their additional and distinctive characteristic is action in the interest of the general public.

A SYNTHESIS AND COMPARISON

As we come to the close of these case studies, it will be useful to step back from the detail and documentation associated with each policy area in order to characterize decisional processes comparatively.

In each of the regions we encounter a guiding theme in the activities of decision makers. Guadalajara presents a general policy of *externally-oriented developmentalism*. Objectives are defined mainly by a *political class* of regional officials in interaction with the incentives and priorities supplied by the federal system. Policy-making is a harmonious activity, largely because the power and authority of the regime is unrivaled. Developmentalism entails pursuing those policies that will reflect best on the region's "progress" according to conventional measures of investment and productivity. This, in turn, has resulted in the infusion of national and foreign interests that dilute the span of control of the regional power structure. Where local initiative prevails, as in the case of urban development, the benefits of policy are more broadly distributed.

The dominant theme in Cali's policy-making process is *ideological elitism*. Nearly universal agreement attaches to the premise that change must come from the top, while protracted conflict stems from the disagreement among status groups as to which should be at the top. Despite periodic intra-elite challenges, an *agrarian-industrial upper class* maintains control and shows signs of absorbing its challengers with generational change. The new elite will differ in style rather than substance, maintaining a scornful view of government and the lower classes.

Monterrey's *industrial-financial upper class* is recently embarked on a new policy of *pragmatic expansionism*. In this effort to maintain the growth rate and simultaneously to save the city from precipitous decline, the historical antagonisms between public and private sectors may be abating. The industrial group continues to dominate with broadly-based support. But the accomplishment of its expansionist goals will require new compromises of its traditional independence with the federal system and the urban non-elite.

The policy-making process in Medellín includes an emphasis on the continuation of industrial growth but is more distinctively captured by the notion of *civic progressivism*. This policy is formulated and implemented by a *public-private coalition of middle- and upper-class groups*. Although sometimes inspired by attitudes of patrimonialism and insular regionalism, this policy is nevertheless aimed at regional development through a broader distribution of economic opportunity.

It will escape no one's attention that these policy-making themes are closely related to the developmental histories of the regions. In many senses policies are not so much rationally or universalistically elected as they are presented to decision-makers in a limited array conditioned by historical influences. Within these limits it is the distinctive contribution of the political process to turn selected resources toward the general goal of economic development. As a result, attention now shifts from the style and content of policy-making to the most fundamental question, "What difference does it make?"

6. The Developmental Record

We come now to the stage of accounting, to a summary presentation of how the four regions rank according to a set of indicators based on both aggregate economic performance and distributional or quality-of-life standards. Our first task will be to synthesize a variety of statistical information under sets of indicators for each of the two facets of development. Next, these data and any patterns they reflect will be characterized in a more discursive style Finally, setting these results against the materials presented in chapters 2 through 5, we shall ask how they reflect contemporary theoretical interpretations and what appear to be the more promising avenues of subsequent theory-building.

In chapter 1, economic development was defined as real increases in material welfare and greater equality in its distribution. Operationally, the intent of this definition is to place equal weight on both the quantitative and qualitative features of economic achievement. Ideally, one would like to have access to a large number of indicators that tap all the conceivably relevant facets of economic life from GNP and electrical consumption to health and leisure. Practically, however, the range of reliably-measured economic indicators in the four regions is rather limited. In an effort to include as many comparable items as possible, a wide variety of sources were consulted, including national censuses, state and local government publications, monthly statistical bulletins, publications of local industrial associations, a number of university-sponsored studies, statistically-based promotional literature, research monographs, and organizational records. After these many volumes and archives had been culled, each datum obtained in the process was itemized and cross-referenced. Then came the difficult task of matching up the data so as to discover those indicators that could be evaluated across cases. Needless to say, a number of choice items that characterized one or two regions had to be dropped when no complementary evidence was available for the others. The net result of this search was three indicators of aggregate economic development: productivity, average income, and industrialization; and six indicators of distributional or quality-of-life development: education, housing and urban services, health, employment, income distribution, and local control of the economy.

Additional measures would have been desirable, and, indeed, some were tried. Public expenditures were considered, but these are impossible to compare across cases with different administrative organization; in one area a single agency will channel all funds in a given undertaking, whereas in another a variety of agencies contribute in amounts that are difficult to ferret out. Many of these kinds of distributional questions require special studies of the kind not reported in the usual national accounts. Nevertheless, we were quite fortunate in locating a number of these special studies that were comparable across cases (e.g., studies of gross regional product, unemployment, and income distribution). Therefore, the nine indicators of economic development are fortunately broader than we might have hoped and, in any event, significantly broader than the typically one-dimensional measurement of this variable.

Many, though not all, of the figures to be cited here were produced by official agencies. As is always the case when dealing with official statistics, certain precautions should be observed and disclaimers entered. At the most general level, these data have to be regarded as self-serving, attempting generally to portray the region in the best possible light as testament to its "dynamic growth potential," or sometimes in the worst when it comes to beseeching needed federal funds.[1] For that reason, official statistics are often of greater utility in the analysis of data-collecting organizations than of the actual state of affairs.[2] In comparative studies it may be safe to assume a constant directional bias toward more optimistic reporting (e.g., unrealistically low estimates of unemployment and high marks for productivity), which would still provide reliable estimates of relative scale location. Such an assumption, however, is not entirely satisfactory in the absence of data on the magnitude of bias.

In this analysis additional problems present themselves. First, "aside from such more-or-less purposeful distortions, data-collection procedures are woefully crude and unsystematic in all but the most advanced nations."[3] Parenthetically, in the attempt to locate as much comparative data as possible one gets the feeling that a good rule-of-thumb measure of development is the availability of carefully-assembled economic accounts. Second, because the comparisons range over two countries and four regions, the comparability of indicators and methods used to generate them is seldom precise. Finally, the unit of analysis employed in this study is a regional area of economic influence, isomorphic with neither the urban center nor the state or department, though it may come closer to the latter. For that reason, and in an attempt to utilize as much data as possible, the analysis is forced to swing between the two levels.

In order to make judicious regional comparisons, several precautionary measures have been employed. First, as noted, a wide variety of sources have been used that frequently provide cross-checks and multiple indicators of items. When a variety of separately-generated measures suggest essentially the same result, confidence in their reliability is enhanced.[4] The variety of available material, along with a certain interpretive expertise one acquires from sifting all of the information and from on-the-spot observation, helps to reduce error. Second, a number of problems related to the noncomparability of time periods and data categories across nations may be eliminated by sticking to within-country comparisons. Although this procedure makes it difficult to rank all four regions on a common scale with respect to each indicator, it does make for judicious point-by-point comparisons that may then be generalized to a common ranking. Finally, the data are not used pretentiously, as would be true of trying to force them into scales, regression equations, or the other statistical models that assume greater measurement precision. Rather, they are presented in individual detail for the purpose of indicating general patterns and patterned differences.

AGGREGATE ECONOMIC INDICATORS

1. *Productivity.* Monterrey's gross regional (state) product is substantially higher than that of Guadalajara, though it is difficult to say exactly how much greater because recent (i.e., post-1955) data from Nuevo León is confined to industrial productivity. Nevertheless, a fairly good estimate is possible with available figures. The contribution of industry to the gross product in Monterrey (4.1 billion pesos in 1960) is nearly three times that of Guadalajara (1.5 billion pesos in 1960). Aggregate value per capita of the net product from industry was approximately 6,800 pesos for Nuevo León in the same year and 3,700 for Jalisco, the national average being about 3,900.[5] These figures on industrial productivity are fairly decisive, since in both states commerce and services make about the same contribution to the gross product, and, although Jalisco has a distinct advantage in agricultural productivity, that advantage is far from sufficient to overcome Nuevo León's global superiority, since within Jalisco industry accounts for more of the gross product than does agriculture.[6] In the early 1960s Nuevo León's gross product from industry, about 40 percent of its total, was nearly equal to Jalisco's total product (approximately 10,000 million pesos).[7] In short, the gross product of Nuevo León is, conservatively, twice that of

Jalisco, and this superiority is redoubled to a 4:1 advantage in terms of per capita gross product, since throughout the sixties the population of Nuevo León was about half that of Jalisco. Both states are growing at about the same rate (10 percent annually in gross industrial product and 4 percent in total gross product per capita), suggesting that the gap is not closing.[8]

Productivity differences in the Colombian cases are less extreme, though Medellín has a clear advantage. Industry in the department of Antioquia in 1965 registered a gross product of 5,629 million pesos against 5,576 million in Valle del Cauca. Differences in aggregate value were 2,711 and 2,438 million respectively.[9] Once again we are somewhat hampered by the absence of a sectoral breakdown of the total gross product for Antioquia, but this is easily overcome. Given the nearly identical distribution of the labor force in Antioquia and Valle del Cauca[10] (e.g., 44 versus 44.2 percent in agriculture and 15.2 versus 17.2 percent in manufacturing respectively) and Antioquia's agricultural importance, particularly in coffee and beef, which rivals the productivity of the traditionally agricultural Valle del Cauca, it is safe to assume that the sectoral breakdown of gross product is comparable for the two regions. Rounding out this picture of sectoral contributions to gross product, other figures show that the value of commercial sales is greater in Medellín than in Cali.[11] These observations, along with the foregoing figures on industrial productivity, suggest that the gross product of Antioquia is higher than that of Valle del Cauca. And, indeed, more direct estimates bear this out. In 1964 the per capita gross regional (department) product was 2,786 pesos in Antioquia against 2,176 in Valle del Cauca or roughly one-third greater in Antioquia.[12] Finally, one study of Valle del Cauca in 1963–1964 indicated a 5 percent reduction in regional gross product, which may have continued.[13]

If attention is focused primarily on the urban centers, these differences in productivity become more substantial, since Medellín and its immediate surroundings embrace 92 percent of the industry in the department, whereas the figure is closer to 60 percent for Cali.[14]

2. *Income.* Data on average income are somewhat more direct. A Mexican national survey in 1960 indicated that average per capita monthly income in Guadalajara was 213 pesos, in Monterrey 347, with a national average of 289. The average yearly family income for sixteen principal cities of the republic was 1,878 pesos, 1,847 in Monterrey and 1,138 in Guadalajara.[15]

Colombian figures are more detailed and show mixed results. For the year 1967 salaried employees in Valle del Cauca averaged 2,415 pesos per month against 2,104 in Antioquia. In the same relationship average hourly wages were 4.89 versus 4.79 pesos.[16] Daily wages for agricultural workers in Cali ranged from 15 to 16.5 pesos and from 13 to 15 pesos in Medellín.[17]

According to these figures, salaries are slightly higher in Cali and Valle del Cauca. However, salaries and wages in manufacturing tend to be higher than others and Antioquia, in 1965, had more people employed in these industries than Valle del Cauca (72,615 versus 51,759).[18] To state it differently, Antioquia had a larger proportion of the labor force in the better-paying jobs, suggesting that more people are making better incomes despite the *averages* that favor Valle del Cauca, and this may reflect distributional inequities greater than those in Antioquia. Again, Medellín's advantage over Cali in this regard is enhanced by its concentration of departmental industry. Moreover, public employees in Antioquia are the best paid in the country, while those in Valle del Cauca rank fifth nationally. In Antioquia departmental employees average 999 pesos per month against 853 in Valle del Cauca; municipal employees earn an average monthly salary of 1,114 and 804 pesos respectively.[19] Given the variation among indicators and types of employment, the most judicious conclusion to be reached here is that incomes in the two regions are not greatly different.

3. *Industrialization.* Conventional measures of industrialization include energy consumption, the proportion of the labor force engaged in manufacturing, and the number and size of industrial establishments. Because available data on this indicator are extensive, all three measures will be employed. As we would expect, the results are quite consistent.

In 1960 Nuevo León consumed 700 million kilowatt hours of electricity, more than three times Jalisco's 212 million.[20] As reported in chapter 2, the percentage of the labor force engaged in manufacturing in Nuevo León was 35.0 against 15.6 in Jalisco for 1960; Guadalajara had 30.9 percent in contrast to 34.3 in Monterrey.[21]

With respect to the number and size of industries, available data are for the adjacent years of 1965 and 1966, a discrepancy of little concern. In 1965 Jalisco reported 8,672 industrial firms employing 75,973 persons and representing 4 billion pesos of invested capital.[22] Nuevo León figures for 1966 show fewer industrial establishments, 5,372, but these employed more people, 112,300, and represented considerably more capital investment, about 14 billion pesos.[23] These figures convey the now familiar fact that Monterrey is a center of large-scale industry, whereas manufacturing in Guadalajara is medium to small (artisan) in scale. A particularly dramatic demonstration of this point is provided by data on industrial enterprises in the top nine branches of production. Here, figures for 1960 show that Monterrey had only 77 firms devoted to its principal manufacturing activities against 253 in Guadalajara. But the value of production of this reduced number of firms was 2 billion pesos a year versus 740 million in Guadalajara, and the capital invested was 2.3 billion versus 584 million.[24]

Thus, in terms of both value of production and capital invested per firm, the size ratio is ten-to-one in favor of Monterrey.

To turn to the Colombian regions, electrical consumption for Cali in 1966 was 569 million kilowatt hours, about half of Medellín's 1,118 million.[25] As indicated in chapter 2, the labor force in manufacturing in Valle del Cauca was 17.2 percent in 1964, slightly larger than Antioquia's 15.2 percent. However, the fact that 92 percent of Antioquia's industrial labor force, as opposed to 60 percent in Valle del Cauca, resides in the immediate vicinity of the regional capital implies greater industrialization in Medellín. Evidence on the number and size of industrial firms supports this conclusion. In 1965 Valle del Cauca had 1,795 industrial enterprises, Antioquia had 1,930. New industrial investment has been greater in Medellín than in Cali, with 226 versus 160 million pesos in 1960 and 625 versus 372 million in 1965.[26]

DISTRIBUTIONAL OR QUALITY-OF-LIFE INDICATORS

1. *Education.* In the Mexican cases Nuevo León and Monterrey excel on a variety of measures related to educational emphasis. At the state level, in 1965 Nuevo León was spending more money on education than Jalisco (118 versus 68 million pesos) and these expenditures represented a larger proportion of state expenditures (55 versus 35 percent), despite the fact that the state population was only half that of Jalisco. As a result, more students completed secondary schools (57,802 versus 43,510),[27] and a substantially larger proportion of the school-age population of the state of Nuevo León was enrolled in school (67.9 versus 41.1 percent).[28]

One reservation about these figures that might be entered is the fact that Jalisco is more rural and, therefore, confronts greater problems in the field of education. A counter-objection would then be that such problems should call for a larger educational budget, but more to the point is the fact that urban differences in educational attainment reflect the same pattern. Census figures for 1960 indicate that Monterrey has a better-educated population than Guadalajara: only 19.1 percent have no education as opposed to 24.4 in Guadalajara; 15.2 percent have six years or more education in Monterrey against only 10.6; in the same relation, the percent literate is 84.8 versus 80.5.[29]

Census figures for 1964 for the departments of Antioquia and Valle del Cauca show nearly identical distributions of the numbers of persons with primary, secondary, and university educations after controlling for population size (Antioquia's population and number of educated persons in the three categories is about 40 percent larger).[30] A recent report from the National Administrative Department of Statistics indicates that Antioquia has more than its expected share of students matriculated in secondary and precollege schools, 58,715 versus 32,786,[31] but the difference is not great after controlling for population size. Other reports attest to a wide gap. In 1963 Cali had 69,225 students enrolled in primary school; 1966 figures for Medellín indicated 121,221—a number large enough to offset the effects of the different dates (the populations of the two cities, of course, are nearly the same).[32] Again, estimates from different years indicate 20 percent of Antioquia's population illiterate against 28 percent for Valle del Cauca.[33] On the basis of the collected evidence it seems fair to conclude that Antioquia and Medellín have a slight advantage in education.

2. *Housing and Urban Services.* In the area of housing and urban services, for the Mexican cases the patterns documented with respect to the first distributional indicator are completely reversed. In Monterrey 41.4 percent of the population lives in one-room dwellings compared to 33.5 in Guadalajara; similarly the proportion living in one- or two-room dwellings is 69.7 versus 59.6. In Guadalajara 16.7 percent of the dwelling units are without piped-in water against 24.7 in Monterrey. The situation is more disparate in the case of sewage facilities, with 20.0 percent of the dwelling units in Guadalajara and 34.4 percent in Monterrey without them.[34] One might argue that these differentials are due to greater demand in Monterrey because of its population size and rate of increase. In fact, the reverse is true, as we have seen: Guadalajara is a larger city and increased faster between 1950 and 1960 (the date of these census figures). In light of this greater demand for housing in Guadalajara, it is interesting to note that the number of inhabitants per dwelling unit was only slightly higher than in Monterrey (5.98 versus 5.69). That is, these figures suggest that the response to housing needs in Guadalajara has been quantitatively and qualitatively greater than in Monterrey. On a statewide basis, some of these differences are reversed (e.g., availability of water and electricity), owing to Jalisco's larger rural sector, but even here Jalisco tops Nuevo León in the quality of construction.[35]

Between 1965 and 1967 the state of Jalisco invested over 100 million pesos in public housing.[36] The budget for the state of Nuevo León in the same years included no such item, and expenditures on related urban services (e.g., potable water, street lighting) were a fraction of the amounts appropriated in Jalisco.[37] One study of the immediate housing needs in Monterrey called for 42,000 new units to solve the problem of dual-family occupancy.[38] As noted in chapter 5, Monterrey is deficient in a number of other urban services (streets, drainage, transportation, recreation) concerning which systematic figures are not kept.

In Colombia, statistical reports on housing for rural and urban areas show Antioquia with a global advantage. In just the urban areas, Antioquia has 50 percent more dwelling units than Valle del Cauca, although the percent urban is similar in the two departments. For the entire population, 73 percent of the dwelling units in Antioquia are private homes as opposed to 55 percent in Valle del Cauca. Similarly, only 1.1 percent are "substandard" against 13.1 in Valle del Cauca.[39] Again as noted in chapter 5, urban services such as electricity, drainage, sewage, potable water, and streets are vastly more available in Medellín.

3. *Health*. Owing principally to the more urban composition of Nuevo León, general health and medical services appear superior to those in Jalisco. The average life expectancy, based on 1960–1965 figures, was 65.5 versus 60.9 years.[40] The proportion of the population reporting weekly consumption of meat, fish, milk, and eggs was 91.9 in Nuevo León versus 74.5 in Jalisco, and 92.2 in Monterrey versus 85.7 in Guadalajara.[41] In 1964 the number of registered illnesses in Jalisco was 288,147 as opposed to 106,137,[42] which is more than what would be expected when comparing population size (and assuming similar age composition). Of course these figures could be interpreted to mean that more people in Jalisco had access to health care facilities, but that seems unlikely in view of the fact that the two states had the same number of hospitals and clinics (44 and 45) and that Nuevo León registered more medical services rendered by the Mexican Institute of Social Security,[43] both of these despite its smaller population.

The department of Antioquia, by the end of 1967, had 5,937 hospital beds as opposed to 3,927 in Valle del Cauca, a ratio consistent with the differences in population size. However, in the similar-sized cities Medellín was far ahead with 2,940 versus 1,707 hospital beds.[44] Even more definitive are departmental figures on the volume of hospital care: Antioquia ranked third nationally and Valle del Cauca fifth.[45]

4. *Employment*. Mexican census figures on unemployment are not very exacting, indicating an implausible 1 percent out of work. Somewhat more useful are figures on the population economically active, with Monterrey reporting 34.4 percent against Guadalajara's 33.8.[46] The percentage of the population in the labor force compared in the same relation, 32.0 versus 29.8.[47] These are essentially the same measure and tell us little about unemployment because they disregard the age structure of the population and the number looking for work. On that latter point the census does report, but the figures are also implausible, indicating 2 to 3 percent looking for work in both states and regional capitals. Other studies showed 3.8 to 5 percent unemployed in Monterrey in 1965.[48] Comparable estimates for Guadalajara are lacking, and the best guess is that both of these cities, experiencing population growth and simultaneous economic expansion, have relatively comparable rates of unemployment that are a good deal higher than the reported estimates.

The Colombian data are much better because they resulted from independent surveys. A university study in 1965 showed 11.8 percent of Cali's labor force unemployed as opposed to 9.7 in Medellín.[49] Samplings on different dates show about a 1 percent margin in the same direction and ranging as high as 13.2 versus 12.0.[50] Census data on the percentage of the population economically active favor Antioquia over Valle del Cauca with 49 versus 41 percent, a margin wide enough to result from something more than the age distribution.[51]

5. *Income Distribution.* Jesús Puente Leyva has written a small but very competent book on the distribution of income in Monterrey. His results indicate that, although income is not quite as concentrated in Monterrey as in Mexico City (Gini coefficients of .36 versus .40), by national standards the distribution is markedly unequal, with the top 20 percent of the population receiving 46.4 percent of the income. Regrettably, the Gini coefficient was not computed for Guadalajara, although it is noted that the .36 figure for Monterrey is high, large cities averaging .35 with the exception of Guadalajara, "whose economic structure results in an especially low coefficient."[52] It would seem that Guadalajara's small-scale and artisan industry is more conducive to equality of income distribution.

In the Colombian cases we have no comparable specific studies of income distribution. Nevertheless, a number of pieces of evidence fit together to reliably suggest a pattern. From a historical standpoint, we have already noted Antioquia's more equalitarian class structure, which includes a rural middle class of smallholders not found in equal numbers in Valle del Cauca. At the other end of the spectrum there appears to be less concentration of wealth among traditional upper classes and, therefore, a larger middle stratum in Antioquia. Average salaries are higher in Valle del Cauca, but this may result from a small number at the very top who raise the mean of a skewed distribution. One survey in Medellín in late 1967 indicated a moderately skewed income structure but one in which the middle range made up 40 percent of the sample and the mean was relatively close to the more populous lower categories.[53] By contrast, a study of Valle del Cauca, without reporting statistical data, noted that "it is known that the distribution of regional income is very unequal and that a profound difference exists between the extremes. There is a concentration of income in a few families and a concentration of families of little income."[54] From these suggestive items it would appear safe to assume that the distribution of income in Antioquia and Medellín is more equitable, although it is difficult to be precise. Here, as elsewhere, the differences are probably less marked than those in the Mexican regions.

6. *Local Control.* The final indicator of qualitative development is local control of economic institutions. It should be stressed that use of this indicator does not require the assumption that nonlocal, particularly foreign,

control is necessarily disadvantageous, although portions of this analysis would argue for its negative effects on local leadership and initiative. The indicator is employed here in a more neutral vein, relying on the fact that arguments in favor of nonlocal investment are based on the exigencies of capital and technical shortages and do not contest the fact that it would be preferable if development could be accomplished under local or national control.

Here all four cases may be compared jointly, since the data came from analyses of Chamber of Commerce records as well as from interviews with corporate directors and perusals of published reports. As we have seen in Cali and Guadalajara, one-half to two-thirds of the top industrial firms are not locally owned or controlled. In Cali, the principal source of nonlocal control is foreign, whereas Guadalajara reflects foreign and national (i.e., Mexico City-Monterrey) influences in about equal measure. Despite proximity to the United States, there is little foreign and no other nonlocal influence in the major enterprises in Monterrey. Medellín, though slightly less autonomous, is still fairly thoroughly controlled by local interests.

SUMMARY AND INTERPRETATION

A good deal of hard and soft data have been presented in this chapter, calling for some convenient summary presentation. Table 31 is provided for that purpose, although, as before, the table merely summarizes the results in a handy form and is not to be understood as the results themselves.

With respect to the aggregate economic indicators, Monterrey's gross product is far and away superior to those of the other regions. In converted national currencies, Valle del Cauca in 1964 had a gross product of roughly 45 million United States dollars, while that of Jalisco in 1967 was about 124 million. On a per capita basis, Jalisco's advantage is closer to two-to-one, about $510 versus $260 gross product per person. In 1964 Antioquia's gross product, though not directly measured in the available data, was about one-third greater than Valle del Cauca's and was growing, which is to suggest that Guadalajara and Medellín (with a somewhat smaller urban population and greater industrial concentration) are quite close on estimates of gross product. With respect to industrialization Medellín is more developed. Even if we take into account differences in absolute scale (of population, financial resources, et cetera) across countries, Medellín is also relatively more advanced in aggregate terms, resulting in its overall ranking above Guadalajara.

Most of the distributional indicators are based on intranational differences due to questions of relative scale and reporting. On all but four of

TABLE 31

A NOTATIONAL SUMMARY OF COMPARATIVE EVIDENCE ON ECONOMIC DEVELOPMENT IN FOUR REGIONS

REGION	ECONOMIC DEVELOPMENT Aggregate Economic Indicators				Distributional—Quality-of-Life Indicators						
	Productivity[a]	Income	Industrialization	Overall Rank[b]	Education	Housing and Urban Services	Health	Employment	Income Distribution	Local Control	Overall Rank
Guadalajara	Md	Md	Md	3	−	+	−[c]	+	+	−	2.5
Monterrey	Hi	Hi	Hi	1	+	−	+	+	−	+	2.5
Cali	Lo	Md	Md	4	−	−	−	−	+	−	4.0
Medellín	Md	Md	Hi	2	+	+	+	+	+	+	1.0

a) Due to differences in dates and categories of reporting, these aspects are most directly interpreted as intranational comparisons, though the other items in the table and the general pattern may be understood as applying to all four cases.

b) The overall rank on productivity is a summary of the three equally-weighted indicators. The gross product of Monterrey and Cali clearly constitute the high and low extremes. Guadalajara's gross product appears slightly higher than Medellín's, but in terms of the relative scale of aggregate industrial achievement Medellín seems to lead.

c) } indicates small discernable differences or inconclusive evidence.

the twelve paired comparisons, marked differences appear. With respect to health, differences in the Mexican cases are clear but possibly spurious outcomes of the rural-urban population structures. In Colombia the differences on the regional level are not substantial. Mexican data on unemployment are inexact and our best guess is that both regions are coping similarly with the problem. So, too, the available data on income distribution in Colombia are sketchy, although there are sufficient clues to warrant confidence in the direction, if not the size, of this difference. The overall rank on distributional aspects of economic development is provided for purposes of this summary discussion and rests on no explicit formula; it simply sums up this didactic presentation of the detailed data analysis. Differences between Cali and Medellín are consistent and easily ranked. Insofar as the evidence is to be trusted, Guadalajara and Monterrey are tied; each excels or lags in different areas, and sometimes the differences on given indicators (e.g., Guadalajara's advantage in housing and services or income distribution and Monterrey's in education and local control) are substantial enough to rule out an equal weighting of items. The distributional advantages of the two regions are complementary.

Although Table 31 sacrifices much of the detail and substance of the results, it does so in the interests of general comparison. Particularly, it allows for the identification of patterns that may be held up against some of the theoretical ideas encountered in earlier chapters.

The initial impression given by the summary results is the absence of any regularity. The cases are not symmetrically arranged, given several instances of small discernible differences and the regular reversals among distributional indicators for Guadalajara and Monterrey. However, this fact, viewed conversely, is of considerable interest. Namely, the results provide plausible evidence that economic development as conventionally defined (i.e., in aggregate measures such as industrialization, GNP, and median income) is *not* regularly associated with "development" in the broader normative sense of the word. Economic growth narrowly defined (or measured) cannot be understood as a correlative (or a surrogate measure) of general improvement in the living standards of a population. In addition to validating the distinction between aggregate and distributional forms of development that underpins this study, the result also suggests certain policy implications. The fact that aggregate economic development is not inimical to a better standard of living is attested to in the case of Medellín. What this suggests is that additional elements must be added, particularly political and social structural factors, in order to arrive at a more complete explanation.

Certain key findings from earlier chapters suggest themselves at this juncture. It will be recalled that chapter 3 demonstrated that power was least concentrated in Guadalajara and progressively more concentrated in Medellín, Cali, and Monterrey in that order. Similarly, in chapter 4 we found that egalitarianism (based on SES) was greatest in Guadalajara, with the other cases following in the same order as above (as was the case with other measures of "openness" in roughly the same order). Now, if we overlay these results with those in table 31 a pattern begins to emerge. Namely *the more diversified* (less "elitist") *the group holding power and the more egalitarian* (open) *the social structure, the greater the quality-of-life or distributional effects of development.* However, the corollary does not hold; *economic development in terms of aggregate or quantitative achievements is not regularly associated with particular structures of class and power.* And, of course, much of the detailed contextual explanation for these generalizations is to be found in our analysis of the styles and priorities of policy-making.

Although, naturally, four cases are far from sufficient for reliable generalization, what this suggests is that development from the standpoint of scale (bigness) may be achievable apart from particular formations of class and power, but development in the distributional or quality-of-life sense seems to require more egalitarian structures of class and power.

If this generalization, despite its limited data base, is true, its theoretical and policy implications would be extensive. They would include, for example, the judgment that, within a given set of resource endowments and national-international constraints, the quantitative or material achievements of a developing area are fairly proscribed and less subject to policy manipulation than many unbridled, achievement-oriented developmental ideologies would suggest. The belief that high productivity, income, and industrialization are simple problems of will and organization may be another ideological illusion with consequences just as perverse as the belief that poverty and inequality are inevitable. Conversely, the suggestion that policy and organization, within the scope of certain resource boundaries, can substantially affect and alter the quality of life experienced in the developmental process is a conclusion of the greatest practical importance. If reasonably accurate, it would suggest that, moral arguments aside, the most effective field of policy intervention is defined by matters of public welfare.

From a theoretical standpoint, these results belie the central tenets of structural-functional or evolutionary views that hypothesize a closely covariant relationship between "structural differentiation" and economic development in the conventional sense. That is, more egalitarian social structures, which are, presumably, more structurally differentiated (specialized), are not coincident with the more "developed" (industrialized) cases in this analysis; they do not "go together" systematically. Moreover, the broad evolutionary themes and alleged trends toward structural homogeneity as a result of economic progress are clearly refuted by these data. The more economically advanced areas of Monterrey and Medellín show little of the similarity in their structures of power, politics, and social class that conventional developmental theory would predict. If anything, the sociopolitical structures of industrialized Monterrey are more similar to those of transitional Cali, whereas Guadalajara and Medellín more closely resemble one another than they do the other cases. If the central thrust of these results is to repudiate evolutionary structural-functional theories, they do not leave us at an impasse. Indeed, where structural-functional analyses fail, neo-Marxist historical interpretations frequently succeed. If it is hypothesized that economic change and modernization will be accompanied by structural differentiation, democratization, secularization, participation, and a decline of "traditionalism," we look in vain for patterns of supportive evidence. If, however, it is hypothesized that the ownership and organization of economic production (agrarian, commercial, industrial) determine class structure, which in turn shapes the distribution of power, content of ideology, and priorities of decision-making, a consistent and reasonable orderliness of patterned differences is rendered. Yet under this theoretical canopy the results offer richer opportunities for interpretation and theory-building. That is the next task.

7. Elites and Economic Development

In this final chapter our attention focuses on matters of theory and explanation. More specifically, since the core of this study deals with the origins and consequences of elites in the developmental process, we shall be concerned with two questions. First, what are the conditions that account for the emergence of distinctive elite structures? Second, what role do elites play in the developmental process and what factors explain their differential capacities for promoting development? Obviously these questions run together and cannot be addressed in the familiar language of cause and effect or of independent and dependent variables. Rather, they yield to a processual analysis that attempts to link a set of historical and structural conditions with activities and their outcomes.

This analytic strategy is not only required, but facilitated, by the political economy of development perspective that was set out in chapter 1 and has guided the study. That framework was based on the utility of five interrelated assumptions concerning key foci in the development process: sequence and timing of change, stratification and power, political processes and the state, the capacity for decision-making, and the interdependence of societal levels of analysis. The raw materials pertinent to each of these foci having been provided, the structure of explanation is prescribed. It entails, in effect, summing up the important substantive findings at each point of the framework and tracing out their contingent interactions vis-à-vis the criterion of economic development.

In chapter 1 we characterized two general theoretical approaches to the sociology of development: conventional, Western evolutionary or structural-functional views and the theory of structural dependency. In the discussion that follows we shall return to these theories by way of critical comparisons between hypotheses that stem from each. The first two sections of this chapter focus on the determinants and consequences of elite organization, primarily from the standpoint of conditions internal to the regions. Since such intrasocietal forces have been the exclusive concern of conventional theory, it is here that we will have occasion to evaluate some of the more widely received explanations of development. Recognizing that the internal-external distinction is only a convenient fiction that allows us to treat separately and sequentially aspects of a complex whole, the discussion next moves to the interface between our regional societies and the constraints imposed upon them by metropolitan or international influences. Accordingly, it is here that we take up theories of structural dependency, building necessarily on the foundation that has been laid.

From a logic-of-inquiry standpoint it is important to recognize that this approach maximizes the objective of theory construction rather than theory testing. We have not set out to rigorously test alternative theoretical formulations—intentionally so, given the diffuse nature of the field and the absence of an adequate body of empirical research. Rather, we have adopted a set of focused and limiting assumptions in the hope of generating a richly documented formulation for subsequent testing. If for no other reason, the four-case comparative design requires this approach. Therefore, we shall compare other theoretical ideas and comment on their utility where they seem to bear directly on the results. But, ultimately, the objective is not to repudiate these alternatives so much as it is to extend them and to generate others.

THE DETERMINANTS OF ELITE STRUCTURE

In a critique of functionalist models of change based on traditional, transitional, and modern stages, Moore notes three problems that characterize most conventional theories of development. First, they exaggerate the uniformity of antecedent conditions and transitional processes leading to modernization. Second, by treating economic factors as prime movers they "understate the extensive interplay between the economy and other aspects of social organization." And, third, they have "little information to offer on the process of transformation, on the sequence, rate, and mechanisms whereby major social institutions and organizations adapt to the altered conditions of life that economic growth entails."[1] In this summary of results with respect to the determinants of elite structure we shall attempt to fill in some of these linkages. From materials presented in chapters 2, 3, and 4 we suggest that a parsimonious set of those aspects of social organization accounting for elite structure includes *ecology-economy*, *class structure*, and *political organization*. Under each of these rubrics characteristic features of the four regions will be recalled briefly. More important, it will be claimed that explanations of the distinctive patterns of elite structure are to be found in the *interaction* among conditions that typify each of these dimensions.

Consider first the question of ecology and economy. A fundamental dichotomy found in the regions was the fact that Monterrey and Medellín were geographically isolated in their beginnings as well as inhospitable to extensive agriculture. These twin "liabilities" proved to be key advantages in that they spared the regions many of the historical burdens of colonial dependence. Guadalajara and, notably, Cali, offered a resource base congenial to extensive agriculture and, consequently, a social organization based on the hacienda system. As a result, in the latter regions their modern development began under the aegis of a colonial elite that suppressed and held in poverty the large majority of the population.

Ecologically, of course, Medellín had the distinct advantage of gold mines, whose initial operation was based on slavery. But the rapid depletion of low-technology mining soon led to small-scale enterprises. Though it was scarcely evident in the early years, Monterrey had a potential locational advantage vis-à-vis mining areas, seaports, and its northern border.

Guadalajara and Cali developed initially as colonial dependencies. Entailed in this system were grossly inequitable patterns of land tenure, agricultural production for export, restrictions on internal trade, and dependence on European imports. Yet certain modifications in these patterns gradually ensued. Guadalajara's urbanization and administrative functions helped engender commercial activity and rustic manufacturing. Similarly, with gains in transportation Cali became an important center of national commerce and distribution. While neither development altered substantially the colonial social organization, they did ameliorate it in the sense of producing some new urban economic classes, notably an urban proletariat and a small middle class.

In a roughly similar period, Monterrey and Medellín were beginning to experience crises in what had been their modest developmental progress. Monterrey's flourishing commerce was threatened by declining markets in the United States, by adjacent mining areas, and by competition from Mexico City and the border towns. Medellín's economy was stagnating as a result of policy blunders at the federal level with respect to free trade and agriculture. Interestingly, in both regions it was the response to the crisis that laid the bases for industrialization. In Medellín the solution came with the introduction of coffee cultivation. Subsequently it was the commercial class, including many coffee brokers, that took advantage of new opportunities (e.g., transportation improvements in the "coffee railways") for industrialization, most spectacularly in the import substitution of textiles. In Monterrey the sequence of change was different and more direct.

Moderately affluent commercial classes now threatened with ruin seized on fortuitous opportunities (e.g., the McKinley Tariff Act and the infrastructure push of the Díaz regime) to implant heavy industrialization. In both cases there was no Toynbee-like mystique in the response to crisis. Rather, economic classes were present that had tasted success, had accumulated modest amounts of capital, and had developed the *organizational mechanisms* (e.g., joint venture corporations, commercial and financial houses, extended family ties) conducive to industrial activity. And in each case these preparatory conditions combined with uniquely fortunate opportunities. This explanation avoids what Bendix calls the "fallacy of retrospective determinism."[2] There was nothing automatic or stage-determined in these experiences of industrialization. Rather, they proceeded from the temporal intersection of sets of social, political, and economic conditions.

At this point in their development the regions had produced distinctive class structures that greatly influenced the contours of elite organization. Of central importance, comparatively, were the wide differences in egalitarianism. Cali's rigid class structure was headed by a small stratum whose original wealth was in large agricultural properties but who increasingly came to dominate commerce and fledgling industries, particularly the sugar mills. The overwhelming majority of the peasantry continued to work as wage labor on the large estates or to cultivate small subsistence plots. Only on the fringes of the valley was there evidence of a reduced middle peasantry. A substantial urban proletariat survived in services, petty commerce, and construction. The urban middle sector was small by comparison, though evident in artisan industries, commerce, and public bureaucracies. Rounding out the agro-business upper class were a few self-made industrialists, but very few in contrast to those with roots in the rural aristocracy. The principal dimensions of class conflict were land tenure and agricultural wages, although the landowners for the most part effectively repressed challenges to their patrimony. Subsequently a limited amount of urban unionization was to produce sharply antagonistic relations with the new industrialists. Finally, there were serious intra–upper-class conflicts between certain urban progressive and rural traditionalist groups.

In the rural sector, prerevolutionary Guadalajara resembled Cali, although the inequities in land tenure patterns were not as vast. In the city, however, a comparatively substantial middle class consisted of artisans, small industrialists, merchants, and bureaucrats in government and education. The church–military–landed upper class was to yield to revolutionary politics.

Industrialization at the hands of a small group of family capitalists in

Monterrey produced a narrow and well-defined upper class. The middle class, such as it was, suffered from the reduced importance of commerce and governmental bureaucracy. Representatives of the middle sector included the minority of urban workers fortunate enough to be employed by the largest industries (i.e., the "labor aristocracy"). Below this stratum existed a comparatively large urban proletariat in unskilled industrial jobs, petty commerce, and services. Individuals, particularly offspring, of this stratum experienced occupational mobility, but the class was regularly populated by urban migrants. With the exception of isolated labor-management disputes, class conflict was rare, a fact that may be explained by the perceived opportunities for migration and occupational mobility.[3]

Like Guadalajara, Medellín exhibited an egalitarian class structure in comparison with the other cases. Historically, the middle sectors arose in small-scale mining, colonization of small-owner agricultural sites, coffee production, and commerce. Distinctive also was an upper class based on commerce and, subsequently, industry. But, unlike what obtained in Monterrey, industrial ownership was fairly diversified and the city boasted a prosperous middle class based on industrial employment as well as an active commercial-service sector. Since the slave rebellions of the early mining days, class conflict has been rare, perhaps as a result of colonization, progressive political reforms, and patrimonial industry.

Implicit in these characterizations of class structure is the influence of our third explanatory consideration, political organization. Most dramatic is the case of Guadalajara, where the interplay of politics and class effectively defines contemporary elite structure. As we have seen, the watershed of the revolution was to displace the ruling class represented by the church, the military, and the large landowners, substituting for this triumvirate a new political elite. Post-revolutionary centralization of power in the one-party state not only dismantled the old social and political order, it also provided the ideological outlines for the new. Development was to be pursued under the aegis of the state, in cooperation with the capitalists wherever possible. The timing of the revolution had a special significance for Guadalajara, for two reasons. First, those institutions it sought to eliminate (e.g., church power, the latifundia) were important in varying degrees in the region. Second, Guadalajara, unlike Monterrey, had no group of formidable industrial capitalists to provide resistance. Consequently, the impact of the revolution was especially forceful.

Under a series of strong governors, programs of urban development were actively pursued. Industrialization, beginning in the 1940s, became the byword for development among these political modernizers, and their first policy priority was to lay-in the necessary infrastructure. As we found in the case studies of decision-making, when the infrastructure requisites failed to stimulate the anticipated local investment, the politicians began to look elsewhere. Their careers depended on making impressive developmental gains as these were defined by the norms of the federal system, namely in such quantitative terms as capital investment, new enterprises, gross product, and so forth. Hence the political decision to seek nonlocal and foreign investors. With respect to elite organization, that decision, in turn, led to the introduction of many powerful external influences over the region's economy and the nature of its development.

Political organization in Monterrey followed a vastly different course. Historical isolation from colonial rule was complemented by a long tradition of strong regional leaders. Notable just prior to the revolution was the close alliance between state government and the industrialists. The revolution had little impact on the region, its class structure, and its political organization. Revolutionary politicians and the Monterrey industrialists chose the path of coexistence and mutual noninterference. The independent regional elite continued to recruit its political leaders and fashion its developmental policies from within.

Once again there are important parallels between the political styles of Monterrey and Medellín. Fundamental is the long tradition of regional independence and strong political leadership. In Medellín these were evident from the early mining laws, colonization and new town legislation, the reform laws of Mon y Velarde, and public corporations in a variety of basic services. In contrast to that of Monterrey, however, this leadership has been more civic-minded and progressive in promoting policies beneficial to a broader range of social classes. Moreover, while the tendency in Monterrey has been to recruit political representatives from the lower echelons of the industrial group, many of Medellín's top economic elite have served in key public posts, regarding it as a civic duty.

Political organization in Cali is best described as conflictual. With the exception of a heavy presence of foreign industrialists, the class structure is unchanged from that described earlier. Political conflicts follow class lines in instances such as land reform, taxation, unionization, and urban land use (e.g., squatter settlements). Intra-elite conflict of the type that characterized the creation of the C.V.C. continues in new initiatives of the development corporation and in efforts to create new organizations. The private sector is regularly at odds with the federal government and withholds its cooperation from local political leaders, who are regarded, with some basis, as ineffectual. In ways similar to that of Guadalajara, but more pronounced, local political initiative in developmental areas is seriously compromised by the influence over the economy held by foreign-owned industries. In short, the pattern is one of political conflict, impotence, and disorganization.

In chapter 3, on the basis of contemporary empirical evidence the four regions were described in terms of the concentration of elite power. Guadalajara's elite was labeled a publicly-directed coalition, Medellín's a privately-directed coalition, Cali's a group of privately-dominated factions, and Monterrey's a privately-dominated pyramid. We may now note the close correspondence between these elite structures and their attendant systems of social stratification. But a straightforward stratification theory of power fails to capture the essentials of an explanation. In Cali, for example, the imposition of colonialism and the hacienda system had consequences for class and elite structures that continue to this day, aided, no doubt, by newer forms of imperialism. From similar beginnings Guadalajara developed more egalitarian class and elite structures through the process of revolutionary intervention. What needs to be stressed, however, is the fact that these critical circumstances represent more than distinctive stratification systems. They entail whole patterns of social organization that shape both the class structure and the change process. To state it differently, class structure is the linchpin in an explanation that proceeds from the most general ecological and economic features of social organization to the more specific political conditions that affect elite structure.

From this standpoint, perhaps the key feature in these accounts of elite structure is what might be called the *organizational modality* of change, that is, both the degree and the quality of organization. The colonial hacienda system and its successors propagated a form of self-sufficiency and isolation from collaborative intercourse. Production was for consumption more than for exchange, and trade was monopolized from the outside. For these historical reasons Cali lacked, and continues to lack, viable forms of organizational cooperation. Conversely, the other regions exhibit historically-conditioned, unique forms of collaborative organization: Guadalajara's one-party political elite, Monterrey's industrial group of family capitalists, and Medellín's joint-venture corporations fashioned in the experiences of mining, coffee production, and textile industrialization. In each of the cases, certain regionally-specific, identifiable circumstances explain both the *degree of organization* or cooperative interdependence of social groups and the *organizing principles* that condition elite structures.

It should be noted that this explanation differs materially from several lines of theorizing about the origins of modernizing elites. One such approach, held by writers like Hagen and Rostow, is that the impetus to development is found in some "deviant minority" or lesser elite whose status and values do not depend upon traditional social structures and who, therefore, are more disposed to innovation.[4] In the regional histories we found no evidence supporting this idea. In Monterrey and Medellín, commercial elites responsible for an earlier period of prosperity responded to economic threats to their privileged positions by promoting industrialization through the adaptation of their own organizations to new demands. Conversely, the Cali experience was one in which a rural aristocracy assumed control of the industrialization process, implanting many of its traditional methods, which left the region vulnerable to foreign penetration. Only in Guadalajara did a new elite assume responsibility for modern development, and, far from constituting a deviant minority, it represented, at least initially, a revolutionary majority.

Another prominent explanation derives from the school of evolutionary functionalists. Important proponents of this approach, such as Hoselitz and Smelser, conceive of the developmental process as "structural differentiation."[5] The absence of development is regarded as something akin to the natural state or the beginning point on a continuum, however irregular. It has no cause but is simply the point at which pre-history merges with the development process. This allows societies to be differentiated by degrees of forwardness and backwardness, lead and lag, or what Frank has called the "gap approach."[6] Once a society is differentiated in this manner, the problem becomes how it bridges the gap, moves in jolts and on tangents along the continuum, or, in short, develops. At this point Parsonian metaphors come in for heavy usage, particularly the idea of structural differentiation, which is at the heart of his own evolutionary perspective. Underdeveloped or traditional societies are said to be undifferentiated structurally; the home is also the work place, religious law is also secular law, the kin group is also the unit of political authority, and so on up the social scale. Role relationships parallel structural differentiation. In less differentiated societies they are more consummatory than instrumental, more particularistic than universalistic, and more ascribed than achieved. Since advanced societies are more differentiated in structures and roles, the analysis of development comes to focus on how these changes occur. According to a recent rendition of this approach, the principal foci of development are role differentiation, structural autonomy, and secularization, although a variety of cognate terms are to be found in other writings of this school.[7] The curious reader who may temporarily set aside his doubts about the caricatured differences between underdeveloped and advanced societies is still haunted by the question of why differentiation takes place. It is to Parsons's credit that he deals with this issue in terms of enhanced "adaptive capacity." Recent developmental theorists have suggested similar mechanisms, such as "changes in the magnitude and content of the flow of inputs which put the existing culture and structure under strain"[8]—or, in both cases, necessity—requiring more specialized roles and structures to adapt to change.

Although the language of structural differentiation has a certain metaphoric appeal, it fails to account for the results of this study in several senses. First, the term itself is vague and a poor substitute for those specific collaborative organizational mechanisms we have stressed here. Second, the evolutionary patterning of social change is simply not found in the historical record. Third, and perhaps most important, structural differentiation bears no systematic relationship to development. Assuming the notion can be operationalized with our evidence, it can be shown that religion and secular concerns did not separate in the industrialization of Medellín; kinship, economic, and political units did not differentiate in Monterrey; Guadalajara's political system amalgamated the functions of the state and the economy. Indeed, in each of these key illustrations it was the absence of differentiation that accounted for the developmental achievement through unique organizational forms. This is not to say that something akin to structural differentiation could not be observed in other aspects of the historical record, the structures of power, or the patterns of decision-making. It is to say that the idea has no regular association with the key features of elite structure and development.

THE CONSEQUENCES OF ELITE ORGANIZATION

Earlier chapters dealt with the consequences of elite organization as reflected in regional ideologies, decision-making styles, and developmental achievements. Ultimately it was found that economic development varies widely in both absolute level and quality. Medellín has accomplished substantial quantitative gains, and these are complemented by high marks on a series of quality-of-life indicators. In absolute terms Monterrey is the most developed of the four regions, but critical measures such as income distribution and urban services reflect the restriction of benefits resulting from its growth. Guadalajara's accomplishments are similarly mixed. Material growth has occurred, though in less spectacular ways. Qualitative advances are more impressive with respect to urban services, income distribution, and employment. But education has lagged and external influences over the region's economy threaten indigenous enterprises and opportunities. In contrast to the other cases, Cali's development has been disappointing on most indicators.

At many junctures we have suggested that these differential accomplishments derive in some significant part from the structure of elites, their ideologies, and their styles of decision-making. This assumption is shared by a number of contemporary theorists. Frequent mention has been made of Hirschman's approach, which views the capacity for decision-making "as the scarce resource which conditions all other scarcities and difficulties in underdeveloped countries."[9] Absent in Hirschman's analysis, however, is any suggestion of the social structural correlates of this capacity. He does speak of "ego-focused" and "group-focused" images of change, but again is silent on their sources. Nevertheless, Hirschman's style is refreshing in that it attempts to break out of vicious circles and deal with organizational concerns.

Nash takes us a step further with the observation that "the more organized the group holding political power, the easier it is to embark on development programs," which is followed by several propositions relating this organization to elite recruitment and ideological cleavage. Similarly, Nash associates underdevelopment with "the polarization of wealth, power, and prestige between classes and social segments."[10] While these propositions may be overly general, they do resemble some of the results of this study. Perhaps more germane to the present analysis is the conflict approach of Horowitz, which emphasizes the connections between economic and political power, elite manipulation and resistance to change, and development resulting from both "mending" and "smashing."[11] Nash's propositions are supported at a very general level, while the Horowitz perspective is sensitive to the basic causal factors and their varying combinations.

Perhaps most pertinent among recent contributions to the field is Geertz's study of two Indonesian towns.[12] Not only does the comparative design have similarities with the present study, but the results suggestively focus on elite and economic organization. Commenting on the less developed of the two towns, Geertz notes that

> . . . the problem of economic development presents itself as an organizational one. . . . What they lack is the ability to mobilize and channel their drive in such a way as to exploit the existing market possibilities. They lack the capacity to form efficient economic institutions. They are entrepreneurs without enterprises.[13]

The town in question is a commercial center containing many petty traders and governed by an insular elite of Islamic merchants. Obstacles to development stem from the unintegrated, individualized market economy of small traders operating independently of any economic organization and spread thin over a wide range of transactions. Despite the fact that both towns experienced Dutch colonialism and Japanese occupation, the more developed of the two survived their disruptive consequences because of its legacy of rule by a nobility. In addition to this centralization of power and authority, Geertz stresses the importance of a form of corporate organization (called the *seka*) that unites groups in residential communities, irrigation societies, religion, voluntary organizations, and kinship groups. The overlapping memberships of these corporate entities produce an organizational network that leaders are able to mobilize in support of local projects. Thus Geertz arrives at an explanation of the social factors responsible for economic development that resembles our previous discussion of organizational mechanisms.

Following the lead of these theorists and our earlier explanation of the determinants of elite structure, it is now possible to suggest a more specific theoretical interpretation of how elites affect development. The explanation contains two elements. The first characteristic of developmental elite structures is that *power has passed from an individualized to an organizational locus.*[14] The historical and circumstantial conditions of this shift vary, as we have seen. But the critical pass occurs when effective decision-making power comes to be more a property of organizations than of individual agents. A corollary to this observation is that organizational power is distributed in some sort of coalition, but unequally distributed *within* that coalition, that is, the coalition has a clearly defined leadership yet is reasonably representative. This generalization corresponds closely to the cases of Guadalajara and Medellín, whose coalitional arrangements were led, respectively, by the public and private sectors while simultaneously embracing a relatively wide range of interests. Although we have not described Monterrey's elite as coalitional in the same sense, it nevertheless seems to qualify under the cautious wording of the generalization, since constraining alliances have been forged with the public sector and the federal government. Moreover, as the studies of decision-making indicate, in each of these cases there is evidence of certain regularized coordinating principles that govern the coalitional arrangements. Cali provides the contrasting case for these generalizations. We would not describe it as a developmental elite, since power is more individual than organizational, and conflict militates against the most elemental coalition arrangements.

The second characteristic of developmental elite structures is the *convergence of power and authority in a network of organizations responsible for decision-making.* That is, in addition to power assuming an organizational locus, the coalition of organizations and its leadership come to be regarded as the rightful agents of economic change. Once again, the routes to this decisive pass are varied. The authority of Guadalajara's political elite derives from the revolution and the centralized, one-party state. In Medellín it stems from a long history of civic reforms. Monterrey's industrial leadership enjoys legitimacy for the material progress and mobility opportunities it has provided. And Cali's failures in this respect result from the narrow distribution of benefits and the persistent conflict between government and private groups.

Summarizing to this point, it is claimed that certain historically- and structurally-conditioned elites play a large role in development and they do so with differential success according to their capacity for decision-making, which is a function of the organizational location of power and authority. A recurrent theme in these pages is the observation that this critical combination of factors may be achieved through different routes. Recently Cole has used the term "functional alternatives" for development to describe this fact.[15] The theoretical point of Cole's analysis, which is shared by the results of this study, is to distinguish the functional alternatives approach from others that he labels historicism, structural modeling, and convergence theory. That is, in contrast to historical particularism and evolutionary (or convergence) theories, it is suggested that unique social structural conditions may combine to produce similar functions for development and, therefore, provide a distinctive basis for theoretical generalization. And that is the sense in which this explanation based on elite organization is offered.

DEPENDENCY AND THE NATURE OF DEVELOPMENT

The previous sections confined themselves to questions of why elite structures were more and less successful in promoting development, without consideration of the nature of that development. Moreover, explanations were sought principally among historical, social, and political conditions internal to the regions. To complete this analysis we must also account for the nature of distinctive developmental experiences in the regions and show how these are determined by the articulation of internal conditions with influences that lie beyond the confines of the local society.

At several earlier points we have discussed theories of structural dependency and their potential application to the regions with respect to the timing of industrialization, external orientation, and foreign investment as factors influencing the nature of economic development. Dependence was defined by Dos Santos as "a situation in which the economy of certain countries is conditioned by the development and expansion of another," resulting in a constrained circumstance in which "some countries (the dominant ones) can expand and can be self-sustaining, while other countries (the dependent ones) can do this only as a reflection of that expansion."[16] Within this perspective Frank has advanced a set of explicit hypotheses[17] that can now be evaluated with our evidence as a first approximation of the explanatory potential of dependency theory. These hypotheses have been discussed in chapter 1. The first is that "the satellites experience their greatest economic development and especially their most classically capitalist industrial development if and when their ties to the metropolis are weakest."[18] Next, the impact of dependency on developing areas will vary historically. Third, the internal structure of elites and privileged sectors will correspond to the material interests fostered by metropolitan ties.

When applied to the four regions, the first hypothesis appears generally true. Monterrey and Medellín experienced their greatest development, which also followed classically capitalist patterns, at a time when the tentacles of international economic control were less extensive than today. In the cases of Guadalajara and Cali, metropolitan and foreign intervention in the regional economy has constrained local initiative and areas of potential development. But in other respects the hypothesis requires careful qualification. Prior to their industrial take-off, both Monterrey and Medellín were less integrated into the colonial economy, and this was to their great advantage. In the late nineteenth century, however, both of these regions began experiencing accelerated development *because of* commercial export ties in minerals, coffee, and textiles with the United States and European nations (Monterrey mostly with the United States and Medellín mostly with Europe). That is, in contrast to the foreign ownership and export-import ties of Guadalajara and Cali today, these ties were minimal; but, in contrast to those in their own past, these export ties of Monterrey and Medellín were decisive stimulants to development. Even more important to the thesis, these new ties did not usher in imperialist domination, but actually allowed regional interests to eclipse foreign groups that were earlier present in mining, railroads, and steel. Finally, during the same pre-twentieth-century period in Guadalajara and Cali, where metropolitan ties generally were less extensive, no impressive growth was taking place. In short, the hypothesis has some global accuracy, but requires qualification on closer historical examination.

This brings us to the second proposition, which, because of its historical thrust, is more suggestive. Monterrey and Medellín developed in an era of less foreign involvement in and control of the economies of Latin American countries than is true today. Moreover, *the nature of the ties*, which were based mainly on trade, was less insidious. As we have seen, once a relatively autonomous developmental process had taken root in these areas, they were less vulnerable to external intervention. Guadalajara and Cali, like much of the developing world we are concerned with today, entered modern growth in the post–World War II period, when both the scope and the strength of metropolitan ties were vastly increased, thus propagating greater dependence. This underscores the importance of the timing and sequence of development as factors accounting for vulnerability to dependency. Yet beyond the fact that recently developing areas face the danger of greater dependence than once was the case, the hypothesis does not carry us very far. From a general standpoint, Guadalajara and Cali have made a number of developmental gains, probably more than have some comparable regions less tied to the international economy. Further, there are important differences between the two regions, suggesting that factors additional to the timing of industrialization vis-à-vis the mechanisms of dependence (i.e., regionally specific factors) play a decisive role in shaping the experience of development.

The third hypothesis on sectoral and elite differentiation captures a good deal of the social inequality found in the four regions. Developmental policies, for example, consistently favored urban over rural interests; power structures consistently overrepresented industrial-financial groups and individuals; decisional priorities generally favored industrial development, foreign investment, and export trade rather than sectoral balance and autonomous growth. These contrasts were especially characteristic of the more recently developing regions. What is critical for the hypothesis, however, is not the existence of these inequalities but their causes—the question of whether they may be attributed largely to the structure of dependency. Here the evidence is highly variable. Cali's agricultural sector, responsive almost exclusively to export markets, and its foreign industry, oriented toward the control of national consumer markets, are choice illustrations of the proposition. But the urban-industrial emphasis of public policy in both of the Mexican regions appears less a result of unchecked capitalist exploitation than of a political solution, right or wrong, to the problems of rapid industrialization and national development. This is not to deny the existence of internal colonialism as a fact and an outcome of deliberate policy. But it is to suggest that the fact and the policy result as much from national and regional structures of power as from the particular exigencies of structural dependence, insofar as these can be separated.

Our objective here is not to reject dependency theory generally or even Frank's particular rendition. Rather, the point is to indicate areas of convergence with this study as well as certain problematic issues. So far, it has been shown that a monolithic view of center-periphery relations must be qualified according to internal factors. This observation, of course, parallels the emphasis that recent dependency theorists place on particular patterns of articulation of "internal" and "external" factors. That is, the imperfect fit of Frank's hypotheses may stem from the failure, as Dos Santos says, "to go beyond a unilateral perspective which limits itself to analyzing the problem from the point of view of the hegemonic centers."[19] As our discussion of this approach in chapter 1 pointed out, several theorists relying on historical and impressionistic evidence have hypothesized that development and underdevelopment are consequences of the ability of different internal elite factions to control the state. Within the ruling class Furtado distinguishes between landowning and urban commercial elites, suggesting that alliances between the latter, "progressive faction of the ruling class" and government were at the root of earlier success in the expansion of exports.[20] In a similar formulation Cardoso concludes that the principal cleavage is between entrepreneurial elites of rural origin and those of the trading and mining sectors. Historical instances of development derived from the "economic action of the non-landowning groups, which succeeded in controlling the state to some extent."[21]

All of these approaches provide us with useful leads, although they are limited in focus (tending to emphasize either metropolitan ties or internal elites) and lack systematically-generated empirical evidence. That is, by drawing on the data from this study we are now in a position to elaborate and give substantive meaning to the interplay of center-periphery relations and the ways these condition the developmental process.

If we abandon the false dichotomy between internal and external influences and focus on the historical process of interaction between these peripheral regions and the metropolitan economic system, we discover that contacts and their consequences are quite varied. A series of circumstances accounts for these differences. From the beginnings of the colonial era Guadalajara and Cali were fashioned as agricultural suppliers based on the *encomienda* system. Trade was unilaterally with Spain rather than interregional, and disadvantaged in the exchange of primary products for European manufactures. This dependent status resulted largely from geographical accidents of regional location and agricultural potential. Conversely, Monterrey and Medellín (after the depletion of low-technology mining profits) offered little attraction to the colonial economy and labored at austere enterprises on the margins of European domination. Again, the principal explanation lay in their geographical remoteness and poverty of resources.

The decisive pass for Monterrey and Medellín came when these relatively autonomous regions hit upon commercial ventures that could be exploited by indigenous groups: trade between the mines and the United States border or gulf seaports in the case of Monterrey and coffee export in that of Medellín. These fledgling efforts at interregional trade posed no threat to the neocolonial patterns of domination, due particularly to the fact that they were occurring at the fringes of the dependent economy. Wallerstein's study of the European world economy documents a similar pattern by which "semi-peripheral" states began to develop through the "technique of mercantilist semi-withdrawal from the world economy."[22] That is, a pattern in which regions less firmly tied to the metropolitan or world economy achieved a more autonomous role in that world system by new mercantilist strategies.

As was suggested in the historical treatment of Monterrey and Medellín, their modern industrial development proceeded in generally similar ways. A once-flourishing trade began to decline, forcing the merchant class to seek new investment opportunities—which, for a variety of fortuitous circumstances coupled with the acquired skills of that class, appeared in the steel and textile fields. By this time, or before, the regions had experienced threats to their autonomy. In Medellín the British had been active in mining with advanced technology and in the construction of the "coffee railways." United States investors had shown an interest in Monterrey's steel industry. Nevertheless, these potential incursions were resisted, for reasons that seem to lie in the political and elite structures. In the first place, each region presented a unified urban, industrial-commercial elite of the type Furtado calls progressive. Unlike those of landed elites, their interests lay less exclusively in export trade and hardly at all in the importation of manufactured goods. Alliances with the metropolitan centers that might suit their interests were clearly circumscribed and centered on exportation of their manufactures in exchange for certain technological equipment and consumer goods.

Equally important, these effective and regionally partisan elites had control of the state or governmental apparatus. Politically they enjoyed a healthy measure of autonomy from their central governments and were represented locally by strong governors who shared their independent interests. Legislation and public infrastructure works encouraged greater local investment. Foreign capital participation was not invited and, where this did occur, subsequent efforts were made to buy it out. In other cases of technological assistance needs, rather than inviting investment they preferred to contract for services. From the standpoint of metropolitan interests it would also appear reasonable to conclude that Monterrey and Medellín did not offer attractive incentives for intervention, initially because of their isolation and the absence of easily exploitable resources, and later because of resident competition in somewhat restricted markets. As we shall see, there were greener pastures.

In the years following World War II, Guadalajara and Cali began experiencing a new form of dependency. Until that time they had continued in the mold of agricultural suppliers for national and export markets, with the urban center serving as a commercial distribution point. Some industry had developed, notably in the processing of agricultural products, and Guadalajara showed signs of greater diversity, given its post-revolutionary efforts to break up the old oligarchy. From the early 1950s onward, Cali came increasingly under the control of foreign investors. Its location and transport facilities lent themselves to the accelerated extraction of primary products. More important, these same characteristics made it an ideal site for new industries that aimed at gaining control of national markets in a variety of fields—pharmaceuticals, food products, soap, rubber, construction materials, and many others. In confirmation, again, of the analyses of Furtado and Cardoso, this new dependency on United States interests stemmed from the fact that they were ushered in by conservative commercial exporters and landowning elites. It was to the advantage of this elite to consolidate their export ties with metropolitan centers and to receive, in the bargain, the broader array of consumer goods that their unusually privileged position afforded. More progressive elements of the elite, the urban industrialists, were either amenable to this drift (since they often simultaneously owned agricultural properties or had class origins in the rural aristocracy) or powerless to resist it because the political system was highly fragmented at the local and national levels and did not provide an instrument for alternative policies.

In this quartet, Guadalajara is unique in its experience with dependency; both the explanation and the extent of the phenomenon are intermediate with respect to the other cases. First, Guadalajara was not a prime site for the location of foreign enterprise. For some time infrastructure services were inadequate and the market the region embraced was relatively small, given what could be reached from the United States border and Mexico City. The latter was overwhelmingly the preferred location for United States investors until its saturation began to deflect certain industries to the provincial centers. Thus, Guadalajara's nonlocal industry represented a "spill-over" of foreign and national interests that encountered declining opportunities in both Mexico City and Monterrey. Another point of contrast was the political elite in Guadalajara, which *did* encourage and plan for foreign investment, but for reasons quite distinct from those of Cali's landowners. Here they took their cues from the powerful central government, followed that example, and represented their "achievements" as developmental gains according to the currency that seemed most negotiable in the contest for federal rewards. In short, much of the reasoning behind the policy was political. To summarize these observations, recent years have witnessed a growing presence of foreign investment in Guadalajara, some of which, in accord with federal preference, is allied with local firms.

These descriptions give an indication of the extent to which each region has acquired ties of dependency to the metropolitan economy as well as the political and economic circumstances that seem to explain the extent of those ties. Next we should consider some of the consequences of dependency observable in the nature of the development experienced by Guadalajara and Cali. But before embarking on that discussion we should stress that the *relative regional autonomy* of Monterrey and Medellín is not to be understood as a situation that places them outside national and international networks of dependency. These regions must contend with such problems to the extent that their national society is exploited by metropolitan interests (for example, by reducing internal markets for their industrial output) and their external trade is constrained by barriers or the competition of transnational firms. For the moment we focus more exclusively on interregional differences.

The consequences of structural dependency have been discussed and documented in a variety of sources and range from increasing monopolization, income inequality, and extraction of national wealth to distortions in class structure and increased unemployment.[23] In this discussion we shall confine ourselves to those consequences of dependency that are clearly documented or reasonably inferred from the evidence presented. These effects will be considered with respect to local elites or styles of decision-making and the economy.

The most obvious consequence of the introduction of metropolitan interests into a region is the reinforcement they provide those elites, usually conservative, that were in some sense responsible for their entrance. They tend to bolster the status quo because of an initial identification of interests and because, once having gained a foothold in the region, they endeavor to retain the good will of local elites through cooperation. Foreign firms and their executives pay good wages, contribute to local causes, join civic associations, and avoid conflict, all as insurance against actions that would jeopardize their continued presence. While these firms and executives prefer to maintain a low profile, the case studies suggested that they interact with local elites, belong to the same groups, and support the same policies. In addition to adding resources to those local elites who welcome these ties, they may also contribute to the tension between the status quo and those progressive or nationalistic elites and their allies in the middle class or small-business sector that suffer from multinational competition.

A second consequence is the fact that local (even national) control over the development decision-making process is sacrificed. Increasingly, the direction taken by the regional economy is less the choice of local policymakers and more a function of the global plans of the transnational corporations. And these may easily conflict, since the multinationals endeavor to maximize corporate profits rather than those of a particular subsidiary. For example, it may be decided from afar that a given subsidiary will lose money for tax purposes, will restrain its production so as not to compete with another subsidiary of the same corporation in a contiguous market, will not reinvest locally, or will reinvest more in the same local enterprise than suits the interests of balanced, diversified growth in the region. The point is that any such decision is less subject to local influence than would be the case for national enterprises. Another way in which local elites sacrifice autonomy derives from the typical aloofness of foreign companies from local political problems. Again in the interests of low visibility, these companies avoid controversial issues, depriving local policy-makers of the support of an important sector of the economy when it comes to making difficult decisions. This problem appeared in the case studies of Cali.

Finally, a heavy foreign presence tends to shape the priorities of decision-making. Having large-scale foreign investments becomes a rationale for attracting more through promotional efforts and provision of the costly infrastructure services they require. This occurred in both regions, although Cali went somewhat further in shaping a substantial part of its educational system around the needs of modern (here largely foreign) firms. For the moment we need not argue that these priorities are wrong, simply that they respond more to the interest of the privileged sectors.

As for the effects of metropolitan ties on the regional economy, the salient characteristic of these enterprises is their noncomplementarity. That is, they tend in the great majority of cases to enter lines of production that existed prior to their entrance and provided for successful local enterprise. In both regions the familiar list of foreign business specialization includes food products, construction materials, retail commerce, and so forth. Rather than introducing economies of scale or new technology, these firms tend to enter already profitable activities and compete with smaller local firms, resulting in a trend toward monopolization. Of course, related to this tendency is the progressive elimination of small local businesses and the sources of employment they provide. A third critical consequence of this pattern of duplication is that even where multinational and local enterprise may be able to coexist the opportunity for creating intersectoral linkages is lost. Unlike new types of industry, these duplications fail to stimulate backward linkages to suppliers of new materials and semifinished goods or forward linkages to new distributors. In short, duplication does not stimulate the economy but instead tends to centralize and monopolize it.

One of the financial consequences, of course, is that multinational firms repatriate profits that might otherwise be reinvested locally, and this loss of investment capital is more than hypothetical when foreign companies displace smaller indigenous ones in the same field of endeavor. Equally important, other research has shown that, rather than alleviating capital shortages by bringing to the regional economy new investment funds, the multinational subsidiaries tend to borrow locally a large portion of their investment. Reports of local banking practices in Cali and Guadalajara suggest that this is true here, meaning that capital shortages are exacerbated while local funds are being used to finance competitors to local enterprise.

Finally, as a reflection of decisional priorities attached to infrastructure works, public investment is increasingly devoted to social overhead expenditures rather than to direct productive activities, particularly in Guadalajara, as we saw in the case studies. These heavy expenditures on sources of power, highways, airports, and so forth benefit most the large and multinational firms. Moreover, when emphasized to the neglect of equally compelling public services and rural development, they contribute to the process of accelerated urbanization and centralization witnessed in these regions.

On balance, then, it would appear that many of the negative impacts of foreign investments anticipated by dependency theory have taken place in Guadalajara and Cali, the most serious being partial usurpation of local decisional power and the structural deformities in the economy produced by multinational competition. What might have taken place in these regions without this intervention is, of course, moot. They cannot be compared directly with the more autonomous regions that, for a set of historical and political reasons, were able to resist dependency. What we can conclude, however, is that levels of dependency can be explained and have major consequences for contemporary developmental experiences.

CONCLUSION

In this discussion we have intentionally pursued explanations for the developmental experience at two levels of analysis. With varying emphasis, essentially the same historical record has been examined from the point of view of elite organization and structural dependency. In effect, that strategy has allowed an evaluation of alternative perspectives that separates the more and less cogent explanatory features of each. Our conclusion, therefore, requires an integration of these theoretical perspectives.

The analysis of elite organization, based primarily on internal characteristics of the regions, led to a general repudiation of conventional theories based on evolutionary principles such as structural differentiation. In opposition to that perspective, the evidence supported an interpretation based on ecological, class, and political determinants of certain organizational modalities by which elites effected development. Although these structurally-rooted organizational mechanisms relied on distinctive principles of coordination, connoted by the term "functional alternatives," they shared two key features: the shift of power from an individual to an organizational locus and the convergence of power and authority in a network of organizations.

More specifically, these features characterized in varying degrees those regions that had experienced development, particularly in the aggregate or quantitative sense. As the evidence summarized in the preceding chapter indicated, however, development in terms of aggregate economic indicators was not systematically associated with improvements in the quality of life. To turn to a more fine-grained explanation of this fact, the reason seemed to lie in the class and economic interests of the elites. In concrete terms, the coalitional elites of Medellín and Guadalajara grew out of relatively egalitarian social class structures and pursued developmental policies that weighted both the quantitative and qualitative aspects of development. Here Monterrey represented the deviant case, although it differed from Guadalajara more on the particular quality-of-life measures where it excelled or lagged than on the overall record. Nevertheless, differences here could be explained by the less egalitarian class structure underpinning Monterrey's industrial elite and the fact that elite policies promoted the general welfare only when their interests coincided. That is, the elite pursued policies of pure self-interest, although these sometimes coincidently benefited the general public. In summary, when we attempt to explain the nature of economic development from this standpoint we must include with the identified features of elite organization the additional considerations of social class and policy *interests*.

Similar refinements apply to the analysis of dependency. The evidence suggested a basic generalization to the effect that regions with fewer ties to the metropolitan centers, ones that turned local advantages to development in an era prior to the most aggressive expansion of Western capitalism, experienced the most development. Here, of course, Medellín and Monterrey recorded impressive records of autonomous development through industrial "miracles" that grew out of early commercial success and effectively precluded metropolitan intervention. In this comparison Guadalajara represents the somewhat deviant case, for, despite its long tutelage under colonial dependency, the revolution produced a new elite seemingly less vulnerable to the imposition of twentieth-century varieties of industrial and technological imperialism. That is, while Cali clearly fit the characterization various theorists have offered of a landed, export-oriented elite whose interests embraced metropolitan intervention, Guadalajara did not, owing to its coalitional political elite. Yet, in the post–World War II years, metropolitan dependency came increasingly to dominate the regional economy, with those adverse effects suggested in several places. Moreover, the explanation for this pattern was apparent, located in the rapid development ambitions of the political elite acting out policies encouraged by the federal government.

Now, in summarizing an explanation of the nature of economic development from the dependency standpoint, we arrive at a conclusion similar to the previous one. That is, the approach is accurate at a generalized level, but to account for the more specific nature of development it must be extended to include considerations based on the character of the elite and the political policies it chooses to follow.

Within any explanation of the nature of economic development, the properties of elite organization and dependency are fundamental, necessary, but not sufficient factors. To these must be added the class interests of the elite as these are reflected in the realm of political policy choices. Elite organization and dependency status provide the basic framework for an analysis of the nature of economic development, but by themselves they do not anticipate variable outcomes. To explain the latter requires more dynamic concepts that lend themselves to capturing the political process in which elite class interests take the form of policy action.

Political class action refers to the process in which the class interests of dominant elements of the elite are formulated in interaction with other elite factions and non-elite groups and are implemented as political policies. The rationale underlying given political class actions serves to elucidate aspects of development that would not be apparent without attention to the policy-making process. For example, the somewhat enigmatic dependency found increasingly in Guadalajara would not have been predicted from social structural considerations alone, but can be understood when the class action of local political elites to encourage foreign investment as a policy advancing their interests (i.e., their standing in the eyes of the federal government) is taken into account. Similar political class action strategies have been characterized in the case studies of Cali's dominant agrobusiness class and Monterrey's industrial class.

Theoretically, then, it can be concluded that a relatively complete explanation of the experience of regional development or underdevelopment requires at least three elements: knowledge of the internal organization of elites (and their class bases), factors (such as the historical timing of development) accounting for dependency status, and the manner in which interests are expressed through political class action. It is the political process that connects the structural attributes of elites and dependency, shaping the nature of their impact on the developmental experience.

This is not to minimize the causal importance of ecological and social structural influences. Geographical location and natural resource endowments obviously have a great deal to do with whether a region will develop and how it will develop in terms of the modes of economic production it can sustain. Similarly, social class structure growing out of the relations of economic production provides the basic outlines of elite organization and the principles that govern that organization. Structural dependency, whether based on colonial imposition or the material interests of certain elements of an indigenous elite, sets severe limits to the possibility and nature of development. Yet, beyond the broad limits of these determining influences, political interests and choices seem to provide the distinctive stamp to the nature of regional development, particularly with respect to its distributional features.

This argument can be carried an important step further. That is, in addition to a focus on the political process and its incremental explanatory potential vis-à-vis structural influences, the political economy of development approach that has guided this study illuminates another processual dimension. Political factors are more than residual explanations, since they interact with structural determinants and mediate their consequences. But even more dramatically, we have seen how political policy acts in *reciprocal causation* on social structural factors. For example, political policies stimulating Medellín's colonization and land tenure patterns through a series of reform laws helped to promote the egalitarian class structure and its important consequences for regional development. Revolutionary politics altered the mode of production and class structure in Guadalajara, just as subsequent political choices explained its growing structural dependency. In the theories reviewed here the political process is too often ignored in deterministic evolutionary and dependency models, or it is given the status of an imponderable intervening variable lying between historical-structural conditions and developmental outcomes. What the political economy framework suggests is that the political process is not an additional "factor" contributing to the explanation of development, but is an integral part of the totality of structural and processual influences that reciprocally produce distinctive patterns of development and underdevelopment.

Bearing in mind the multiple influences of the developmental process and their reciprocal interaction, we may draw from the evidence several propositions for subsequent evaluation. Regions such as Medellín that combine egalitarian social structures, relatively autonomous control over the economy, and powerful coalitional elites tend to develop in terms of both material achievements and the distribution of an enhanced standard of living. In the absence of egalitarian social structures and a diversified elite, autonomy may lead to aggregate economic progress but not necessarily to distributional gains, as the case of Monterrey suggests. Conversely, a relatively egalitarian social structure and coalitional elite may produce development in the quality of life but limited economic growth to the extent that autonomy is sacrificed to metropolitan interests, as in the case of Guadalajara. Finally, the Cali experience suggests that restrictive social structures, ties of dependency, and narrow, conflictual elites result in continuing underdevelopment.

These general propositions are offered in the spirit of advancing inquiry and should not be taken as permanent characterizations of the four regions. They may be compared with other research discoveries or assessed in new comparative work, provided it is understood that the regions continue to change. Standing back from the material presented and the various ways in which it has been systematized, we can see that contemporary events suggest new dilemmas for developing regions. Prominent among the changes that have been witnessed in the period since this research began has been the accelerated expansion of metropolitan ties between Latin America and the United States in the form of transnational corporations and new political encroachments. Similarly, Western European and Japanese investors have shown increasing interest in the continent, which is no longer a United States preserve. As we would expect, Guadalajara and Cali have become even more closely dependent on the exterior and more underdeveloped as a result. Equally important, the historical advantages of autonomous development in Monterrey and Medellín are rapidly being eroded as foreign enterprises within their national borders exploit opportunities that might have fallen to indigenous groups. By the late 1960s industrial production in Cali, based substantially on multinational firms, had drawn even with Medellín and threatened to surpass it. Monterrey's metropolitan area was becoming saturated with industry and new ventures were moving to other cities, where they encountered multinational competitors.

Faced with such threats to their continued development, regional elites, however unified, would seem powerless to expand. The result may soon be stagnation in these regions or at least a homogenization of their once distinctive development with that of the rest of their nations. To the extent that this may occur, many of the regionally-specific developmental strategies documented here will assume only historical interest.

At the same time, certain intellectual and nationalistic elites throughout the underdeveloped world are becoming increasingly conscious of the inequalities they have suffered at the hands of transnational corporations and the trade and aid policies of the metropolitan powers. In the last few years this consciousness has been expressed in a variety of actions ranging from nationalization and the renegotiation of contracts with foreign corporations to producer associations and regional trade and political organizations. Clearly one cannot predict the outcome of this movement, and there are likely to be many outcomes, including a reduction of exploitation on the one hand and forcible repression, economic threats, or more subtle forms of imperialism on the other. Yet it seems certain that the underdeveloped nations will, in the immediate future, be attempting to devise strategies to regain and hold economic independence as a basis for promoting more efficacious development.

Although this study of four rather unique regions in Latin America is limited in its generalizability, I hope that it has some relevance for contemporary developmental problems. New opportunities for regional development still exist despite the encircling tendencies of international capital. More important, political strategies for achieving autonomy as a basis for true development and fundamental changes in the world economic order may find informative the record of how social structures and political decisions variously succeeded in that effort.

Notes

1. THE ORGANIZATION OF INQUIRY

1. Irving Louis Horowitz, *Three Worlds of Development: The Theory and Practice of International Stratification*, p. ix.

2. Gabriel A. Almond and James S. Coleman, eds., *The Politics of the Developing Areas.*

3. Some important works representing this orientation include: Gabriel A. Almond and G. Bingham Powell, Jr., *Comparative Politics: A Developmental Approach*; David E. Apter, *The Politics of Modernization*; S. N. Eisenstadt, *Modernization: Protest and Change* and *Essays on Sociological Aspects of Political and Economic Development*; Bert F. Hoselitz, *Sociological Aspects of Economic Growth*; Marion J. Levy, Jr., *Modernization and the Structure of Societies: A Setting for International Affairs*; Lucian W. Pye, *Aspects of Political Development*; Wilbert Moore, *Social Change* and "Social Aspects of Economic Development," in *Handbook of Modern Sociology*, edited by R. E. L. Faris; Neil J. Smelser, *The Sociology of Economic Life*; J. P. Nettl, *Political Mobilization: A Sociological Analysis of Methods and Concepts*; Warren F. Ilchman and Norman Thomas Uphoff, *The Political Economy of Change.*

4. David C. McLelland, *The Achieving Society*; Everett E. Hagen, *On the Theory of Social Change*; John H. Kunkel, *Society and Economic Growth.*

5. Paul Baran, *The Political Economy of Growth*; Andre Gunder Frank, *Capitalism and Underdevelopment in Latin America: Historical Studies of Chile and Brazil*; Celso Furtado, *Economic Development of Latin America: A Survey from Colonial Times to the Cuban Revolution* and "Development and Stagnation in Latin America: A Structuralist Approach," *Studies in Comparative International Development* 1 (1965): 159–175; Raúl Prebisch, *Nueva política comercial para el desarrollo*; Frantz Fanon, *The Wretched of the Earth*; Robert I. Rhodes, ed., *Imperialism and Underdevelopment: A Reader*; Maurice Zeitlin, *Revolutionary Politics and the Cuban Working Class*; James F. Petras, *Politics and Social Structure in Latin America.*

219

6. Moore, "Social Aspects of Economic Development," in *Handbook of Modern Sociology*, ed. by R. E. L. Faris.

7. Albert O. Hirschman, *The Strategy of Economic Development*, p. 1.

8. Levy, *Modernization and the Structure of Societies*, p. 11.

9. Moore, "Social Aspects of Economic Development," p. 889.

10. Cf. Herbert R. Barringer, George I. Blanksten, and Raymond W. Mack, eds., *Social Change in Developing Areas: A Reinterpretation of Evolutionary Theory*, and all of the authors cited in note 3.

11. See Daniel Lerner, *The Passing of Traditional Society: Modernizing the Middle East*; Almond and Powell, *Comparative Politics*; Eisenstadt, *Modernization: Protest and Change*; A. F. K. Organski, *The Stages of Political Development*.

12. Cf. Clark Kerr, et al., *Industrialism and Industrial Man*; Joseph A. Kahl, *The Measurement of Modernism: A Study of Values in Brazil and Mexico*; Alex Inkeles, "The Modernization of Man," in *Modernization: The Dynamics of Growth*, edited by Myron Weiner, and "Making Men Modern: On the Causes and Consequences of Individual Change in Six Developing Countries," *American Journal of Sociology* 75 (September 1969): 208–225.

13. Among the more prominent critiques of this idea are: Reinhard Bendix, "Tradition and Modernity Reconsidered," *Comparative Studies in Society and History* 9, no. 3 (1967): 292–346; Joseph R. Gusfield, "Tradition and Modernity: Misplaced Polarities in the Study of Social Change," *American Journal of Sociology* 72 (January 1967): 351–362; Andre Gunder Frank, "The Sociology of Development and the Underdevelopment of Sociology," *Catalyst* 3 (Summer 1967): 20–73.

14. Furtado, "Development and Stagnation in Latin America."

15. Theotonio Dos Santos, "The Structure of Dependence," *American Economic Review* 38 (August 1973): 424–438.

16. Thomas S. Kuhn, *The Structure of Scientific Revolutions*.

17. Prebisch, *Nueva política comercial*.

18. Gunnar Myrdal, *Rich Lands and Poor: The Road to World Prosperity*.

19. Moore, "Social Aspects of Economic Development."

20. Frank, "The Development of Underdevelopment," *Monthly Review* (September 1966), reprinted in *Latin America: Underdevelopment or Revolution*, edited by Andre Gunder Frank.

21. Dos Santos, "La Crise de la théorie du développement et les relations de dépendence en Amérique Latine," *L'Homme et la Société* 12 (April, May, June 1969), translated and quoted in Philip Ehrensaft, "Semi-Industrial Capitalism in the Third World; Implications For Social Research in Africa," *Africa Today* 18, no. 1 (January 1971): 40–67.

22. Ibid., p. 60.

23. Furtado, "Development and Stagnation," p. 160.

24. Fernando Henrique Cardoso, "The Entrepreneurial Elites of Latin

America," *Studies in Comparative International Development* 2 (1966): 156.

25. E.g., Paul Singer, "Migraciones internas en America Latina: Consideraciones teóricas sobre su estudio," in *Imperialismo y urbanización en América Latina*, edited by M. Castells.

26. E.g., Manuel Castells, "La urbanización dependiente en América Latina," in *Imperialismo y urbanización*, edited by M. Castells.

27. E.g., John W. Gartrell, "Development and Social Stratification in South Indian Agrarian Communities," paper presented at the VIII World Congress of Sociology, Toronto, August 1974.

28. E.g., Giovanni Arrighi, "Labor Supplies in Historical Perspective: A Study of the Proletarianization of the African Peasantry in Rhodesia," in *Essays on the Political Economy of Africa*, edited by Giovanni Arrighi and John S. Saul.

29. E.g., Rodolfo Stavenhagen, "Classes, Colonialism, and Acculturation: A System of Inter-Ethnic Relations in Mesoamerica," in *Masses in Latin America*, edited by Irving Louis Horowitz.

30. Moore, "Social Aspects of Economic Development," p. 887.

31. Bendix, "Tradition and Modernity," p. 294.

32. James O'Connor, "The Meaning of Economic Imperialism," in *Imperialism and Underdevelopment: A Reader*, edited by Robert I. Rhodes.

33. Castells, "La urbanización dependiente en América Latina."

34. Dos Santos, "The Structure of Dependence."

35. Hoselitz, *Sociological Aspects of Economic Growth*, pp. 48–49.

36. Bendix, "Tradition and Modernity."

37. Manning Nash, "Some Social and Cultural Aspects of Economic Development," *Economic Development and Cultural Change* 7 (January 1959): 137–150.

38. Horowitz, *Three Worlds of Development*, p. 214.

39. Ibid., p. 419.

40. Moore, "Social Aspects of Economic Development," p. 907.

41. Hirschman, *The Strategy of Economic Development*, pp. 26–27.

42. *Economic Survey of Latin America, 1965*, p. 14.

43. Everett E. Hagen and Oli Hawrylyshyn, "Analysis of World Income and Growth, 1955–1965,"*Economic Development and Cultural Change* 18, no. 1, part 2 (October 1969): 94.

44. See the extensive literature on regional economics, e.g., William Alonso, "Urban and Regional Imbalances in Economic Growth," *Economic Development and Cultural Change* 17 (October 1968): 1–14; J. G. Williamson, "Regional Patterns," *Economic Development and Cultural Change* 13, part 2 (July 1965); Jane Jacobs, *The Economy of Cities*; Lloyd Saville, *Regional Economic Development in Italy*.

45. See, for example: Hagen, *On the Theory of Social Change*; Edward Ban-

field and Laura Fosano Banfield, *The Moral Basis of a Backward Society*; Clifford Geertz, "Social Change and Economic Modernization in Two Indonesian Towns: A Case in Point," in Hagen, op. cit.; Arnold M. Rose, "Sociological Factors Affecting Economic Development in India," *Studies in Comparative International Development* 3 (1967–1968): 169–183; Arnold Rivkin, ed., *Nations by Design: Institution Building in Africa*; Bert F. Hoselitz, "The Role of Cities in the Economic Growth of Underdeveloped Countries," *Journal of Political Economy* 61 (1953): 195–208; Leo F. Schnore, "The Statistical Measurement of Urbanization and Economic Development," *Land Economics* 37 (August 1961): 229–244.

46. Horowitz, "Sociological Priorities for the Second Development Decade," *Social Problems* 19 (Summer 1971): 138.

47. John Walton, "A Methodology for the Comparative Study of Power: Some Conceptual and Procedural Applications," *Social Science Quarterly* 52 (June 1971): 39–60.

48. Authors emphasizing the egalitarian and volitional consequences of development include W. Arthur Lewis, *The Theory of Economic Growth*, and David E. Apter, *Choice and the Politics of Allocation: A Developmental Theory*.

2. SOCIAL STRUCTURE AND ECONOMIC GROWTH IN FOUR CITIES OF LATIN AMERICA

1. María Teresa Gutiérrez, *Geodemografía del Estado de Jalisco*.

2. The phrase is borrowed from Charles C. Cumberland's book *Mexico: The Struggle for Modernity*, an excellent general work that will be called upon frequently in this discussion.

3. See Stanley M. Elkins, *Slavery: A Problem in American Institutional and Intellectual Life*. The concept, of course, comes from Erving Goffman, *Asylums*.

4. Victor Alba, *The Mexicans: The Making of a Nation*, pp. 38–39.

5. Hubert Herring, *A History of Latin America*, pp. 256–257.

6. The first set of estimates are derived from Henry G. Ward, *Mexico in 1827*, and reported in Alejandra Moreno Toscano, "Cambios en los patrones de urbanización en México, 1810–1910," University of Wisconsin-Milwaukee, Center for Latin American Studies, Center Discussion Paper No. 28. The more conservative figures are from Luis González y González, "La situación social de Jalisco en vísperas de la Reforma," in *La Reforma en Jalisco y el Bajío*, pp. 34–41.

7. *Noticia de Jalisco*, p. 24.

8. Cumberland, *Mexico: The Struggle for Modernity*, p. 136.

9. Luis Pérez Verdía, *Historia particular del Estado de Jalisco*, II, 188.

10. Cumberland, *Mexico: The Struggle for Modernity*, p. 129.

11. This estimate is reported in González y González, "La situación social de Jalisco," p. 35.

12. Ibid., pp. 38–39.

13. Mariano Bárcena, *Descripción de Guadalajara en 1880*, pp. 147–166.

14. Gutiérrez, *Geodemografía del Estado de Jalisco*, p. 62.

15. José G. Zuno, *Historia de la Revolución en el Estado de Jalisco*, p. 38.

16. Ibid.

17. Joe C. Ashby, *Organized Labor and the Mexican Revolution under Lazaro Cardenas*, p. 6.

18. J. Angel Moreno Ochoa, *Diez años de agitación política en Jalisco, 1920–1930*, p. 237.

19. Nathan L. Whetten, *Rural Mexico*, pp. 272–273.

20. Whetten, *Rural Mexico*; Eyler N. Simpson, *The Ejido: Mexico's Way Out*, p. 40.

21. All these figures are based on official Mexican statistics as compiled in the works of Whetten and Simpson.

22. Cf. Luis Unikel, "The Process of Urbanization in Mexico: Distribution and Growth of Urban Population," in *Latin American Urban Research*, edited by Francine F. Rabinovitz and Felicity Trueblood, I, 258–285.

23. *Jalisco ofrece*, p. 29.

24. Eliseo Mendoza, "Perspectivas industriales del Estado de Jalisco," in *Desarrollo integral de Jalisco*, V, 62–68.

25. *Examen de la situación económica de México*, 41, no. 479 (October 1965): 18–23, and 42, no. 483 (February 1966): 13–19.

26. Andrés Montemayor Hernández, *Historia de Monterrey*, pp. 76–79.

27. Isidro Vizcaya Canales, *Los orígenes de la industrialización de Monterrey, 1867–1920*, p. iv.

28. Montemayor Hernández, *Historia de Monterrey*, p. 108.

29. Vizcaya Canales, *Los orígenes de la industrialización de Monterrey*, p. 19.

30. Montemayor Hernández, *Historia de Monterrey*, p. 164.

31. Ibid., p. 167.

32. Daniel Cosío Villegas, ed., *Historia moderna de México*, II, 576.

33. José P. Saldaña, *Apuntes históricos sobre la industrialización de Monterrey*.

34. Ibid.

35. Samuel N. Dicken, "Monterrey and Northeastern Mexico," *Annals of the Association of American Geographers* 29 (June 1939): 139.

36. Saldaña, *Apuntes históricos*.

37. "Cervecería Cuauhtémoc, S. A.: Su desarrollo y su aspecto social," *Mañana* 1228 (March 11, 1967): 55–59.

38. See Joseph R. Gusfield, "Tradition and Modernity: Misplaced Polarities in the Study of Social Change," *American Journal of Sociology* 72 (January 1967): 351–362.

39. Vizcaya Canales, *Los orígenes de la industrialización de Monterrey*, p. 70.

40. Saldaña, *Apuntes históricos*, p. 30.

41. Montemayor Hernández, *Historia de Monterrey*, p. 277.

42. Saldaña, *Apuntes históricos*, p. 26.

43. Vizcaya Canales, *Los orígenes de la industrialización de Monterrey*, p. 78.

44. Montemayor Hernández, *Historia de Monterrey*, pp. 320–322.

45. Ibid., pp. 344–456.

46. Ibid., pp. 351–354.

47. Saldaña, *Contemporaneas*, quoted in ibid., p. 373.

48. Frank R. Brandenberg, *The Making of Modern Mexico*, p. 267.

49. Derived from Montemayor Hernández, *Historia de Monterrey*, p. 374.

50. Unikel, "The Process of Urbanization in Mexico," p. 270.

51. Ibid., pp. 284–285.

52. Jorge Balán, Harley L. Browning, and Elizabeth Jelin, *Men in a Developing Society: Geographic and Social Mobility in Monterrey, Mexico*, chapter 2.

53. Máximo de León Garza, *Monterrey: Un vistazo a sus entrañas*, p. 279.

54. Jesús Puente Leyva, *Distribución del ingreso en un área urbana: El caso de Monterrey*.

55. Elizabeth Jelin de Balán, "Movilidad intrageneracional," in *Movilidad social, migración y fecundidad en Monterrey metropolitano*, pp. 203–274.

56. Raymond E. Crist, *The Cauca Valley, Colombia: Land Tenure and Land Use*, p. 14.

57. Donald J. Lloyd-Jones, "The Potential Development of the Upper Cauca Valley, Colombia," p. 18.

58. Ibid., p. 19.

59. See Albert O. Hirschman, *Journeys toward Progress: Studies of Economic Policy-Making in Latin America*, pp. 155–160ff.

60. These population figures are from Crist, *The Cauca Valley*, pp. 43–49.

61. William Paul McGreevey, *An Economic History of Colombia, 1845–1930*, p. 258.

62. Everett E. Hagen, *On the Theory of Social Change: How Economic Growth Begins*, p. 364.

63. Lloyd-Jones, "Potential Development," p. 147.

64. *El por qué de un plan de desarrollo económico y social para el Departamento del Valle del Cauca*, p. 35.

65. *Cali y el Valle de Cauca*, p. 15.

66. Ibid., chapter 8.

67. Lloyd-Jones, "Potential Development," pp. 151–152.

68. Cole Blasier, "Power and Social Change in Colombia: The Cauca Valley," *Journal of Inter-American Studies* 8 (July 1966): 399–425.

69. *Colombia Today* 5, no. 11 (1970).

70. *Cali y el Valle del Cauca*, pp. 67–69.

71. *Revista de la Superintendencia de Sociedades Anónimas, 1965*.

72. This was done in connection with the present study and, like other investigations, is not definitive because the figures are self-reported and the chamber records somewhat incomplete.

73. Antonio J. Posada and Jeanne de Posada, *La C.V.C.: Un reto al subdesarrollo y al tradicionalismo*, p. 58.

74. Jan L. Flora, *Elite Solidarity and Land Tenure in the Cauca Valley of Colombia*.

75. Everett Hagen places a good deal of emphasis on the Antioqueño case in developing his theory of status withdrawal and creativity in his book *On the Theory of Social Change*, chapter 15. Andre Gunder Frank simply mentions in passing that Antioqueño development may be due to its isolation from the kind of "structural dependency" that, according to his analysis, is at the root of Latin American underdevelopment. Cf. "The Development of Underdevelopment" in Frank, *Latin America: Underdevelopment or Revolution*, p. 11.

76. James J. Parsons, *Antioqueño Colonization in Western Colombia*, p. 44.

77. Ibid., p. 46.

78. Ibid., pp. 55, 65–66.

79. McGreevey, *An Economic History of Colombia*, pp. 190–193.

80. Luis H. Fajardo, *Social Structure and Personality: The Protestant Ethic of the Antioqueños*, p. 69.

81. See Alvaro López Toro, *Migración y cambio social en Antioquia durante el siglo diez y nueve*, p. 58.

82. Parsons, *Antioqueño Colonization*, p. 10⊦.

83. Parsons estimates that by 1949 Antioquia produced two-thirds of the gold mined in Colombia and that three-fourths of that came from foreign-owned companies. Ibid., p. 57.

84. López Toro, *Migración y cambio social*, p. 69.

85. Frank Safford, "Foreign and National Enterprise in Nineteenth Century Colombia," *Business History Review* 34 (Winter 1965): 503–526.

86. Safford, "Significación de los Antiqueños en el desarrollo económico colombiano," *Anuario Colombiano de Historia Social y la Cultura*, pp. 49–69. Reprinted in Latin American Series, no. 281, p. 64.

87. McGreevey, *An Economic History of Colombia*, p. 69.

88. Ibid., pp. 196–197.

89. Hagen, *On the Theory of Social Change*, p. 359.

90. Parsons, *Antioqueño Colonization*, p. 173.

91. Luis Ospina Vásquez, *Industria y Protección en Colombia, 1810–1930*, p. 340.

92. See Safford, "Foreign and National Enterprise."

93. McGreevey, *An Economic History of Colombia*, p. 204.

94. For a discussion and case study rebuttal of this line of thinking see Manning Nash, *Machine Age Maya: The Industrialization of a Guatemalan Community*.

95. Gusfield, "Tradition and Modernity," and Reinhard Bendix, "Tradition and Modernity Reconsidered," *Comparative Studies in Society and History* 9, no. 3 (1967): 292–346.

96. Parsons, *Antioqueño Colonization*, p. 177.

97. *Medellín: Estudio general de la ciudad y su area circundante, 1969*, pp. 11–15.

98. Juan Felipe Gaviria Gutiérrez, "La industria en Antioquia," *Revista Trimestral* 6 (June 1968): 3–18.

99. *Medellín*, pp. 37–38.

100. *Cifras comparativas y algunos coeficientes de la industria manufacturera en Colombia, 1964–1965*, pp. 14–15.

101. The figures for Bogotá (Cundinamarca) are higher in both respects, 813 corporations with 180 (22.2 percent) of foreign origin. Cf. *Revista de la Superintendencia de Sociedades Anónimas, 1965*, p. 32.

102. "El Secreto de Coltejer: Modernización y 40,000 accionistas," *Progreso: Revista del Desarrollo Latino-Americano* (November-December 1967): 57–58.

103. Among the four regions in this study, only Antioquia has attracted the serious attention of developmental theorists. On the surface these interpretations abound in diversity. Some observers stress the character and traditionalism of the Antioqueño, his proclivity for hard work, frugality, and entrepreneurship (e.g., Harold P. Eder, *Colombia*). Marxists such as López Toro and Luis Eduardo Vieto Arteta (*Ensayos sobre economía colombiana*) emphasize economic organization and its social class consequences. A third group, including Hagen and Ospina Vásquez, would call attention to the social psychological dynamics of "status withdrawal." And to these we should add what McGreevey calls a "garden variety economic explanation." Yet this diversity of opinion exists on the surface. A more careful analysis of the solid historicism of Parsons, Ospina Vásquez, Safford, López Toro, and McGreevey yields differences mainly in emphasis. In his thoroughgoing critique of Hagen's thesis (on "status withdrawal") Safford demonstrates that the Antioqueños were not an ethnic (Basque) minority, did not suffer disrespect at the hands of other Colombians, and acquired their unique reputation in the country after, rather than before, their

celebrated economic achievements. For Safford, as we have noted, the key factor in Antioqueño development was gold mining as an "entrepreneurial school" (of joint ventures and corporate-like "societies of equals") and as a source of liquid financial resources, and these insofar as they provided the impetus to commerce and finance. The crux of the current dispute is whether this may not be reaching a bit too far back in time. McGreevey acknowledges (as does Hagen) the importance of mining and joint ventures but questions their prominence as fundamental causes. "Certainly mining ventures were important to the Antioqueños, but Safford and more recently Alvaro López have exaggerated their importance. Mining technology, for example, was not of the kind which would produce the side effects Hagen, Ospina Vásquez, Safford and López attribute to it. . . . If for no other reason, the temporal break between indigenous mining enterprise in the middle of the nineteenth century and the establishment of large manufacturing plants for cotton textiles is altogether too great." (McGreevey, *An Economic History of Colombia*, pp. 191–192). But on that score McGreevey's well-taken objection is better directed at Hagen and Ospina Vásquez than at Safford and López Toro, since the latter emphasize, not mining *per se*, but its stimulus to commerce. Nevertheless, McGreevey goes on to suggest a highly plausible explanation based on trade, the social organization of production, and economic interdependence. Actually McGreevey has two theories, a "theory of transition" based on population growth and a less explicit theory of socio-economic structure, not to mention several brilliant theoretical digressions into the growth patterns of agrarian societies and export economies. After all this, the great irony of his book is that it ends on a forcefully atheoretical note. "But the basic ingredient of the transition was the will to make it. Having recognized that element of motivation and will, the economist reaches the end of his own range of expertise" (p. 304). McGreevey's pessimism aside, the Antioqueño case and his own material are rich in theoretical insights that we shall explore in a comparative framework after presenting the data from this study.

3. COMPARATIVE PERSPECTIVES ON THE STRUCTURE OF POWER

1. Floyd Hunter, *Community Power Structure: A Study of Decision Makers.*
2. Robert S. Lynd and Helen M. Lynd, *Middletown in Transition*; W. Lloyd Warner, *The Social Life of a Modern Community.*
3. This literature is summarized in several sources that include extensive bibliographies: Michael Aiken and Paul E. Mott, eds., *The Structure of*

Community Power; Charles M. Bonjean, Terry N. Clark, and Robert L. Lineberry, eds., *Community Politics: A Behavioral Approach*; Frederick Wirt and Willis Hawley, *The Search for Community Power*.

4. Nelson W. Polsby, *Community Power and Political Theory*; Thomas J. Anton, "Power, Pluralism, and Local Politics," *Administrative Science Quarterly* 7 (March 1963): 425–457; Charles M. Bonjean and David M. Olson, "Community Leadership: Directions of Research," *Administrative Science Quarterly* 9 (December 1964): 278–300; as well as the sources listed in note 3.

5. Robert A. Dahl, *Who Governs?: Democracy and Power in an American City*.

6. Robert R. Alford, *Bureaucracy and Participation: Political Cultures in Four Wisconsin Cities*, p. 194.

7. John Walton, "Substance and Artifact: The Current Status of Research on Community Power Structure," *American Journal of Sociology* 71 (January 1966): 430–438; Michael Aiken, "The Distribution of Community Power: Structural Bases and Social Consequences," in Aiken and Mott, *The Structure of Community Power*, pp. 487–525; James E. Curtis and John W. Petras, "Community Power, Power Studies and the Sociology of Knowledge," *Human Organization* 29 (Fall 1970): 204–218; Spencer H. Hildahl, "A Note on ' . . . A Note on the Sociology of Knowledge,' " *Sociological Quarterly* 11 (September 1970): 405–415.

8. Among the more outstanding multi-method studies are: Robert E. Aggar, Daniel Goldrich, and Bert E. Swanson, *The Rulers and the Ruled: Political Power and Impotence in American Communities*, and Robert Presthus, *Men at the Top: A Study in Community Power*. Recent large-scale comparative analyses include: Terry N. Clark, "Community Structure, Decision Making, Budget Expenditures, and Urban Renewal in 51 American Communities," *American Sociological Review* 33 (August 1968): 576–593, and Michael Aiken and Robert R. Alford, "Community Structure and Innovation: The Case of Urban Renewal," *American Sociological Review* 35 (August 1970): 650–665.

9. Aiken and Alford, "Community Structure"; Walton, "The Vertical Axis of Community Organization and the Structure of Power," *Social Science Quarterly* 48 (December 1967): 353–368; Aiken, "The Distribution of Community Power."

10. Perhaps the earliest effort in this area was Delbert C. Miller's comparison of Bristol, England, with Seattle: "Decision-Making Cliques in Community Power Structures: A Comparative Study of an American and an English City," *American Journal of Sociology* 64 (November 1958): 299–310. Several studies of European cities are reported in *The New Atlantis* 2 (Winter 1970).

11. William V. D'Antonio and William H. Form, *Influentials in Two Bor-*

der Cities: A Study in Community Decision-Making; Orrin E. Klapp and L. Vincent Padgett, "Power and Decision-Making in a Mexican Border City," *American Journal of Sociology* 65 (January 1960): 400–406.

12. Klapp and Padgett, "Power and Decision-Making."

13. Lawrence S. Graham, *Politics in a Mexican Community.*

14. Gary Hoskin, "Power Structure in a Venezuelan Town: The Case of San Cristóbal," in *Case Studies in Social Power*, edited by Hans-Dieter Evers.

15. George F. Drake, *Elites and Voluntary Associations: A Study of Community Power in Manizales, Colombia.*

16. Richard R. Fagen and William S. Tuohy, *Politics and Privilege in a Mexican City.*

17. D'Antonio and Form, *Influentials in Two Border Cities.*

18. Miller, *International Community Power Structures: Comparative Studies in Four World Cities.*

19. José Fernando Ocampo, *Dominio de clase en la ciudad colombiana.*

20. H. E. Torres-Trueba, "Factionalism in a Mexican Municipio: A Preliminary Study of the Political, Economic, and Religious Expressions of Factionalism in Zacapoaxtla, Puebla," *Sociologus* 19, no. 2 (1970): 134–152.

21. Ronald H. Ebel, "The Decision Making Process in San Salvador," in *Latin American Urban Research*, vol. 1, edited by Francine F. Rabinovitz and Felicity M. Trueblood.

22. Antonio Ugalde, *Power and Conflict in a Mexican Community: A Study of Political Integration.*

23. On the definitional question see Robert Bierstedt, "An Analysis of Social Power," *American Sociological Review* 15 (December 1950): 730–738; Clark, *Community Structure and Decision-Making: Comparative Analyses*; Robert A. Dahl, "The Concept of Power," *Behavioral Science* 2 (July 1957): 201–215; Richard M. Emerson, "Power Dependence Relations," *American Sociological Review* 27 (February 1962): 31–40; Talcott Parsons, "On the Concept of Power," *Proceedings of the American Philosophical Society* 107 (June 1963): 232–262; Dennis H. Wrong, "Some Problems in Defining Social Power," *American Journal of Sociology* 73 (May 1968): 673–681.

24. Charles E. Merriam, *Political Power.*

25. James G. March, "The Power of Power," in *Varieties of Political Theory*, edited by David Easton.

26. See, for example, William Kornhauser, " 'Power Elite' or 'Veto Groups'?" in *Culture and Social Character*, edited by Seymour M. Lipset and Leo Lowenthal.

27. Parsons, "On the Concept of Power"; Wrong, "Some Problems"; Max Weber, *The Theory of Social and Economic Organization*; Harold Lasswell and Abraham Kaplan, *Power and Society: A Framework for Political Inquiry*;

Peter Blau, *Exchange and Power in Social Life*; Edward W. Lehman, "Toward a Macrosociology of Power," *American Sociological Review* 34 (August 1969): 453–465.

28. Weber, *The Theory of Social and Economic Organization*, p. 180.

29. See Reinhard Bendix, *Max Weber: An Intellectual Portrait*, chapter 9.

30. Amitai Etzioni, *A Comparative Analysis of Complex Organizations*.

31. C. Wright Mills, *The Sociological Imagination*.

32. Lehman, "Toward a Macrosociology of Power," pp. 454–455.

33. Bendix, *Max Weber*, p. 290.

34. Lehman, "Toward a Macrosociology of Power," p. 456.

35. Marvin E. Olsen, ed., *Power in Societies*, p. 74.

36. L. Vaughn Blankenship, "Community Power and Decision Making: A Comparative Evaluation of Measurement Techniques," *Social Forces* 43 (December 1964): 207–216.

37. See chapter 2 for an explanation of this more-and-less extensive design. Here the results obtained in all four regions will be treated comparably since there is good evidence for the reliability of influential nominations between positional and influential groups. For example, in Cali and Guadalajara, where the two sets of nominators could be compared, rank order correlations between their nominators were high, +.82 and +.85 respectively. Also, patterns identified in the initial stages of the extensive method were not altered in subsequent investigation; simply more detail was uncovered.

38. The term "influential" designates those persons most frequently nominated as key figures in the regional political economy or the economic development work in the area. Thus, these are not to be understood as "general influentials" but ones important in the concrete tasks of the economy and politics. Nevertheless, given the great salience of these matters in developing areas, these persons are probably also the "most important people in town" from a variety of standpoints. A cutoff point of 4 or 5 nominations was used as the arbitrary lower limit of the influential group, since this formed a natural breaking-point, after which a very large number of people were mentioned. It should be stressed that the cutoff is arbitrary and artificial in the sense of simply rendering the analysis more manageable through concentration on a small group. Thus, no claim is or need be made that these are *the* important people. For the purposes of this analysis, all we need to and do claim is that the group is representative of the kinds of people that wield power.

39. The disproportionate representation of industrial occupations in all of these lists can be appreciated by comparing the occupational distribution of the total labor force presented in chapter 2.

40. For example, there tends to be a rapid turnover in local and state administrations. Only very recently have there been cases of these admin-

istrations completing their formal period of tenure, which is a mere two years. Typically, government officials do not have previous experience in public life and, before long, return to positions in the private sector.

41. These sociometric data on acquaintance and joint participation are based on small N's in that not all influentials completed the item. The average was based on summing all reported instances of close acquaintance and mutual participation and dividing by the number of respondents.

4. LEADERS AND LEADERSHIP IDEOLOGIES

1. Max Weber, *The Protestant Ethic and the Spirit of Capitalism.*
2. Reinhard Bendix, *Max Weber: An Intellectual Portrait*, p. 46.
3. Irving Louis Horowitz, *Three Worlds of Development: The Theory and Practice of International Stratification*, p. 38.
4. Joseph R. Gusfield, "Tradition and Modernity: Misplaced Polarities in the Study of Social Change," *American Journal of Sociology* 72 (January 1967): 358.
5. Chapter 1 provides more detailed information on the criteria for inclusion in the leadership sample or universe. Essentially the two chief administrative officers of all public agencies and private interest groups with even an indirect connection with developmental problems were interviewed. Completed interviews with this designated universe exceeded 90 percent in each city.
6. Using gamma as a measure of association the coefficients representing the relationship between age and professional experience are Guadalajara .41, Monterrey .33, Cali .39, and Medellín .62.
7. Floyd Hunter, *Community Power Structure: A Study of Decision Makers*, p. 79.
8. Occupational levels are described in the legend to table 22.
9. This analysis is, of necessity, somewhat crude. A more sophisticated study of occupational mobility would have to take into consideration intergenerational changes in the entire labor force distribution as well as the differences between parental occupational level and that of all children of the family, which would require a study in itself. Though the data here are crude, their plausibility is enhanced by a convergence of separate indicators. For an excellent discussion of the methodological problems in this area see Otis Dudley Duncan, "Methodological Issues in the Analysis of Social Mobility," in *Social Structure and Mobility in Economic Development*, edited by Neil J. Smelser and Seymour Martin Lipset, pp. 51–97.
10. Karl Mannheim, *Ideology and Utopia: An Introduction to the Sociology of Knowledge*, p. 2.

11. Cutoff points for these rank-ordered lists were set at places where a large gap in the number of nominations occurred.

12. Other authors who regard the scope of government as a fundamental indicator of political-economic ideology include Harry G. Johnson, "The Ideology of Economic Policy in the New States," in *Economic Nationalism in Old and New States*, edited by Harry G. Johnson, pp. 124–141, and Robert E. Agger, Daniel Goldrich, and Bert E. Swanson, *The Rulers and the Ruled: Political Power and Impotence in American Communities.*

13. For example, measures of association (gamma) for "position" by "scope of government" in Guadalajara and Cali, where influential samples were drawn, are small, $-.12$ and $-.09$ respectively. In other words, within regions position is not an important determinant of ideology, allowing us to compare freely the four samples. The question of socioeconomic status as a determinant of ideology will be taken up separately.

14. See data in Agger, Goldrich, and Swanson, *The Rulers and the Ruled.*

15. See Horowitz, *Three Worlds of Development.*

16. See Johnson, "The Ideology of Economic Policy."

17. These two items are well suited to combination in one "ideological index" since they entail to a reasonable extent criterion validity and are themselves only moderately correlated, thus tapping different dimensions of the phenomenon of ideology. The coefficients of association (gammas) between scope of government and foreign investment in the four regions are Guadalajara .21, Cali .30, Monterrey .43, and Medellín 0.

18. The measure gamma is to be interpreted as the extent to which one may better predict a respondent's ideological orientation by virtue of knowing his position, the region he comes from, or his SES. For a discussion of such "proportional reduction in error" measures see Herbert L. Costner, "Criteria for Measures of Association," *American Sociological Review* 30 (June 1965): 341–353. Because of the necessarily crude level of measurement of these attitudinal data, the tabular presentation and ordinal level measures were deemed more appropriate than parametric or correlational statistics, which involve several assumptions not met here.

5. DECISIONS FOR DEVELOPMENT

1. Harold Lasswell, *Politics: Who Gets What, When and How.*

2. Albert O. Hirschman, *Journeys Toward Progress: Studies of Economic Policy-Making in Latin America* and *Development Projects Observed.*

3. The idea is borrowed from Irving Louis Horowitz, "Consensus, Conflict, and Cooperation: A Sociological Inventory," *Social Forces* 41 (December 1962): 177–188.

4. *Plan Lerma, Asistencia técnica.*

5. Hirschman, *The Strategy of Economic Development*, chapter 5. As Hirschman correctly predicts this fact has made Guadalajara particularly attractive to foreign investors.

6. See *Planeación y urbanización; Jalisco, Renovación urbana; Ley de Planeación y urbanización del Estado de Jalisco.*

7. Alberto Ortiz Nava, *Evolución de protecciónes legales de las inversiones extranjeras en México*, pp. 99–103.

8. *Sugerencias para el establecimiento de nuevas industrias en Jalisco.*

9. "Business Shakes Up a Lotus Land," *Business Week* (January 13, 1968): 90.

10. Robert D. Lamont, "Mexico's Awakening Giant," *Mexican-American Review* (May 1966).

11. Bessie Galbraith Sours, "Jalisco: Mexico's 'Golden West,' " *Mexican-American Review* (January 1968): 10–12.

12. Adolf B. Horn, Jr., "Executive Living," *Mexican-American Review* (May 1966): 51–54.

13. Edward L. Thomas, "Booming Guadalajara Welcomes U.S. Investors," *San Diego Union* (March 15, 1968).

14. Lamont, "Mexico's Awakening Giant."

15. Analyses supporting this claim are extensive. Two useful collections of articles dealing with the approach are *Imperialism and Underdevelopment: A Reader*, edited by Robert I. Rhodes, and *The Political Economy of Development and Underdevelopment*, edited by Charles K. Wilber.

16. Eleazar Santiago Cruz, "Antecedentes del Plan Agrícola Jalisco," in *Desarrollo integral de Jalisco*, vol. 3, *Desarrollo agropecuario.*

17. *Jalisco ofrece.*

18. Pablo González Casanova, *La democracia en México*, p. 277.

19. Andre Gunder Frank, "Mexico: The Janus Faces of Twentieth-Century Bourgeois Revolution," in *Latin America: Underdevelopment or Revolution*, edited by Andre Gunder Frank, pp. 298–317; Robert I. Rhodes, "Mexico—A Model for Capitalist Development in Latin America?" *Science and Society* 34 (Spring 1970): 61–77; Kenneth F. Johnson, *Mexican Democracy: A Critical View*, pp. 89–97.

20. Paul L. Yates, *El desarrollo regional de México.*

21. Rhodes, "Mexico—A Model?" p. 66.

22. Charles J. Erasmus, *Man Takes Control*, pp. 221–224.

23. Mario M. Carrillo Huerta, "La introducción del crédito al sector agrícola: Problemas y perspectivas."

24. Ibid.

25. See Marnie W. Mueller, "Changing Patterns of Agricultural Output and Productivity in the Private and Land Reform Sectors in Mexico, 1940–60," *Economic Development and Cultural Change* 18 (January 1970): 252–

266; R. S. Weckstein, "Evaluating Mexican Land Reform," *Economic Development and Cultural Change* 18 (April 1970): 391–409; Roldolfo Stavenhagen, "Classes, Colonialism, and Acculturation," *Studies in Comparative International Development* 1 (1965): 53–77.

26. See Antonio J. Posada F. and Jeanne de Posada, *La C.V.C.: Un reto al subdesarrollo y al tradicionalismo*, pp. 65–66.

27. For a description of David Lilienthal's Development and Resources Corporation see *Business Week*, August 12, 1967.

28. Posada and Posada, *La C.V.C.*, pp. 71–75.

29. Jan Leighton Flora, *Elite Solidarity and Land Tenure in the Cauca Valley of Colombia*.

30. *Colombia: Estadísticas agropecuarias, 1950–1966*.

31. Flora, *Elite Solidarity*.

32. See Hirschman, *Journeys Toward Progress*, chapter 2.

33. John Phelan, "Prospects for Political Stability in Colombia With Special Reference to Land Reform," and the accompanying critiques of that paper by Charles W. Anderson and William P. Glade.

34. *Seis años de reforma social agraria en Colombia, 1962–1967*.

35. Roderick F. O'Connor, "This Revolution Starts at the Top," *Columbia Journal of World Business* 1 (Fall 1966): 41.

36. See *Programa de magister en administración industrial*. This fact of participation by so many of the leadership sample may provide a better explanation for the frequent mention of this project than its actual accomplishments.

37. O'Connor, "This Revolution," pp. 43–45.

38. Ibid., p. 42.

39. See "Fifteen Reported Killed as Students Battle Colombian Troops," *New York Times* (February 27, 1971), p. 5. Actually in this incident it was closer to one killed, but student complaints then, as in 1968 when the training of U.S. Peace Corps volunteers on a contract basis rather than Colombian students led to demonstrations, centered on the low priorities given to mass public education.

40. *Seminario de exportaciónes de A.F.E.M.* and *Primer diálogo y análisis sobre exportación*.

41. *Ley de fomento industrial y desarrollo económico*.

42. "La descentralización industrial en Nuevo León," *Boletín COFIDE* 3 (April 1969).

43. Jorge Balán, Harley L. Browning, and Elizabeth Jelin, *Men in a Developing Society: Geographic and Social Mobility in Monterrey, Mexico*, chapter 6.

44. *Apuntes para el plano regulador de la Ciudad de Monterrey*, p. 3.

45. Guillermo Cortés Melo, *La planificación en provincia: La experiencia de Nuevo León*.

46. E. Livardo Ospina, *Una vida, una lucha, una victoria: Monografía histórica de las empresas y servicios públicos de Medellín*, pp. 100–101.

47. *Empreses públicas de Medellín: Su organización, servicios que presta*, p. 9.

48. Ibid., p. 11.

49. Ibid.

50. It should be noted that while this analysis follows the project nominations of respondents that put great stock in EEPP, six other important municipal and departmental agencies also deal in public works and beneficiary-assessed urban improvements.

51. *¿Qué es el Instituto para el Desarrollo de Antioquia?*

52. Ibid., p. 8.

53. *Codesarrollo, VI Asamblea 1968*.

54. Perhaps indicative of progressive civic policy in Medellín is the fact that the red light district operates openly in a proscribed area and is, therefore, subject to some regulation. Although this study lists some 7,376 women (where "persons" would be more appropriate) engaged in prostitution and an estimated 13,000 "clandestine harlots," it is doubtful that the incidence of prostitution is any greater than in other large cities. What distinguishes Medellín in this connection is its recognition of this fact of life and its efforts to control it in a sensible way, as the study itself demonstrates.

6. THE DEVELOPMENTAL RECORD

1. See Albert B. Biderman, "Social Indicators and Goals," in *Social Indicators*, edited by Raymond A. Bauer.

2. See John I. Kitsuse and Aaron V. Cicourel, "A Note on the Use of Official Statistics," *Social Problems* 11 (Summer 1963): 131–139.

3. Marvin E. Olsen, "Multivariate Analysis of National Political Development," *American Sociological Review* 33 (October 1968): 704.

4. See Paul F. Lazarsfeld, "The Interchangeability of Indicators," in *The Language of Social Research*, edited by Paul F. Lazarsfeld and Morris Rosenberg.

5. "Monterrey: Aspectos económicos y sociales," *Examen de la Situación Económica de México* 41, no. 479 (October 1965): 18–23; "Guadalajara," *Examen* 42, no. 483 (February 1966): 13–19.

6. *Jalisco: Presencia industrial*.

7. Ibid.; *Invest in Nuevo León*.

8. *Invest in Nuevo León*.

9. Juan Felipe Gaviria Gutiérrez, "La industria en Antioquia," *Revista Trimestral* 6 (June 1968): 3–18; *Cali y el Valle del Cauca*.

10. See tables in chapters 5 and 6.

11. *Cali y el Valle del Cauca*, p. 56; *Medellín: Estudio general de la ciudad y su área circundante, 1969*, p. 34.

12. *El estado actual del desarrollo de Antioquia*, p. 163; *El por que de un plan de desarrollo económico y social para el departamento del Valle del Cauca*, p. 7.

13. *El por que de un plan de desarrollo*, p. 6.

14. Gaviria, "La industria en Antioquia," p. 13; chapter 5, above.

15. *Las dieciséis ciudades principales de la República Mexicana: Ingresos y egresos familiares*.

16. *Boletín Mensual de Estadística* 206 (May 1968): 193.

17. Ibid., 205 (April 1968): 135, 142.

18. *Cali y el Valle*; *Medellín: Estudio general*.

19. *Informe al Congreso Nacional, 1967*, p. 139.

20. *(VII) Censo industrial, 1961*, p. 604.

21. *(VIII) Censo general de población, 1960, Estado de Jalisco* and *Estado de Nuevo León*.

22. *Jalisco ofrece*, p. 29.

23. *Directorio industrial de Nuevo León, 1968*, p. xix.

24. "Monterrey: Aspectos económicos" and "Guadalajara."

25. *Cali y el Valle del Cauca*, p. 31, and *Medellín: Estudio general*, p. 22.

26. *Medellín: Estudio general*.

27. *Anuario estadístico de los Estados Unidos Mexicanos, 1964–65*, pp. 189–261.

28. *Examen* 42, no. 485 (April 1966): 15 and no. 487 (June 1966): 17.

29. *(VIII) Censo general de población, Jalisco* and *Nuevo León*.

30. *(XIII) Censo nacional de población, Resumen general*, pp. 30, 80, 82.

31. *Boletín Mensual de Estadística* 206 (May 1968): 200–202.

32. *Cali en cifras*, p. 33; *Antioquia: Síntesis socio-económica*, p. 72.

33. *Antioquia: Síntesis*, p. 71; Alberto Sandoral, *Estudio geo-económico del Valle del Cauca*, cited in Antonio J. Posada F. and Jeanne de Posada, *La C.V.C.: Un reto al subdesarrollo y al tradicionalismo*, p. 52.

34. *(VIII) Censo general de población, Monterrey* and *Jalisco*.

35. *Examen* 42, no. 485 (April 1966): 15 and no. 487 (June 1966): 17.

36. *Memoria de Jalisco, 1964–70*.

37. *Finanzas públicas del Estado de Nuevo León*.

38. *El problema de la vivienda en Monterrey*.

39. *Boletín Mensual de Estadística* 205 (April 1968): 12–13.

40. *Examen* 42, no. 485 (April 1966): 15 and no. 487 (June 1966): 17.

41. *(VIII) Censo general*, pp. 428–429.

42. *Anuario estadístico*, p. 143.

43. Ibid., pp. 181, 184.

44. *Boletín Mensual de Estadística* 206 (May 1968): 20 and 48.

45. *Informe al Congreso Nacional*, p. 38.

46. *(VIII) Censo general.*
47. *Las dieciséis ciudades principales,* p. 30.
48. *Ocupación y salarios en Monterrey metropolitano, 1966,* p. 6; Elizabeth Jelin de Balán, "Fuerza de Trabajo," in *Movilidad social, migración y fecundidad en Monterrey metropolitano,* p. 163.
49. *Empleo y desempleo en Colombia,* p. 16.
50. Robert L. Slighton, *Urban Unemployment in Colombia: Measurement, Characteristics, and Policy Problems,* p. 16.
51. *(XIII) Censo nacional.*
52. Jesús Puente Leyva, *Distribución del ingreso en un área urbana: El caso de Monterrey,* p. 67.
53. *Medellín: Estudio general,* p. 16.
54. *El por que de un plan de desarrollo,* p. 52.

7. ELITES AND ECONOMIC DEVELOPMENT

1. Wilbert E. Moore, "Social Aspects of Economic Development," in *Handbook of Modern Sociology,* edited by R. E. L. Faris, p. 886.
2. Reinhard Bendix, *Nation-Building and Citizenship: Studies of our Changing Social Order,* pp. 13, 208.
3. Jorge Balán, Harley L. Browning, and Elizabeth Jelin, *Men in a Developing Society: Geographic and Social Mobility in Monterrey, Mexico,* chapter 11.
4. Everett E. Hagen, *On the Theory of Social Change;* Walt W. Rostow, "The Take-Off into Sustained Growth," *The Economic Journal* 66 (March 1956): 25–48.
5. Bert F. Hoselitz, *Sociological Factors in Economic Development;* Neil J. Smelser, *The Sociology of Economic Life.*
6. Andre Gunder Frank, "The Sociology of Development and the Underdevelopment of Sociology," *Catalyst* (Summer 1967): 20–73.
7. Gabriel A. Almond and G. Bingham Powell, Jr., *Comparative Politics: A Developmental Approach;* S. N. Eisenstadt, *Modernization: Protest and Change.*
8. Almond and Powell, *Comparative Politics,* p. 35.
9. Albert O. Hirschman, *The Strategy of Economic Development,* p. 27.
10. Manning Nash, "Some Social and Cultural Aspects of Economic Development," *Economic Development and Cultural Change* 7 (January 1959): 137–150.
11. Irving Louis Horowitz, *Three Worlds of Development: The Theory and Practice of International Stratification.*
12. Clifford Geertz, *Peddlers and Princes: Social Development and Economic Change in Two Indonesian Towns.*
13. Geertz, "Social Change and Economic Modernization in Two Indo-

nesian Towns: A Case in Point," in *On the Theory of Social Change: How Economic Growth Begins* by Everett E. Hagen, p. 389.

14. For a similar distinction between "intermember" and "systemic" arrangements of power and their consequences see Edward W. Lehman, "Toward a Macrosociology of Power," *American Sociological Review* 34 (August 1969): 453–465.

15. Robert E. Cole, "Functional Alternatives and Development: An Empirical Example of Permanent Employment in Japan," *American Sociological Review* 38 (August 1973): 424–438.

16. Theotonio Dos Santos, "The Structure of Dependence," *American Economic Review* 60 (May 1970): 231.

17. Frank, "The Development of Underdevelopment," *Monthly Review* (September 1966), reprinted in Frank, *Latin America: Underdevelopment or Revolution.*

18. Ibid., p. 9.

19. Dos Santos, "La crise de la théorie du développement et les relations de dépendence en Amérique Latine," *L'Homme et la Société* 12 (April, May, June 1969), translated and quoted in Philip Ehrensaft, "Semi-Industrial Capitalism in the Third World; Implications for Social Research in Africa," *Africa Today* 18 (January 1971): 55.

20. Celso Furtado, "Development and Stagnation in Latin America: A Structuralist Approach," *Studies in Comparative International Development* 1 (1965): 160.

21. Fernando Henrique Cardoso, "The Entrepreneurial Elites of Latin America," *Studies in Comparative International Development* 2 (1966): 156.

22. Immanuel Wallerstein, *The Modern World-System: Capitalist Agriculture and the Origins of the European World-Economy in the Sixteenth Century.*

23. See Frank, *Capitalism and Underdevelopment in Latin America: Historical Studies of Chile and Brazil*; Giovanni Arrighi and John S. Saul, eds., *Essays on the Political Economy of Africa*; Ronald Müller, "The Multinational Corporation and the Underdevelopment of the Third World," in *The Political Economy of Development and Underdevelopment*, edited by Charles K. Wilber.

Bibliography

Agger, Robert E.; Goldrich, Daniel; and Swanson, Bert E. *The Rulers and the Ruled: Political Power and Impotence in American Communities*. New York: Wiley, 1964.

Aiken, Michael. "The Distribution of Community Power: Structural Bases and Social Consequences." In *The Structure of Community Power*, edited by Michael Aiken and Paul E. Mott, pp. 487–525. New York: Random House, 1970.

————, and Alford, Robert R. "Community Structure and Innovation: The Case of Urban Renewal." *American Sociological Review* 35 (August 1970): 650–665.

————, and Mott, Paul E., eds. *The Structure of Community Power*. New York: Random House, 1970.

Alba, Victor. *The Mexicans: The Making of a Nation*. New York: Praeger, 1967.

Alford, Robert R. *Bureaucracy and Participation: Political Cultures in Four Wisconsin Cities*. Chicago: Rand McNally, 1961.

Almond, Gabriel A., and Coleman, James S., eds. *The Politics of the Developing Areas*. Princeton, N. J.: Princeton University Press, 1960.

————, and Powell, G. Bingham, Jr. *Comparative Politics: A Developmental Approach*. Boston: Little, Brown, 1966.

Alonso, William. "Urban and Regional Imbalances in Economic Growth." *Economic Development and Cultural Change* 17 (October 1968): 1–14.

Antioquia: Síntesis socio-económica. Medellín: Departamento Administrativo de Planeación, Gobernación de Antioquia, 1968.

Anton, Thomas J. "Power, Pluralism, and Local Politics." *Administrative Science Quarterly* 7 (March 1963): 425–457.

Anuario estadístico de los Estados Unidos Mexicanos, 1964–1965. Mexico City: Secretaría de Industria y Comercio, 1967.

Apter, David E. *Choice and the Politics of Allocation: A Developmental Theory.* New Haven: Yale University Press, 1971.

————. *The Politics of Modernization.* Chicago: University of Chicago Press, 1967.

Apuntes para el plano regulador de la Ciudad de Monterrey. Monterrey: Instituto de Estudios Sociales de Monterrey, 1950.

Arrighi, Giovanni. "Labor Supplies in Historical Perspective: A Study of the Proletarianization of the African Peasantry in Rhodesia." In *Essays on the Political Economy of Africa,* edited by Giovanni Arrighi and John S. Saul. New York: Monthly Review Press, 1973.

————, and John S. Saul, eds. *Essays on the Political Economy of Africa.* New York: Monthly Review Press, 1973.

Ashby, Joe C. *Organized Labor and the Mexican Revolution under Lazaro Cardenas.* Chapel Hill: University of North Carolina Press, 1963.

Balán, Jorge; Browning, Harley L.; and Jelin, Elizabeth. *Men in a Developing Society: Geographic and Social Mobility in Monterrey, Mexico.* Austin: University of Texas Press, 1973.

Banfield, Edward C., and Banfield, Laura Fosano. *The Moral Basis of a Backward Society.* Glencoe, Ill.: The Free Press, 1958.

Baran, Paul. *The Political Economy of Growth.* New York: Monthly Review Press, 1957.

Bárcena, Mariano. *Descripción de Guadalajara en 1880.* Guadalajara: Ediciones IIC, 1880.

Barringer, Herbert R.; Blanksten, George I.; and Mack, Raymond W., eds. *Social Change in Developing Areas: A Reinterpretation of Evolutionary Theory.* Cambridge, Mass.: Schenkman, 1965.

Bendix, Reinhard. *Max Weber: An Intellectual Portrait.* New York: Anchor Books, 1962.

————. *Nation-Building and Citizenship: Studies of our Changing Social Order.* New York: Wiley, 1964.

————. "Tradition and Modernity Reconsidered." *Comparative Studies in Society and History* 9, no. 3 (1967): 292–346.

Biderman, Albert B. "Social Indicators and Goals." in *Social Indicators,* edited by Raymond A. Bauer, pp. 68–153. Cambridge: M.I.T. Press, 1966.

Bierstedt, Robert. "An Analysis of Social Power." *American Sociological Review* 15 (December 1950): 730–738.

Blankenship, L. Vaughn. "Community Power and Decision Making: A Comparative Evaluation of Measurement Techniques." *Social Forces* 43 (December 1974): 207–216.

Blasier, Cole. "Power and Social Change in Colombia: The Cauca Valley." *Journal of Inter-American Studies* 8 (July 1966): 399–425.

Blau, Peter. *Exchange and Power in Social Life*. New York: Wiley, 1964.

Boletín Mensual de Estadística 205 (April 1968) and 206 (May 1968). Departamento Administrativo Nacional de Estadística, Bogotá.

Bonjean, Charles M.; Clark, Terry N.; and Lineberry, Robert L., eds. *Community Politics: A Behavioral Approach*. New York: The Free Press, 1971.

————, and Olson, David M. "Community Leadership: Directions of Research." *Administrative Science Quarterly* 9 (December 1964): 278–300.

Brandenberg, Frank R. *The Making of Modern Mexico*. Englewood Cliffs, N. J.: Prentice-Hall, 1964.

"Business Shakes Up a Lotus Land." *Business Week*, January 13, 1968, p. 90.

Business Week. August 12, 1967.

Cali en cifras. Bogotá: Departamento Nacional de Estadística, 1965.

Cali y el Valle del Cauca. Cali: Asociación Nacional de Industriales, n.d.

Cardoso, Fernando Henrique. "The Entrepreneurial Elites of Latin America." *Studies in Comparative International Development* 2 (1966): 147–158.

Carrillo Huerta, Mario M. "La introducción del crédito al sector agrícola: Problemas y perspectivas." Unpublished paper, Universidad Autónoma de Guadalajara, 1968.

Castells, Manuel. "La urbanización dependiente en America Latina." In *Imperialismo y urbanización en America Latina*, edited by Manuel Castells, pp. 7–26. Barcelona: Editorial Gustavo Gili, 1973.

(VIII) Censo general de población, 1960, Estado de Jalisco and *Estado de Nuevo León*. Mexico City: Secretaría de Industria y Comercio, 1963.

(VII) Censo industrial, 1961. Mexico City: Secretaría de Industria y Comercio, 1965.

(XIII) Censo nacional de población, Resumen general. Bogotá: Departamento Administrativo Nacional de Estadística, 1967.

"Cervecería Cuauhtémoc, S. A.: Su desarrollo y su aspecto social." *Mañana* 1228 (March 11, 1967): 55–59.

Cifras comparativas y algunos coeficientes de la industria manufacturera en Colombia, 1964–1965. Bogotá: Departamento Administrativo Nacional de Estadística, 1967.

Clark, Terry N. *Community Structure and Decision Making: Comparative Analyses*. San Francisco: Chandler, 1968.

————. "Community Structure, Decision Making, Budget Expenditures, and Urban Renewal in 51 American Communities." *American Sociological Review* 33 (August 1968): 576–593.

Codesarrollo, VI Asamblea, 1968. Medellín: Codesarrollo, 1968.

Cole, Robert E. "Functional Alternatives and Development: An Empirical Example of Permanent Employment in Japan." *American Sociolog-*

ical Review 38 (August 1973): 424–438.

Colombia: Estadísticas agropecuarias, 1950–1960. Cali: Universidad del Valle y el Instituto Colombiano Agropecuario, 1966.

Colombia Today 5, no. 11 (1970).

Cortés Melo, Guillermo. *La planificación en provincia: La experiencia de Nuevo León.* Paper presented at the V Congreso Nacional de Arquitectos de México, n.d.

Cosío Villegas, Daniel, ed. *Historia Moderna de México.* Vol. 2, *La República restaurada; La vida económica.* Mexico City: Editorial Hermes, 1955.

Costner, Herbert L. "Criteria for Measures of Association." *American Sociological Review* 30 (June 1965): 341–353.

Crist, Raymond E. *The Cauca Valley, Colombia: Land Tenure and Land Use.* Baltimore: Waverly Press, 1952.

Cumberland, Charles C. *Mexico: The Struggle for Modernity.* New York: Oxford University Press, 1968.

Curtis, James E., and Petras, John W. "Community Power, Power Studies and the Sociology of Knowledge." *Human Organization* 29 (Fall 1970): 204–218.

Dahl, Robert A. "The Concept of Power." *Behavioral Science* 2 (July 1957): 201–215.

————. *Who Governs?: Democracy and Power in an American City.* New Haven: Yale University Press, 1961.

D'Antonio, William V., and Form, William H. *Influentials in Two Border Cities: A Study in Community Decision-Making.* Notre Dame, Ind.: University of Notre Dame Press, 1965.

"La descentralización industrial en Nuevo León." *Boletín COFIDE* 3 (April 1969).

Dicken, Samuel N. "Monterrey and Northeastern Mexico." *Annals of the Association of American Geographers* 29 (June 1939): 139.

Las dieciséis ciudades principales de la República Mexicana: Ingresos y egresos familiares. Mexico City: Secretaría de Industria y Comercio, 1960.

Directorio industrial de Nuevo León, 1968. Monterrey: Comisión de Fomento Industrial y Desarrollo Económico del Estado de Nuevo León, 1968.

Dos Santos, Theotonio. "La crise de la théorie du développement et les relations de dépendence en Amérique Latine." *L'Homme et la Société* 12 (April, May, June 1969). Translated and quoted in Philip Ehrensaft, "Semi-Industrial Capitalism in the Third World: Implications for Social Research in Africa." *Africa Today* 18 (January 1971): 40–67.

————. "The Structure of Dependence." *American Economic Review* 38 (August 1973): 424–438.

Drake, George F. *Elites and Voluntary Associations: A Study of Community Power in Manizales, Colombia.* Madison: Land Tenure Center, 1970.

Ebel, Ronald H. "The Decision Making Process in San Salvador." In *Latin American Urban Research*, vol. 1, edited by Francine F. Rabinovitz and Felicity M. Trueblood. Beverly Hills: Sage Publications, 1971.

Economic Survey of Latin America, 1965. New York: United Nations, 1967.

Eder, Harold P. *Colombia.* London: T. Fisher Unwin, 1938.

Eisenstadt, S. N. *Essays on Sociological Aspects of Political and Economic Development.* The Hague: Mouton, 1961.

————. *Modernization: Protest and Change.* Englewood Cliffs, N. J.: Prentice-Hall, 1966.

Elkins, Stanley M. *Slavery: A Problem in American Institutional and Intellectual Life.* Chicago: University of Chicago Press, 1959.

Emerson, Richard M. "Power Dependence Relations." *American Sociological Review* 27 (February 1962): 31–40.

Empleo y desempleo en Colombia. Bogotá: Ediciones Universidad de los Andes, 1968.

Empresas públicas de Medellín: Su organización, servicios que presta. Medellín: Empresas públicas de Medellín, 1968.

Erasmus, Charles J. *Man Takes Control.* Indianapolis: Bobbs-Merrill, 1961.

El estado actual del desarrollo de Antioquia. Medellín: Instituto para el desarrollo de Antioquia, 1969.

Etzioni, Amitai. *A Comparative Analysis of Complex Organizations.* New York: The Free Press, 1961.

Examen de la Situación Económica de México 42, no. 485 (April 1966): 15; 42, no. 487 (June 1966): 17. Banco Nacional de Méxio, Mexico City. *See also* "Monterrey: Aspectos económicos y sociales"; "Guadalajara."

Fagen, Richard R., and Tuohy, William S. *Politics and Privilege in a Mexican City.* Stanford: Stanford University Press, 1972.

Fajardo, Luis H. *Social Structure and Personality: The Protestant Ethic of the Antioqueños.* Cali: Universidad del Valle, 1969.

Fanon, Frantz. *The Wretched of the Earth.* New York: Grove Press, 1966.

"Fifteen Killed as Students Battle Colombian Troops." *New York Times* (February 27, 1971), p. 5.

Finanzas públicas del Estado de Nuevo León. Monterrey: Centro de Investigaciones Económicas, Universidad de Nuevo León, 1967.

Flora, Jan L. *Elite Solidarity and Land Tenure in the Cauca Valley of Colombia.* Latin American Studies Program Dissertation Series, Cornell University, 1971.

Frank, Andre Gunder. *Capitalism and Underdevelopment in Latin America: His-*

torical Studies of Chile and Brazil. Rev. ed. New York: Monthly Review Press, 1969.

————. "The Development of Underdevelopment." In *Latin America: Underdevelopment or Revolution,* edited by Andre Gunder Frank, pp. 3–17. New York: Monthly Review Press, 1969.

————. "Mexico: The Janus Faces of Twentieth-Century Bourgeois Revolution." In *Latin America: Underdevelopment or Revolution,* edited by Andre Gunder Frank, pp. 298–317. New York: Monthly Review Press, 1969.

————. "The Sociology of Development and the Underdevelopment of Sociology." *Catalyst* (Summer 1967): 20–73.

Furtado, Celso. "Development and Stagnation in Latin America: A Structuralist Approach." *Studies in Comparative International Development* 1 (1965): 159–175.

————. *Economic Development of Latin America: A Survey From Colonial Times to the Cuban Revolution.* New York: Cambridge University Press, 1970.

Gartrell, John W. "Development and Social Stratification in South Indian Agrarian Communities." Paper presented at the VIII World Congress of Sociology, Toronto, August, 1974.

Gaviria Gutiérrez, Juan Felipe. "La industria en Antioquia." *Revista Trimestral* 6 (June 1968): 3–18.

Geertz, Clifford. *Peddlers and Princes: Social Development and Economic Change in Two Indonesian Towns.* Chicago: University of Chicago Press, 1963.

————. "Social Change and Economic Modernization in Two Indonesian Towns: A Case in Point." In *On the Theory of Social Change: How Economic Growth Begins* by Everett E. Hagen, pp. 385–407. Homewood, Ill.: Dorsey Press, 1962.

Goffman, Erving. *Asylums.* Garden City, New York: Anchor Books, 1961.

González Casanova, Pablo. *La Democracia en México.* Mexico City: Ediciones ERA, 1965.

González y González, Luis. "La situación social de Jalisco en vísperas de la Reforma." In *La Reforma en Jalisco y el Bajío,* pp. 24–31. Guadalajara: Librería Font, 1959.

Graham, Lawrence S. *Politics in a Mexican Community.* Gainesville: University of Florida Press, 1968.

"Guadalajara." *Examen de la Situación Económica de México* 42, no. 483 (February 1966): 13–19. Banco Nacional de México.

Gusfield, Joseph R. "Tradition and Modernity: Misplaced Polarities in the Study of Social Change." *American Journal of Sociology* 72 (January 1967): 351–362.

Gutiérrez, María Teresa. *Geodemografía del Estado de Jalisco.* Mexico City: Universidad Nacional Autónoma de México, 1968.

Hagen, Everett E. *On the Theory of Social Change: How Economic Growth Begins.* Homewood, Ill.: Dorsey Press, 1962.

————, and Hawrylyshyn, Oli. "Analysis of World Income and Growth, 1955–1965." *Economic Development and Cultural Change* 18, no. 1, part 2 (October 1969): 1–96.

Herring, Hubert. *A History of Latin America.* Rev. ed. New York: Knopf, 1961.

Hildahl, Spencer H. "A Note on ' . . . A Note on the Sociology of Knowledge.' " *Sociological Quarterly* 11 (September 1970): 405–415.

Hirschman, Albert O. *Development Projects Observed.* Washington, D.C.: The Brookings Institution, 1967.

————. *Journeys toward Progress: Studies of Economic Policy-Making in Latin America.* New York: Twentieth Century Fund, 1963.

————. *The Strategy of Economic Development.* New Haven: Yale University Press, 1958.

Horn, Adolf B., Jr. "Executive Living." *Mexican-American Review* (May 1966): 51–54.

Horowitz, Irving Louis. "Consensus, Conflict, and Cooperation: A Sociological Inventory." *Social Forces* 41 (December 1962): 177–188.

————. "Sociological Priorities for the Second Developmental Decade." *Social Problems* 19 (Summer 1971): 137–144.

————. *Three Worlds of Development: The Theory and Practice of International Stratification.* 2nd ed. New York: Oxford University Press, 1972.

Hoselitz, Bert F. "The Role of Cities in the Economic Growth of Underdeveloped Countries." *Journal of Political Economy* 61 (1953): 195–208.

————. *Sociological Aspects of Economic Growth.* Glencoe, Ill.: The Free Press, 1960.

Hoskin, Gary. "Power Structure in a Venezuelan Town: The Case of San Cristobal." In *Case Studies in Social Power,* edited by Hans-Dieter Evers. Leiden, Belgium: Brill, 1969.

Hunter, Floyd. *Community Power Structure: A Study of Decision Makers.* Chapel Hill: University of North Carolina Press, 1953.

Ilchman, Warren F., and Uphoff, Norman Thomas. *The Political Economy of Change.* Berkeley and Los Angeles: University of California Press, 1971.

Informe al Congreso Nacional, 1967. Bogotá: Departamento Administrativo Nacional de Estadística, 1967.

Inkeles, Alex. "Making Men Modern: On the Courses and Consequences of Individual Change in Six Developing Countries." *American Journal of Sociology* 75 (September 1969): 208–225.

————. "The Modernization of Man." In *Modernization: The Dynamics of Growth,* edited by Myron Weiner. New York: Basic Books, 1966.

Invest in Nuevo León. Monterrey: Comisión de Fomento Industrial y Desarrollo Económico del Estado de Nuevo León, 1964.

Jacobs, Jane. *The Economy of Cities*. New York: Vintage Books, 1970.

Jalisco ofrece. Guadalajara: Departamento de Economía del Gobierno del Estado, 1968.

Jalisco: Presencia industrial. Guadalajara: Departamento de Economía del Estado, 1968.

Jalisco, Renovación urbana. Guadalajara: Junta General de Planeación y Urbanización del Estado de Jalisco, 1968.

Jelin de Balán, Elizabeth. "Fuerza de trabajo." In *Movilidad social, migración y fecundidad en Monterrey metropolitano*. Monterrey: Centro de Investigaciones Económicas, Universidad de Nuevo León, 1967.

———. "Movilidad intrageneracional." In *Movilidad social, migración y fecundidad en Monterrey metropolitano*, pp. 203–274. Monterrey: Centro de Investigaciones Económicas, Universidad de Nuevo León, 1967.

Johnson, Harry G. "The Ideology of Economic Policy in the New States." In *Economic Nationalism in Old and New States*, edited by Harry G. Johnson. Chicago: University of Chicago Press, 1967.

Johnson, Kenneth F. *Mexican Democracy: A Critical View*. Boston: Allyn and Bacon, 1971.

Kahl, Joseph A. *The Measurement of Modernism: A Study of Values in Brazil and Mexico*. Austin: University of Texas Press, 1968.

Kerr, Clark, et al. *Industrialism and Industrial Man*. Cambridge, Mass.: Harvard University Press, 1960.

Kitsuse, John I., and Cicourel, Aaron V. "A Note on the Use of Official Statistics." *Social Problems* 11 (Summer 1963): 131–139.

Klapp, Orrin E., and Padgett, L. Vincent. "Power and Decision-Making in a Mexican Border City." *American Journal of Sociology* 65 (January 1960): 400–406.

Kornhauser, William. " 'Power Elite' or 'Veto Groups'?" In *Culture and Social Character*, edited by Seymour M. Lipset and Leo Lowenthal. New York: The Free Press, 1961.

Kuhn, Thomas S. *The Structure of Scientific Revolutions*. Chicago: University of Chicago Press, 1962.

Kunkel, John H. *Society and Economic Growth*. New York: Oxford University Press, 1970.

Lamont, Robert D. "Mexico's Awakening Giant." *Mexican-American Review* (May 1966).

Lasswell, Harold. *Politics: Who Gets What, When and How*. New York: McGraw-Hill, 1936.

———, and Kaplan, Abraham. *Power and Society: A Framework for Political Inquiry*. New Haven: Yale University Press, 1950.

Lazarsfeld, Paul F. "Problems in Methodology." In *Sociology Today*, edited by Robert K. Merton, Leonard Broom, and Leonard S. Coltrell, Jr., pp. 39–78. New York: Basic Books, 1959.

Lehman, Edward W. "Toward a Macrosociology of Power." *American Sociological Review* 34 (August 1969): 453–465.

León Garza, Máximo de. *Monterrey: Un vistazo a sus entrañas*. Monterrey: Imprenta Linotipográfica, 1968.

Lerner, Daniel. *The Passing of Traditional Society: Modernizing the Middle East*. Glencoe, Ill.: The Free Press, 1958.

Levy, Marion J., Jr. *Modernization and the Structure of Societies: A Setting for International Affairs*. Princeton, N. J.: Princeton University Press, 1966.

Lewis, W. Arthur. *The Theory of Economic Growth*. Homewood, Ill.: Irwin, 1955.

Ley de fomento industrial y desarrollo económico. Decreto no. 21, December 29, 1964. Monterrey: Gobierno del Estado de Nuevo León, 1964.

Ley de planeación y urbanización del Estado de Jalisco. Guadalajara: Gobierno del Estado, 1959.

Livardo Ospina, E. *Una vida, una lucha, una victoria: Monografía histórica de las empresas y servicios públicos de Medellín*. Medellín: Empresas Públicas de Medellín, 1966.

Lloyd-Jones, Donald J. "The Potential Development of the Upper Cauca Valley, Colombia." Ph.D. dissertation, Columbia University, 1961.

López Toro, Alvaro. *Migración y cambio social en Antioquia durante el siglo diez y nueve*. Bogotá: Universidad de los Andes, 1970.

Lynd, Robert S., and Lynd, Helen M. *Middletown in Transition*. New York: Harcourt Brace, 1937.

McGreevey, William Paul. *An Economic History of Colombia, 1845–1930*. New York: Cambridge University Press, 1971.

McLelland, David C. *The Achieving Society*. Princeton, N. J.: Van Nostrand, 1961.

Mannheim, Karl. *Ideology and Utopia: An Introduction to the Sociology of Knowledge*. New York: Harvest Books, 1936.

March, James G. "The Power of Power." In *Varieties of Political Theory*, edited by David Easton, pp. 39–70. Englewood Cliffs, N. J.: Prentice-Hall, 1966.

Medellín: Estudio general de la ciudad y su área circundante, 1969. Medellín: Asociación Nacional de Industriales, 1969.

Memoria de Jalisco, 1964–70. Guadalajara: Departamento de Economía del Estado de Jalisco, 1970.

Mendoza, Eliseo. "Perspectivas industriales del Estado de Jalisco." In *Desarrollo integral de Jalisco*, vol. 5, pp. 62–68. Guadalajara: VIII Jornadas de la Alianza para el Progreso, 1967.

Merriam, Charles E. *Political Power.* New York: Collier Books Edition, 1964.

Miller, Delbert C. "Decision-Making Cliques in Community Power Structures: A Comparative Study of an American and an English City." *American Journal of Sociology* 64 (November 1958): 299–310.

———. *International Community Power Structures: Comparative Studies in Four World Cities.* Bloomington: Indiana University Press, 1970.

Mills, C. Wright. *The Sociological Imagination.* New York: Oxford University Press, 1959.

Montemayor Hernández, Andrés. *Historia de Monterrey.* Monterrey: Asociación de Editores y Libreros de Monterrey, 1972.

"Monterrey: Aspectos económicos y sociales." *Examen de la Situación Económica de México* 41, no. 479 (October 1965): 18–23. Banco Nacional de México.

Moore, Wilbert. "Social Aspects of Economic Development." In *Handbook of Modern Sociology,* edited by R. E. L. Faris, pp. 882–911. Chicago: Rand McNally, 1964.

———. *Social Change.* Englewood Cliffs, N. J.: Prentice-Hall, 1963.

Moreno Ochoa, J. Angel. *Diez años de agitación política en Jalisco, 1920–1930.* Guadalajara: Galería de Escritores Revolucionarios Jaliscienses, 1959.

Moreno Toscano, Alejandro. "Cambios en los patrones de urbanización en México, 1810–1910." Center Discussion Paper No. 28. University of Wisconsin–Milwaukee, Center for Latin American Studies.

Mueller, Marnie A. "Changing Patterns of Agricultural Output and Productivity in the Private and Land Reform Sectors in Mexico, 1940–1960." *Economic Development and Cultural Change* 18 (January 1970): 252–266.

Müller, Ronald. "The Multinational Corporation and the Underdevelopment of the Third World." In *The Political Economy of Development and Underdevelopment,* edited by Charles K. Wilber, pp. 124–151. New York: Random House, 1973.

Myrdal, Gunnar. *Rich Lands and Poor: The Road to World Prosperity.* New York: Harper and Row, 1957.

Nash, Manning. *Machine Age Maya: The Industrialization of a Guatemalan Community.* Chicago: University of Chicago Press Edition, 1967.

———. "Some Social and Cultural Aspects of Economic Development." *Economic Development and Cultural Change* 7 (January 1959): 137–150.

Nettl, J. P. *Political Mobilization: A Sociological Analysis of Methods and Concepts.* New York: Basic Books, 1967.

Noticia de Jalisco. Guadalajara: Dirección de Promoción Económica, 1959.

Ocampo, José Fernando. *Dominio de clase en la ciudad colombiana*. Medellín: Oveja Negra, 1972.

O'Connor, James. "The Meaning of Economic Imperialism." In *Imperialism and Underdevelopment: A Reader*, edited by Robert I. Rhodes, pp. 101–150. New York: Monthly Review Press, 1970.

O'Connor, Roderick F. "This Revolution Starts at the Top." *Columbia Journal of World Business* 1 (Fall 1966): 41.

Ocupación y salarios en Monterrey metropolitano, 1966. Monterrey: Centro de Investigaciones Económicas, Universidad de Nuevo León, 1966.

Olsen, Marvin E. "Multivariate Analysis of National Political Development." *American Sociological Review* 33 (October 1968): 699–712.

———, ed. *Power in Societies*. New York: Macmillan, 1970.

Organski, A. F. K. *The Stages of Political Development*. New York: Knopf, 1967.

Ortiz Nava, Alberto. *Evolución de protecciones legales de las inversiones extranjeras en México*. Mexico City: Facultad de Derecho, UNAM, 1966.

Ospina Vásquez, Luís. *Industria y protección en Colombia, 1810–1930*. Medellín: Editorial Santa Fe, 1955.

Parsons, James J. *Antioqueño Colonization in Western Colombia*. Berkeley: University of California Press, 1949.

Parsons, Talcott. "On the Concept of Power." *Proceedings of the American Philosophical Society* 107 (June 1963): 232–262.

Pérez Verdía, Luis. *Historia particular del Estado de Jalisco*. 2nd ed. 2 vols. Guadalajara: Impresa Gráfica, 1951.

Petras, James F. *Politics and Social Structure in Latin America*. New York: Monthly Review Press, 1970.

Phelan, John. "Prospects for Political Stability in Colombia with Special Reference to Land Reform." Discussion Paper No. 1, Land Tenure Center. Madison: University of Wisconsin, January 1963.

Planeación y urbanización. Guadalajara: Colegio de Arquitectos de Jalisco, 1969.

Plan Lerma, Asistencia técnica. Guadalajara: Plan Lerma, 1966.

Polsby, Nelson W. *Community Power and Political Theory*. New Haven: Yale University Press, 1963.

El por qué de un plan de desarrollo económico y social para el Departamento del Valle del Cauca. Cali: Centro de Investigaciones sobre Desarrollo Económico, Universidad del Valle, 1966.

Posada F., Antonio J., and Posada, Jeanne de. *La C.V.C.: Un reto al subdesarrollo y al tradicionalismo*. Bogotá: Tercer Mundo, 1966.

Prebisch, Raúl. *Nueva política comercial para el desarrollo*. Mexico City: Fondo de Cultura Económica, 1961.

Presthus, Robert. *Men at the Top: A Study in Community Power*. New York:

Oxford University Press, 1964.

Primer diálogo y análisis sobre exportación. Monterrey: Asociación para el Fomento de Exportaciones Mexicanos, 1968.

El problema de la vivienda en Monterrey. Monterrey: Centro de Investigaciones Económicas, Universidad de Nuevo León, 1967.

Programa de magister en administración industrial. Cali: Universidad del Valle, Facultad de Ciencias Económicas, 1968.

Puente Leyva, Jesús. *Distribución del ingreso en un área urbana: El caso de Monterrey.* Monterrey: Siglo Veintiuno, 1969.

Pye, Lucian W. *Aspects of Political Development.* Boston: Little Brown, 1966.

¿Qué es el Instituto para el desarrollo de Antioquia? Medellín: IDEA, 1968.

Revista de la Superintendencia de Sociedades Anónimas, 1965. Bogotá: Imprenta Nacional, 1967.

Rhodes, Robert I., ed. *Imperialism and Underdevelopment: A Reader.* New York: Monthly Review Press, 1970.

—————. "Mexico—A Model for Capitalist Development in Latin America?" *Science and Society* 34 (Spring 1970): 61–77.

Rivkin, Arnold, ed. *Nations by Design: Institution Building in Africa.* New York: Doubleday, 1968.

Rose, Arnold M. "Sociological Factors Affecting Economic Development in India." *Studies in Comparative International Development* 3 (1967–1968): 169–183.

Rostow, Walt W. "The Take-off into Sustained Growth." *The Economic Journal* 66 (March 1956): 25–48.

Safford, Frank. "Foreign and National Enterprise in Nineteenth Century Colombia." *Business History Review* 34 (Winter 1965): 503–526.

—————. "Significación de los Antioqueños en el desarrollo económico colombiano." In *Anuario Colombiano de Historia Social y la Cultura.* Bogotá: Universidad Nacional de Colombia, 1967. Reprinted in Latin American Series, no. 281. Berkeley: Center for Latin American Studies, University of California.

Saldaña, José P. *Apuntes históricas sobre la industrialización de Monterrey.* Monterrey: Centro Patronal de Nuevo León, 1965.

Sandoral, Alberto. *Estudio geo-económico del Valle del Cauca.* Cali: Instituto Vallecaucano de Estadística, 1960.

Santiago Cruz, Eleazar. "Antecedentes del Plan Agrícola Jalisco." In *Desarrollo integrado de Jalisco,* vol. 3, *Desarrollo agropecuario.* Guadalajara: VIII Jornadas de la Alianza Para el Progreso, 1967.

Saville, Lloyd. *Regional Economic Development in Italy.* Durham, N. C.: Duke University Press, 1967.

Schnore, Leo F. "The Statistical Measurement of Urbanization and Economic Development." *Land Economics* 37 (August 1961): 229–244.

"El secreto de Coltejer: Modernización y 40,000 accionistas. *Progreso: Revista del Desarrollo Latino-Americano* (November-December 1967): 57–58.

Seis años de reforma social agraria en Colombia, 1962–1967. Bogotá: Instituto Colombiano de la Reforma Agraria, 1968.

Seminario de exportaciones de A.F.E.M. Monterrey: Asociación para el Fomento de Exportaciones Mexicanas, 1967.

Simpson, Eyler N. *The Ejido: Mexico's Way Out.* Chapel Hill: University of North Carolina Press, 1937.

Singer, Paul. "Migraciones internas en América Latina: Consideraciones teóricas sobre su estudio." In *Imperialismo y urbanización en América Latina*, edited by Manuel Castells, pp. 27–54. Barcelona: Editorial Gustavo Gili, 1973.

Slighton, Robert L. *Urban Unemployment in Colombia: Measurement, Characteristics, and Policy Problems.* Santa Monica, Cal.: Rand Corp., 1968.

Smelser, Neil J. *The Sociology of Economic Life.* Englewood Cliffs, N. J.: Prentice-Hall, 1963.

———, and Lipset, Seymour Martin, eds. *Social Structure and Mobility in Economic Development.* Chicago: Aldine, 1966.

Sours, Bessie Galbraith. "Jalisco: Mexico's 'Golden West.' " *Mexican-American Review* (January 1968): 10–12.

Stavenhagen, Rodolfo. "Classes, Colonialism, and Acculturation." *Studies in Comparative International Development* 1 (1965): 53–77.

Sugerencias para el establecimiento de nuevas industrias en Jalisco. Guadalajara: Departamento de Economía, Gobierno del Estado, 1967.

Thomas, Edward L. "Booming Guadalajara Welcomes U.S. Investors." *San Diego Union* (March 15, 1968).

Torres-Trueba, H. E. "Factionalism in a Mexican Municipio: A Preliminary Study of the Political, Economic, and Religious Expressions of Factionalism in Zacapoaxtla, Puebla." *Sociologus* 19, no. 2 (1970): 134–152.

Ugalde, Antonio. *Power and Conflict in a Mexican Community: A Study of Political Integration.* Albuquerque: University of New Mexico Press, 1970.

Unikel, Luis. "The Process of Urbanization in Mexico: Distribution and Growth of Urban Population." In *Latin American Urban Research*, vol. 1, edited by Francine F. Rabinovitz and Felicity Trueblood, pp. 258–285. Beverly Hills: Sage Publications, 1970.

Vieto Arteta, Luís Eduardo. *Ensayos sobre economía colombiana.* Medellín: Oveja Negra, 1969.

Vizcaya Canales, Isidro. *Los orígenes de la industrialización de Monterrey, 1867–1920.* Monterrey: Instituto Tecnológico y de Estudios Superiores de Monterrey, 1969.

Wallerstein, Immanuel. *The Modern World-System: Capitalist Agriculture and the Origins of the European World-Economy in the Sixteenth Century*. New York: Academic Press, 1974.

Walton, John. "A Methodology for the Comparative Study of Power: Some Conceptual and Procedural Applications." *Social Science Quarterly* 52 (June 1971): 39–60.

———. "Substance and Artifact: The Current Status of Research on Community Power Structure." *American Journal of Sociology* 71 (January 1966): 430–438.

———. "The Vertical Axis of Community Organization and the Structure of Power." *Social Science Quarterly* 48 (December 1967): 353–368.

Warner, W. Lloyd. *The Social Life of a Modern Community*. New Haven: Yale University Press, 1941.

Weber, Max. *The Protestant Ethic and the Spirit of Capitalism*. New York: Scribner's, 1958.

———. *The Theory of Social and Economic Organization*. New York: Oxford University Press, 1947.

Weckstein, R. S. "Evaluating Mexican Land Reform." *Economic Development and Cultural Change* 18 (April 1970): 391–409.

Whetten, Nathan L. *Rural Mexico*. Chicago: University of Chicago Press, 1948.

Wilber, Charles K., ed. *The Political Economy of Development and Underdevelopment*. New York: Random House, 1973.

Williamson, J. G. "Regional Patterns." *Economic Development and Cultural Change* 13, Part II (July 1965).

Wirt, Frederick, and Hawley, Willis. *The Search for Community Power*. Englewood Cliffs, N. J.: Prentice-Hall, 1968.

Wrong, Dennis H. "Some Problems in Defining Social Power." *American Journal of Sociology* 73 (May 1968): 673–681.

Yates, Paul L. *El desarrollo regional de México*. Mexico City: Banco de México, 1961.

Zeitlin, Maurice. *Revolutionary Politics and the Cuban Working Class*. Princeton, N. J.: Princeton University Press, 1967.

Zuno, José G. *Historia de la Revolución en el Estado de Jalisco*. Mexico City: Biblioteca del Instituto Nacional de Estudios Históricos de la Revolución Mexicana, 1964.

Index